FINDING MY HUMANITY

FINDING MY HUMANITY

I AM BECAUSE YOU ARE

RYAN UBUNTU OLSON

NEW DEGREE PRESS

COPYRIGHT © 2023 RYAN UBUNTU OLSON

All rights reserved.

FINDING MY HUMANITY

I Am Because You Are

ISBN   979-8-88926-916-8 *Paperback*
        979-8-88926-959-5 *Ebook*

ADVISORY

This book is meant to be for all people, everywhere. The stories found within are real. Out of an abundance of caution, in the hopes of speaking to the wider truths this memoir is meant to reveal to those who peruse through its pages, some characters and settings have been altered or rearranged to offer protection and anonymity to those whom the story engages.

In today's world, to experience love in certain forms is still shameful for some. It is made even worse when revealing that love is met with shame and scorn from society, even codified into laws, which in turn repress and criminalize people simply for sharing who they really are within the world and finding love and connection with their fellow human beings, forced behind closed doors or into dark shadows away from the prying eye of the public.

Additionally, this memoir details accounts of stigma, discrimination, violence, suicide, and death. Bullying, harassment, mocking, scorn, and even murder are realities too many are forced to face while striving to honor their eternal truths and are also a part of what makes their efforts so heroic.

Please be advised.

To my father. To my mother. To my sister.
May you eternally know the profound love I have always had for you.

To my grandparents, Frank and Shirley, my guardian angels
I know you are there. I feel your presence every day.

To the loves of my life
*May you know the causality of your love
in the expanse of the universe.*

To my family, by blood and by choice
*May you know the ongoing power of your
guidance, care, and support.*

To Tommy Ray, Matthew Shepard, Arch, and Anita Datar
You will never be forgotten.

To those bursting with magic inside, still afraid
to let the world see your greatest gifts
*May you peruse through these pages and find a glimmer of hope
for what could be if you dare let your light burn brightly*

TABLE OF CONTENTS

PREFACE	11
INTRODUCTION	15

PART I. DIFFERENCE	**27**
SAFETY AT HOME	29
LEARNING NOT TO CRY	39
SERVICE TO OTHERS	47
BULLIED AND BROKEN	59
A CLIMATE OF FEAR	73
A NEW BEGINNING, A SECOND CHANCE	83
NEW SCHOOL, NEW REALITY	95

PART II. GATES	**107**
A GATE OPENS	109
A WORLD TOO PERFECT	123
BECOMING AN ACCIDENTAL ACTIVIST	135
FIGHTING DRAGONS	151
DEEP SECRETS AND HOMOPHOBIC REALITIES	161
NATIONALLY RECOGNIZED	175
PRAY THE GAY AWAY	185
AN ODE TO FAMILY	199
CIRCUMNAVIGATING THE GLOBE	203
NDIBONA UBUNTU KUWE	217

PART III. ABYSS	**231**
LIFE UPENDED	233
NUMB	241
CLOSE	249

VILLAGE LIFE	257
ABANDONED AND ESTRANGED	269
OVERCOMING DARKNESS	279
PART IV. PERSEVERANCE	**291**
CLINTON SCHOOL	293
LGBTI HUMAN RIGHTS IN KENYA	303
RELIGIOUSLY BASED HOMOPHOBIA AT THE UNITED NATIONS	311
GLOBAL ADVOCACY THROUGH THE INTERNATIONAL DAY AGAINST HOMOPHOBIA, TRANSPHOBIA, AND BIPHOBIA	317
PART V. ACTION	**325**
DIVING INTO DEVELOPMENT	327
FINDING OMAR	337
PARADIGMS FOR UNDERSTANDING GENDER AND SEXUAL DIVERSITY	353
WHAT MIGHT THE FUTURE HOLD?	363
EPILOGUE: WITH GREAT PRIVILEGE, COMES GREAT RESPONSIBILITY	375
ACKNOWLEDGMENTS	379
APPENDIX	383

PREFACE

Dr. Niobe Way

Connection that entails listening with curiosity helps us recognize our common humanity. Yet we often don't listen to each other and thus perpetuate a crisis of connection in which we increasingly disconnect from ourselves and each other. The crisis of connection is a consequence of a hypermasculine culture that privileges all things and people deemed masculine over all things and people deemed feminine. Yet humans are both *hard* and *soft,* and thus a culture that only promotes the former and disparages the latter gets in the way of human thriving.

Boys and men suffer from this culture or nature clash as society asks them to forgo their *soft* sides in the name of manhood. However, their *feminine* side (e.g., sensitivity, vulnerability, empathy) is necessary for forming a human connection. The consequence of living in such a culture that genders core human capacities and needs and makes feelings *girly* and *gay* a crisis of connection is that it often leads to depression, anxiety, loneliness, suicide, and violence, particularly among boys and men.

The solution to the crisis of connection is to create a culture that values what all humans want and need, which is each other, and recognizes that both sides of our humanity, the hard and the soft, are equally necessary for thriving regardless of our identities.

Judy Shepard

We must erase hate. So much of the world today centers around an epidemic of violence driven by hatred toward others, often based on meritless aspects of our individual identities that fail to see the underlying humanity in every person. Even when laws are passed, and hearts and minds are changed, not all are.

We must work to overcome the intolerance and ignorance that breeds so many stereotypes and prejudices within our world. We must work together to advance the rights of those targeted for simply being who they are and who are denied fundamental freedoms for loving who they love.

It's important to be who you are. We don't just tolerate people; we must accept people. We must replace hate with understanding, compassion, and acceptance.

Mungi Ngomane

The Southern African philosophy of ubuntu calls for living a life of courage, compassion, and connection where the inherent worth and dignity of every human being is recognized, beginning with ourselves. It is then in living that life, a life guided by ubuntu, that we recognize we are all inextricably linked. Our humanity is bound up within one another's. I am because you are.

Ubuntu encourages us to step outside of ourselves to acknowledge our true humanity. As the Xhosa proverb says,

"Umntu ngumntu ngabantu"

"A person is a person through other persons."

Ubuntu is ever present in times of great human suffering. It is reaching out to fellow human beings to provide and find comfort, solace, and a sense of belonging. We are, after all, made for one another.

David Kuria

In Kenya, the fullness of my humanity is not always recognized. Yet while I continue to face discrimination, heartache, and more, I remain hopeful.

LGBTI Kenyans are not only criminalized in my country, but increasingly, there is a growing wave to enact even more stringent laws, including the death penalty over and above the fourteen-year prison sentence prescribed in the penal codes we inherited after colonization by the British. These laws provide fertile ground for blackmail, extortion, and violence to proliferate. They also silently communicate to LGBTI people that we are not fully human. We are a mistake and cannot, therefore, be part of the loving human community.

Yet we remain resilient, knowing that our fundamental human rights as human beings are deserving of respect and dignity. These rights are found within the very universal declaration of human rights my country endorsed decades ago, and while these rights may not be realized for people like me, within my lifetime, *Finding My Humanity* inspires me to hope and aspire for their realization for those who will come after me.

Beyond the legal environment, I know many LGBTI Kenyans who are beautiful, bright, and have boldly lived and loved out loud as they are. Their perpetual light has added shape and form to our world, and regardless of the oppression they face, I have nothing but faith in the work they will undertake.

Alok Menon

"One piece of me marvels at the miracle that we are, in fact, both here and queer. That despite every attempt to evict us from existence, we remain inexorable. One ginormous beauty mark on an ugly, ugly world.

Another piece of me grieves it, how much here hurts. In this country, that tells us we are free. Free to be banned when we write. Free to be criminalized when we perform. Free to be beaten on its streets without redress. I want to address that we have more rights and more wrongs than ever, and it feels wrong how the right weaponizes words like "family" and "freedom" against us.

And I wonder, do we see it in ourselves, our freedom? For so long, LGBTQ people have sought to convince the world of our humanity. This was a project destined to fail. It relies on the incorrect premise that we are broken. A belief that ensures that our claims always remain aspirational and our worthiness conditional. We are not broken. A society that winnows down the wonders of the world into binaries is.

Yet we spend our entire lives apologizing and accommodating, exonerating, and exculpating, insisting we are not the monsters in their closets, not the collapse of their civilizations, not their cartoon villains, not their stranger danger, emphasizing so much of what we are not, that we neglect to actually express what we are.

What we are is free. We are not targeted because we fail. Fail to be men. Fail to be women. Fail to be normal. But because we are free. But do we see it in ourselves, our freedom?

… I'm trying to do the rebellious act of loving myself in a world that hates me. Or rather, I am trying to do the rebellious act of admitting that sometimes I am the world that hates me… We must develop a vision of ourselves outside of ourselves. We must learn to love queerness in a society structured against us. We must remember what it's like to be free." (Vaid-Menon 2023)

INTRODUCTION

What would the world be like without a me, a you, an us, or a them?

I began writing this memoir from a plane bound for Johannesburg, South Africa, where I was joined by over a dozen of my closest friends and close confidants from throughout my life to celebrate my fortieth birthday, a day I never thought I'd live to see. Something worth celebrating after all that might not have been.

On the plane, there were individuals from all walks of life, each with their own journey. Old, young, and everything in between. Gendered, racialized, sexualized, disability-impacted, and othered bodies traveling five hundred miles an hour thirty-six thousand feet in the air across a never-ending ocean and a vast continent below.

To think the recirculated air we breathed dinosaurs, pharaohs, or moguls inhaled thousands of years ago, and what started it all was billion-year-old stardust, which found its way to this planet from far beyond our galaxy somewhere out in the universe. Yet somehow, we all exist on this pale blue dot known as Earth, bound by this time and place before us.

Some on the plane were returning home to where they'd lived their whole lives. Others were traveling to a foreign land they'd never been to before. And still others were passing through on the way to another destination.

Each person carries a past, present, and future, all bundled up within and before them, just like me, just like all those who came before and who will come after. The summation of it all and each tiny moment within is incomprehensible for just one person to ever fully grasp, but it exists, nonetheless.

As just another person sitting on the plane and looking back on my life, it's hard to believe I'm still here. I was once a sullen little boy, feeling so alone and afraid of my own shadow, which made me who I am, and found myself not wanting to wake up anymore. To die and leave peacefully behind a world not meant for me, or so I thought. I believed something was wrong with me because I was different from the other little boys my age. I was sensitive. I had feelings. I cared deeply for my friends. Yet my tenderness seemed to be at odds with the world, especially as I realized my more fluid gender and sexuality.

I feel blessed to have experienced a profound transformation in my life decades ago when I fell in love for the first time, which shifted the fear I had of myself. My newly discovered capacity to love another human being, my desire to know them and connect with them in every way, helped shed light within what I once falsely considered the darkest recesses of my heart, unlocking a well of emotion I had been taught to suppress. I realized the love within me I was so afraid of feeling actually was present in all people everywhere, and wasn't it a shame people could be so fearful of something that had the possibility to bring such a bright light to all who felt it? It was indeed what made us all human—our ability to love.

When I realized my capacity to love was instead a profound gift within me, I started evangelizing to the world. "Can't you see? This is me. This is you. This is us. This is them. Why are you so afraid?"

I've spent the past few decades striving to illuminate that humanity for others to see as a globally recognized gender and human rights advocate pushing for social change to embrace our collective capacity to love all people everywhere, in all their diversity.

I've traveled to over sixty countries and interacted with thousands of individuals from all walks of life. I've worked at the happiest place on Earth in Florida, lived a village life in The Gambia, West Africa, and helped shed light on these fundamental human qualities in places like Nairobi, Kenya, Kingston, Jamaica, New Delhi, India or Phnom Penh, Cambodia. I've traced the steps of pioneers advancing civil rights throughout the Deep South of the United States, spoken up in crowded rooms at the United Nations in New York, and held my breath in prayer for lives lost to hatred and bigotry around the world.

I've laughed with children and the elderly alike, gained the confidence of my peers, and stared into a seemingly endless abyss and seen light. I've broken bread with world leaders and public figures and have been moved profoundly by countless individuals whose names and likenesses may never make up the pages of a history book but nonetheless have lived prolific lives and whose very existence has given me a greater glimpse into that which we are all connected to—a shared humanity. All because I dared to love in ways once forbidden to me.

An innate part of ourselves knows somehow, someway, we are connected to something bigger. This knowing tugs at us, moves and shapes us, nagging at us to pay attention, refusing to leave us alone. The more we ignore it, the stronger it pushes.

When we are denied these aspects of ourselves or must keep them hidden for fear of abandonment, we miss out on the greater aspects of who we are as human beings.

As I've grown and evolved, I realized my differences weren't really that different after all. To love and to feel was a fundamental aspect of who we all are. In fact, it was something most people I've met have also ached for. My story was like others who had walked different but similar paths, including those who had traversed different geographies or had come to this point in time and space from a different origin. We found ourselves in one another's orbits, sitting next to each other on a plane, passing one another on the street, or shaking immovable mountains alongside one another.

While working in Ghana, I befriended two men who were "best friends to all who knew them." We attended several events together where I met their wives, their children, and their surrounding community members. They were heralded as future leaders of their country and seemed to have it all.

As time passed and we became closer, they disclosed to me they were secretly in a romantic relationship. Trusting me, they shared how they felt forced to concoct entire lives to fit into their cultural context while hiding the deep and beautiful love they shared behind closed doors. Then, meeting me, they were curious about how I could express my energy so openly—something they were still too timid to do.

In that unique cultural, social, and political context, they were forced to suppress such a profound aspect of who they were, all for the song and dance of putting on a good show (Isaack 2018). One of them told me, "It is out of our cultural duties that we must marry and have children. It is the expectation of us as men."

I had to respect this. But I also wondered, what if the world had been open to and embraced wholeheartedly the clear love they had between them? Would their lives be the same? What lives might their wives have been able to live? If their community had embraced their inner truths, would they still be openly celebrated within their community?

Through the remnants of colonialism, many Ghanaians saw homosexuality as taboo and sinful. As a result, it was still criminalized with up to fourteen years in prison, a leftover British Penal Code even the Brits had removed decades before in their own country (Gupta 2008). To survive, those who experienced same-sex attraction or wanted to express the totality of who they were had to create alternative arrangements to be presentable in the eyes of society—marriage, kids, going to church, etc.

I'm not sure what I would have done had I had to live in such a reality. Would I have even made it at all?

There are countless others I've met all around the world who find themselves in similar circumstances. They've been forced to navigate the familial, social, political, and cultural realities imposed upon them while suppressing their capacities to love and live freely and equally, fully as themselves.

Their hidden lives reminded me of when I had to hide who I was and the love I felt. If I had continued that path, I also might have had a wife, children, and a hidden life.

Too often, around the world, including in the United States, we force young people to deny their feelings and curiosity simply because we may call them boys. We deny them their intellect and enterprise simply because we may call them girls. We measure the level at which they experience human connection and codify it into predefined categories that label and confine those feelings to the limitations we claim for them.

"Don't get too close!" some say. We discipline them because they don't fit our modern conventions or culturally ascribed social constructions of binary gender roles even we don't fully comprehend. "You're acting girly. You're a boy." "No, you can't wear pants. You're a girl." "You can't play sports because you are trans." At some level, these social conventions restrict us all, not just some of us.

We cast one another into spells of good and evil, light and darkness, and right and wrong. This manifests itself in everything we go on to do. In doing so, we damage our own collective spirits and energies, limiting our capacities to love to the core of what makes up our humanity.

Those who find themselves on the outside might subtly be quieted within conversations among friends, shunned within their broader communities, or even criminalized by the State for simply being themselves.

In turn, those of us who feel different in one way or another may internalize these impositions and lose a sense of ourselves as we struggle to fit into the world around us. We silence that little voice tugging at our innate desires simply because we are made to feel like there is something wrong within us. At worst, we may experience ostracization, violence, or even death should we be discovered.

We may hold back from taking risks to pursue something we genuinely want. We fear what might be on the other side of that gate if we pass through and truly choose that part of ourselves, for we have been made to feel shame and fear for what we could be. We may limit the potential of our being, afraid to explore and discover who we really are, including our connection to others.

We may even hate ourselves and wonder why we are even here at all, as I once did.

We misunderstand our innate need for connection and belonging and push it away because we've been told it is harmful. We weaken our collective consciousness when we should be cultivating a shared meaning and purpose in our ever-changing, complex, and pluralistic world.

Social constructions of gender, sexuality, race, ability, age, religion, identity, politics, or religion constrain what we might become as individuals and as a human species. As such, that which we repress are things that not only inform our individual lives but better the whole of us. In fact, our collective future depends on our ability to see each other wholly and, indeed, is worth fighting for.

In 2018, I was reminded of this when I traveled to Cuba, where I joined a four-day US Congressional Delegation, or CODEL, made up of Congressional Staffers, community leaders, and other human rights defenders while we explored the distinct LGBTI social movements there as they honored the International Day Against Homophobia, Transphobia, and Biphobia, a day in May commemorating the removal of same-sex attraction as a mental disorder from the World Health Organization.

We joined dozens of celebrations—from nationally televised shows to galas, pride parades, and dances—and met with dozens of activists. Just like all social movements, these advocates had different tactics, strategies, and aims to advance LGBTI rights within their country.

We spoke with them about their lives and the significance of their experiences as queer people. We learned about the intersections of their activism as they faced everyday discrimination and sought to have their lives recognized by the Cuban State.

In certain ways, they expressed it was okay to be gay in Cuba. Still, it wasn't okay to question the government or exist far away from what the government had prescribed or preordained as *acceptable*. Freedom and self-expression, self-organization, or public advocacy for those who strayed away from this acceptable way of being were often forcibly repressed.

We learned of the treatment LGBTI people had historically received in the country. In the 1950s and 1960s, like in the United States, individuals were accused of being gay to smear their good names as a part of the earlier days when the communist regime pillaged the once democratically elected government (Acosta 2010).

To be gay meant you were aligned with the Americans and working against the State.

During the height of the HIV/AIDS crises in the 70s and 80s, HIV-positive individuals and outed gay men were forced into quarantine to live out their days well before any treatment was available. Activists who dared press too hard were harassed, jailed, or even disappeared. To this day, advancing one's equal rights in that country can come at a great cost (Pink News 2016).

Despite the harsh environment, such resilience was present within the advocates we met. They simply wanted the right to claim their self-evident truths. Not to hide in shame or to love in darkness but to live and love out loud as their whole selves.

I was so inspired by all those I met. For each person to step forward, be themselves, and find strength in such a controlled environment meant their silence was not an option. To survive, they had to fight for their rights and their fundamental freedoms to exist, precisely what had compelled me into activism over a decade and a half before.

From being a token gay at a private catholic school addressing the unequal treatment of LGBTI students to working to remove harmful policies affecting millions of LGBTI people in various contexts around the world, I, too, have fought for those self-evident truths that too many fear. My existence. My truth. My humanity—indeed, our humanity. There has been no other choice.

As I ponder the extraordinary journey I've lived thus far, I think about all the tiniest moments that make up the summation of my life and make it all worth fighting for. From moments of kindness by complete strangers to the profound wisdom of mentors, sage guides, friends, and family, to the deep love and intimacy I have shared with the loves of my life, I have felt overwhelmed with an abundance of love, light, and purpose within my life.

I've also overcome extreme odds, forced to claim my truth despite many obstacles, including stigma, discrimination, and fear for my physical safety. I've been made to doubt my very existence. I've constantly had to ask myself, "What does it all mean? Do I belong here? Am I meant to be in this life? At this time and in this place? Am I possibly from another era? Decades long ago or one far into the future?"

Through many twists and turns and acts of fate, moments of profound beauty and instances of silent suffering, and everywhere in between, I've found myself fighting another version of the same fight, a battle I've now recognized as not solely my own. The right to exist. The freedom to live and to boldly love in a shape and manner that reflects the greatest sum of our parts. You. Me. Us. Them. Human.

I can't avert my eyes from all I have seen. I can't change what has been illuminated before me or that which has offered me hope and inspiration. I can't pretend that what makes me come alive and brings me authentic joy has only been derived from within. Instead, my perception has included the profound gifts of connection, love, hope, and curiosity that cannot be unfelt or unseen and is something I must share with the whole of the world.

Our capacity to love is at the core of my humanity and what I believe is at the core of all people everywhere. Giving freely and without expectation the full bounty of my love and embracing that vulnerability within me has allowed me to tap into what is within us all. Isn't that what we all want?

I was reminded of this recently when I served as the best man in two of my close friends' wedding, Chad and Gabe. They had built a beautiful, symbiotic relationship during their four-year courtship. Chad and Gabe were a great complement to one another. I was so happy for them.

Their wedding was deeply moving. Chad and Gabe exchanged vows, expressing their profound love for one another, sporadically choking up in tears throughout the ceremony. Their families were there, offering their love and support in the best ways they knew how.

At the reception, someone asked the maid of honor and me to offer a few musings to those in attendance. So naturally, I couldn't help but remark on what a rare opportunity it was to celebrate such love in this time and place. After all, it was a moment that might never have happened just a decade before.

"I've traveled the world and worked with individuals who couldn't even dare speak about who they were. They had to love in darkness. I've worked with countless advocates who have had to come out of the shadows to fight simply to exist. So many have suffered and died for merely speaking up. Yet here I stand, offering my well-wishes to my best friends on their wedding day and the life ahead of them, something just a few years before wouldn't have been possible here in the United States. Something many had fought and died for in previous lives.

When I see Chad and Gabe standing here today, knowing all the things they've faced, indeed so many just like them have had to work toward just to get here today, I am honored to call you husbands.

And it's true. So many might not have made it to this moment. To boldly live and love as Chad and Gabe had is a feat in and of itself. It is something to celebrate and fill each and every one of us with pride. It is a true reclamation of our right to love, something far too many still fear and run away from.

Evangelicals often discuss the need to speak *God's truth* to the masses through evangelism. But they often interpret this as literally quoting a Bible, translated from Aramaic into English from a time thousands of years ago, positioned only in one corner of the globe.

I want to recapture the notion of evangelism, far and away from a religious connotation. We must hear one another's stories. We must learn one another's truths, to have empathy and compassion for each other's pain and suffering while also finding joy and hope in one another's light. The space between us, the world around us, has all the answers we may be looking for if we better understand, listen, and find value in our shared humanity.

To do so, we must evangelize as we uncover all that we find divine within our lives, the greater truths our unique realities offer us from the distinct time, place, and geography of our lived experiences.

What might we gain if we spoke into the world that which we have seen, felt, and understood as our greatest purpose and possibility within this finite moment in time and space?

If I could go back and share with the sullen little boy I was, who dreamed of not waking up, I'd show him the best was yet to come. All he had endured and transcended was part of a much bigger and broader purpose. His pain and loneliness might hold something capable of unlocking secrets to the universe that all of humanity might benefit from.

What have you born witness to that you feel you can't look away from but must reclaim for the greater good of all of humanity? What stories would you feel compelled to share with the wider world because of your lived experiences? What answers might you be continuing to search for that could be found sitting within the person next to you on a plane, even someone you might have dismissed or forgotten because you too easily judged them?

For me, this memoir is just that. The brightest light for which I have seen but for which I cannot avert my eyes. It is rising out of a cave's shadows to see the illumination of life before me, giving me bountiful gifts and an acute awareness that we are not alone as I once felt. We have shared strength and possibility when we learn from one another and build from our darkness; when we grow together; when we see in one another that which we have always known and deeply felt—our shared humanity.

This is my journey and how I started to discover the humanity within us all.

In me. In you. In us. In them.

ACT ONE

DIFFERENCE

Hatred paralyzes life; love releases it. Hatred confuses life, love harmonizes it. Hatred darkens life; love illuminates it.
—MARTIN LUTHER KING JR.

Our deepest fear is not that we are inadequate. Our deepest fear is that we are powerful beyond measure. It is our light, not our darkness that most frightens us.
—MARIANNE WILLIAMSON

Boys are human too. They want the same things that everyone wants which is close, intimate connections with other people. The culture of masculinity that denies that desire gets in the way.
—DR. NIOBE WAY

SAFETY AT HOME

I wasn't always afraid of my own shadow.

In fact, I was a gregarious kid, very much alive and engaged in my surroundings. I loved the freedom of exploring life in all its technicolor.

I grew up in Fort Collins, Colorado, nestled in the foothills of the Rocky Mountains dividing the western United States from the rest. The town itself was a quintessential American town developed around its agricultural roots and the local college, Colorado State University. Its downtown area inspired Walt Disney's design of Mainstreet USA at his beloved Disneyland in California (Francaviglia 1996).

My family lived in a neighborhood south of the university, in a small three-bedroom home with a large pond just behind our house. A bike path passed by, one I would use to discover the city, fueled by my never-ending curiosity about the world around me.

I grew up in the protective bubble of my family's love, away from national politics or international debate. Life was simple.

I never needed heroes growing up. My family already inspired me with the abundance of knowledge, compassion, and love they so freely gave. I could not have been more valued as a child nor grown up in a more loving home.

I could explore the world wholly and fully as who I was, producing a profound wonder within me. I also felt a deep connection to our surrounding friends and family.

My mom Beth, an effervescent and perpetually positive woman, is the embodiment of kindness and caring.

From comforting my sister and me when we were sick to sharing her enthusiasm for life as a magnanimous figure representing love and light in her every action, she was my beacon of hope in the world.

Raised by my grandparents, Frank, and Shirley, in Albuquerque, New Mexico, alongside her four siblings, she had a lot on her shoulders as the eldest daughter. She was a perfect child, or so my grandmother always lovingly declared.

She and her brothers went to a private catholic school, St. Pius. According to my uncle Keith, she had the "effortless ability to garner the admiration of everyone around her." From playing Eve, in *Adam and Eve*, to serving on the student council, to playing ping pong and softball on the respective high school teams, my mom seemed to do it all. She was named Most Charming Miss in New Mexico by a local news station and was ranked nationally in ping pong in 1976, one of the things I love to brag about to this day.

In college, she became a student leader serving as a resident advisor in her residence hall, became a student council member, and was a champion for women's rights through her role as vice president of the Associated Women Students at New Mexico State University. She once led a sit-in at the boy's dorm to protest the unfair treatment of young women on campus who had to be home by 10 p.m. on weekdays while the boys had no curfew.

In her junior year, she met and fell in love with my father, Barry, a freshman, when she embarked on a National Student Exchange to Bozeman, Montana. They met roller skating, where she helped my dad learn to skate because he had trouble standing. They'd always cheekily say, "He fell for her."

My dad had a more reserved demeanor but was equally loved by his peers, many of whom looked up to him for his kindness and intelligence. He grew up in a two-room schoolhouse with his parents, Faye and Bob, and two siblings on the eastern border of Montana in a small town, Dagmar, made up of just about one hundred people.

His parents taught all the kids from the surrounding towns for much of their lives while driving a semitruck during the summers. My grandma Faye taught grades first through fourth, and my grandpa Bob taught grades fifth through eighth before they would head off to the high school in the next town over. My grandparents were also the bus driver, the cook, the custodian, the principal, the guidance counselor, and everything a school provides.

My dad's parents were stoic, proud people, their demeanor based on our Scandinavian roots, which certainly provided a stricter upbringing for my dad and his siblings.

Like my mom, my dad was also quite active in his community.

In high school, he was an all-star athlete playing football and basketball, serving on the student council, and participating in other social activities. He was revered and well-liked by most with whom he interacted, winning several awards for his athletic prowess.

He chose to go to the *big city* of Bozeman for college to discover life and learn more about who he was. When he met my mom, he became enamored by her big outlook on life, which seemed otherworldly.

From the stories they told, my parents had a classic love story.

My mom was the charming new girl on campus when she came on her exchange. Everyone loved her, and she had many doting admirers. She even turned down a few proposals. My dad was one of those doting men and would write my mom beautiful letters, play songs for her on his guitar, and express grand gestures of his love.

When my mom returned to New Mexico, my dad drove sixteen hours down from Montana multiple times to meet her and her family. Her sisters lovingly referred to him as *Saint Barry*. He eventually proposed.

For their honeymoon, they traveled throughout Europe. My dad lost his luggage and wore the same clothes for much of the trip. To everyone they knew, they were the perfect couple.

They moved to Fort Collins after my mom entered a graduate program and secured a job as student activities program director at Colorado State University. My dad took a job at a local high school thirty minutes away as a math teacher. He also became the coach of several sports programs, including the girls' basketball team, which he would go on to coach for nearly two decades.

My sister, Sarah, and I were born at Poudre Valley Hospital a few years later.

My sister and I were best friends. She shadowed me for the first decade of her life. She was such a loving, caring person and equally curious and adventurous about the world as I was. We'd get into many adventures together throughout our colorful childhood.

As children, we were full of creativity and had a zest for life. We grew up in the eighties and nineties when kids still had room to roam neighborhoods, play in creeks, and imagine the world free from a constant barrage of everything coming at you all at once.

We were always getting into all sorts of mischief or, should I say, me getting us into mischief. We'd build forts, put on elaborate plays, make breakfast in bed for my parents, and sell lemonade and cookies on the city bike path behind our neighborhood. One of our favorite treats was to shine our Britelight on our parents as they tenderly held each other in our living room, dancing to the latest country songs from Brooks and Dunn, Dolly Parton, or their favorite, John Denver. We'd go to the local drive-in theater, look through picture books our grandparents would send us, and imagine ourselves in some of the world's most wondrous places—from the Pyramids of Giza in Egypt to Machu Pichu in Peru or the Taj Mahal in India.

Whenever it was supper time, our mom or dad would yell to us, playing on our makeshift raft on the small pond behind our home, "Ryan Michael, Sarah Dawn, it's time for dinner!" We ate a lot of frozen dinners and poured pounds of sugar on our already sugar-filled cereal. We'd have Fudgsicles on a hot day and cocoa on a cold winter's night.

Working in higher education, my mom developed student programming and oversaw the student government. She often brought us to her events—from hypnotists to musicians and various activities enjoyed by the student body.

She would often sit with us to bring our understanding of others facing discrimination to our attention, building our social justice awareness. We'd participate in activities like wearing yellow ribbons for veterans or collecting canned goods and donating them to our nearby food bank.

She once sat us both down to watch the Brown Eyes, Blue Eyes experiment (Elliott 2016). The experiment documented a fourth-grade classroom in Michigan that recorded a teacher's efforts to educate her students about racial discrimination. The teacher split the class in two, one side blue-eyed and the other brown-eyed. For the first part of the day, the blue-eyed kids had privileges and could do more than the brown-eyed children. Then, in the afternoon, the roles were reversed.

So many little things happened during the experiment. The children became little monsters to each other. Yet when the children debriefed the day, they began to recognize the harm in seeing one another as less than others.

My mom used the documentary to talk with us about what we felt and understood about the impacts of being different and how we must treat others respectfully, specifically about racial injustices ever present throughout the country.

My mom was a person who had my soul from the beginning. Someone I could always turn to. She offered me space to build my emotional and spiritual understanding of the world, never pushing me but asking poignant questions that gave me guidance and support. Her emotional intelligence offered me an awareness of the world and myself that I don't think I would otherwise have, particularly in allowing me to deeply feel and express my emotions in both words and actions.

She would calmly explain away my fears and soothe my suffering whenever I felt at odds with the world. Later in life, she would explain how it was her philosophy to talk to children as adults to improve their language skills and enhance their cognitive and emotional capabilities. As a person who believed in gender equality, she always wanted to give my sister and me a real opportunity to be ourselves, express who we truly were, and confront traditional gender norms, which hurt both boys and girls.

"Ryan, use your words. Could you help me to understand your feelings? Why do you feel that way? It's okay to feel," she would say comfortingly when I became upset. My dad always supported her in this way and often complemented her through his own actions.

While more stoic, my dad more often expressed his emotions through his actions as opposed to his words but in just as rich of ways as my mom. I respected him for the ways he brought himself into the world, even though they were in contrast to the effervescent and tender love my mom would give. He consistently demonstrated his upstanding character and love for us through his beautiful actions and how he showed up for us in small and magnanimous ways.

When I sometimes had trouble understanding my dad's quiet demeanor or stoic façade, my mom would take my hurt and help explain the subtle ways in which my dad cared.

"See how your dad holds you close when you are scared? How he picks you up from school? How he sings you lullabies at bedtime with his guitar? How he scares away the monsters in your closet? He may not always say he loves you, but you can see he does."

My sister and I always loved when he would sing us songs like Billy Joel's "Lullaby" or Jimmy Buffet's "A Pirate Looks at Forty." Songs I love to this day because they remind me of him.

Growing up as a former athlete, my dad taught my sister and me to play sports. He often served as a coach or our biggest fan on the sidelines as we went from sport to sport, whether it was basketball, softball, or what would become my ultimate passion, soccer. He built up our skills and capabilities from an early age. Through sport, he also taught us the importance of rigorous practice, teamwork, and leadership.

As a girl's high school basketball coach, my dad made us a part of his world, and we were his biggest fans.

My mom would drive us to every game, no matter which city in Colorado it was in. Sometimes the games would be hours away, and we were always there. It was what we did for him, always supporting his passion for the game. My sister and I would sit on the bench to cheer on his players. My mom would help throw after-game punch and cookie gatherings with the players and parents—regardless if they won. I even got a technical once for shouting "boo" during free throws. His teams were all like older sisters to us and my greatest heroes. They often babysat us.

When his team went to the state championships, I dressed up in the same tux as my dad and his coaching staff like a little team mascot. When they won, we all celebrated in style like a big family.

When the games were over, Sarah and I always begged to drive home with my dad to spend time with him. While we loved connecting with our mom, the car rides home were some of the few times we got with just our dad.

When we were in the car, he would talk with us about the players and the game's outcomes. Sometimes it was just about listening to music with him on the drive home, but they were moments we shared and reveled in.

He'd play songs like "What if Jesus Came Back Like That" by Collin Raye. The song asked fundamental questions of accepting and embracing the authentic ways others bring themselves into the world. Indeed, what would we do if Jesus came back and looked like a person we commonly pass or ignore in our communities? Would we still hear the message?

In my dad's own way, it was how we connected, how he showed us who he was and instilled in us his principles and values like my mom did when she showed us the brown-eyed, blue-eyed experiment. Just spending time with him meant the world to us.

What I knew deep down then and carry with me to this day was how much our family loved each other and how that love has spread itself out across my life.

My parents also knew it takes a village to do just about anything. So we were fortunate to find lifelong family friends in our neighborhood who would become our chosen family: the Stills and Samars.

We first met the Stills when we moved into our neighborhood in the late eighties. That day, the landscaping company was still laying sod on our new yard late into the evening, and my mom and I were outside checking on the day's work when we met our new neighbors, Robyn and her daughter Melissa.

With Melissa standing behind her mom and I standing behind mine, they began talking about a shared fence. Robyn's husband, Michael, was just inside the house and gave us a quick wave of hello. They were the friendliest people whom we'd go on to share so many memories with. A few years later, they would also have another daughter, Caitlin, who we all felt was our little sister and were protective of.

While my parents both worked, they needed a babysitter to watch us. My mom found Diane, who would watch us after school every day and whom my mom had also recommended to the Stills. She was a living version of Mary Poppins and offered a loving environment for us to thrive as children. She, too, had a daughter Amy who was my age. So, Sarah, Melissa, Amy, Caitlin, and I, along with a handful of other children, grew up under the care of the three families.

We shared so many childhood adventures together.

We'd dress up, play make-believe, and scare ourselves on thunderous days just outside. We found a magical oasis on the pond behind our houses to explore and discover nature, where hundreds of geese, ducks, and other critters called home. We'd catch crawdads and snapping turtles with pieces of ham from our refrigerator as we explored the crevasses of the banks of the rivers that fed into the pond.

We got into trouble together too. We'd teepee our parents' bedrooms, concoct a mud-filled witches brew, or loudly scream late into the night for no reason. Sarah and Melissa once cut all the lilacs off Diane's Lilac tree. I dented the washing machine when I kicked a soccer ball, pretending it was a goal.

I'd find myself tearing up at a Disney movie or crying at some innocuous thing. But my tears were always comforted by the loving embrace of our families.

Most importantly, we always found ourselves laughing all the time. We were all just ourselves, as ourselves, without a care in the world or any judgment.

Our families would often go on day trips to the nearby mountains. We took several road trips together as well. One year, we camped in Yellowstone National Park, hiking on the trails and boating on the local lakes. Another time we went to Disneyland and Universal Studios in California. We were all so excited. I remember riding the Jungle Cruise and being enthralled by the skipper at the front of the boat on the humorous adventure.

Themed birthdays were always a big event for us. Our families made a point to mark significant moments in one another's lives with creativity and flair. Throughout our friendships, we all bonded in different ways at different times when we needed one another the most.

I was always so happy around them. Our relationships formed a baseline of what friendships ought to be for me and what ultimate happiness ought to look like. It's what I have measured all other friendships against—authentic, radiant joy. We've maintained that love to this day.

I had a beautiful, creative, and imaginative upbringing. I was allowed to play, explore, discover, and feel in the most authentic ways. I developed a deep connection to those I would come to love and consider family both through blood and those considered chosen. I didn't have a care in the world.

This foundation of love and support would provide sanctuary to me during some of the darker moments of my life as I slowly began to learn boys aren't supposed to cry.

LEARNING NOT TO CRY

I had the most incredible family, came from the most loving home, and was surrounded by the most caring and accepting people. But that didn't mean the world outside was equally as accepting.

When I started elementary school, I was well-liked by my teachers and adults. I was known for being a polite little boy who expressed himself in various ways. We learned our ABCs and watched caterpillars become butterflies and seeds grow into sprouts.

At recess, I played various sports every day, especially those my father taught me. Basketball, football, and soccer were my favorites. Like most little boys my age, I dreamed of being a famous athlete like Michael Jordan, Scottie Pippen, or Stacey Howard—one of my favorite players from my dad's basketball team.

I quickly found myself naturally sticking out. I couldn't help it, even if I tried.

This same little boy who loved sports was also artistic and creative. I drew everything from dinosaurs to mountains to portraits, which covered my bedroom walls. A large picture I drew in art class with two classmates even won an award and was hung at a local community arts center.

I also loved the performing arts, playing make-believe, and singing in our school choir.

As a deeply feeling child, I cried at little things that moved me. I even cried just at the sight of other children crying too. It was as if I felt their pain.

In second grade, we were each asked to take turns starting the day with a unique talent. I chose to sing the National Anthem and once wore a beret from France that my grandmother got for me to show off to the class.

In the fourth grade, I tried out for and got the lead role in the school-wide play, *The Nutcracker*. Our fantastic music teacher, Mrs. Ewing, had a different song for every grade. The entire elementary was involved, from little kindergarten flowers to first-grade gingerbread people, second-grade mice, third-grade ornaments, and fourth-grade candy canes. They would sing a song and do a little dance while I and a few others acted out our parts during the interludes. I memorized all my lines and added a little flare to the role.

It was my first time in front of over a thousand parents and fellow students, and I loved every part of it. I was a natural and grew quite comfortable speaking in front of such an audience, which would serve me well later in life. I didn't mind the attention. In fact, because I already stuck out, it felt quite natural.

As a sensitive soul, I gradually became more aware of being different, as did the other children. It's as if there was something on my face everyone saw but me.

When there would be difficulties with other children, I would easily have my feelings hurt. Early on, I didn't have the language to describe my difference, making me sadder and sadder. I couldn't understand why.

Despite my active participation in school and various friendships with other children, I started to experience feelings of profound loneliness. I often wondered why I seemed so different from my peers.

I quickly began to learn about the unspoken rules of being a boy.

I received messages all around me that having feelings and emotions was unusual. It wasn't something I was supposed to express. At least, it was what we were told boys shouldn't do. It was reinforced in small and not-so-small ways as I grew and interacted with other children.

From segregation between boys and girls regarding how we were taught to separate activities in the gym, where we sat, or the types of stories read to us by the teachers, I found myself conflicted.

I liked all sorts of things—from creative activities to sports and playing house with my stuffed animals to going on rugged adventures on my bike around my neighborhood—but I had to choose.

My best friends were girls, including my sister. My heroes were women, like my mom, aunts, and the girls on my dad's basketball team. Other boys were my friends who I played in after-school recreation leagues with. My father was my idol. I'd never given it a second thought there was a distinct difference between us all, let alone in how I was supposed to express myself or even who I was.

This realization ate away at me, making me unsure of myself. Was I different? Was something wrong with me? At recess, I started to repeat the words to the children's song, "Nobody likes me, everybody hates me, I'll just go eat worms." According to my mom, I even once said I wanted to kill myself. I don't know of any exact circumstance that led me to start saying this, but even from this early age, I understood I was cut from a different cloth.

Understandably, my parents were concerned for my well-being after being informed by a guidance counselor I was singing sad songs about loneliness. So, I joined the school counselor and other little children my age at lunchtime meetings once a week. The group was called the *Friendship Group*.

When I entered the room, it was an eclectic mix of seemingly broken kids. Some had anger issues I saw at recess or in the classroom, pushing around and yelling at other kids. Others would curse and shout and act out of line. Some were bullies. Others were somewhat shy and disheveled. All were lonely, like me.

We would talk about our feelings and share what we were going through. Being a part of the group only made it more apparent what I sensed about myself was, in fact, true. I was different. Each kid was broken, bruised, or buried in their own unique world. I in no way related to them, yet I was one of them.

As I returned to my classes, I continued to navigate my relationships with my peers. In those days, relationships among all the kids were complicated yet simple. You liked someone. You became friends. You liked someone else's friend and learned to navigate this as you were socialized.

This happened between girls and between boys and between boys and girls. Everyone navigated relationships, learning how to be friends with others.

As boys and girls, we played the typical children's games. We'd pretend to be a mom and a dad or to have tiny crushes on each other. It was all performative, something I did and understood at the time as just what you did. It meant nothing to me other than pretending. I didn't have associated feelings connected to it, but I participated like it was another game. I'd pretend to like a girl. Have crushes—all of it.

I also started to develop deep friendships with other boys in my classes. To me, it wasn't any different than what the other boys were experiencing, too, who became my friends. It just naturally happened as we became closer to each other.

During this time, I became particularly drawn to some of the boys I made friends with within my school. So, I'd cycle through *close* male friends.

I distinctly remember entering my first-grade classroom at the start of the year and peeking into the other class next door. I noticed the beauty of a specific boy. I wasn't necessarily thinking sexually in any way I was aware of. Nevertheless, something struck me about him and made me curious about who he was. Whenever I entered my class, I always looked for him, even though I didn't know who he was.

I soon learned his name and naturally initiated a conversation, which became a friendship. We'd hang out after school, play basketball, and share our interests, all after simply being drawn to him at the start of the year before even knowing his name.

This would frequently happen with the other boys I would meet. I'd just gravitate toward someone, and then we'd become friends.

I would call them my *best friends*, feeling confident they felt the same way. Our friendships, however brief, always felt inseparable. I found myself caring for them deeply. There was always a shared intimacy in the most innocent of ways. A bond as natural as any elementary school relationship ever was. It was who I was and what friendships were all about to me.

In some cases, my emotional attachments became complicated. For example, there once was a boy named Jose, whom I grew close to in the second grade. We both loved basketball and played at every lunchtime recess. We'd fend off the basketball hoop by beating all the other kids in a two-on-two game to fifteen. We even beat the fourth graders once, which we were especially proud of. This formed a unique bond between Jose and me, which I cherished.

One day, I had to stay in to do something during part of the lunch recess. When I finished, I went to the playground and saw Jose playing basketball with another boy from our class, Billy!

As innocent as it was, my little heart broke. I was so hurt and started crying.

When we returned to our classroom, our teacher Mrs. Arnold saw I was sad and pulled us outside to discuss what was wrong.

With tears streaming down my face, I sobbed, "Jose played with Billy and not me during lunchtime, which hurt my feelings."

Mrs. Arnold quickly did her best to help all three of us make amends, and then we all hung out for the rest of the year. However brief, it was a devastating moment to me, and for the life of me, I can't recall why.

While I knew I was different in my personality and the way I expressed myself, I had no reason to believe my feelings for the other boys were necessarily different. I just presumed everyone felt the way I did.

In many ways, my feelings and sentiments were reciprocated through my many friendships. We didn't sit around talking about our feelings with each other. We just became closer and closer until we weren't close anymore. This sentimentality would evolve over the years from just the way things were to what made me stick out even further.

In second grade, I neither understood what sexuality was nor had the language available to describe what I was experiencing. This gave way by the fourth grade, though, when I started to associate the word *gay* with myself.

A distinct moment when this happened was when my sister and I were being driven home by our babysitter and her friend from a trip to the Denver Zoo.

After the long day, my sister and I were asleep in the backseat while my babysitter and her friend chatted it up in the front seat as they drove us home. Half asleep, I listened to their conversation, complaining about their dating lives.

"I can't find any good men!" the babysitter's friend said.

"I know! And all the hot ones are always gay!" she exasperated. What I recall most was my association with the word gay.

At that moment, I understood it as it applied to me. Similar to when a person hears their name and associates it with themselves. When someone says "Ryan," I know it's me. I heard that word and knew they were talking about people like me. I'm sure at recess, I had heard it mentioned, maybe in passing while watching television with my parents. Or even in conversations they would have with friends or family.

I don't recall having shame around the word gay other than knowing, at such a young age, not to say anything about it.

In fourth grade, gender roles between boys and girls weren't as distinct despite starting to rear their ugly heads in very subtle ways.

I still played basketball every day with the boys at recess. I also had a lot of close girlfriends I would play other games with. But, as the sensitive little boy who still cried at little things here and there, I was often laughed at by others in my class. My difference became more noticeable, and my loneliness only grew.

Some days I wouldn't play basketball, but I would just walk around the perimeter of the schoolyard alone in my sadness. Tension was building within me. My difference was becoming something more than just different but possibly shameful.

In one of those moments, walking around in my thoughts around the playground, I was approached by a small group of children whom I considered close friends. There were two girls and two boys. I was on a city recreation league with the two boys, Christopher and Steven. In fact, I secretly had tiny crushes on them without fully understanding why.

At first, I was delighted to see them.

"Hey, Ryan," Christopher said.

"Hey," I excitedly replied.

"We have a game we want to play with you," he said.

Naturally, I innately trusted him and assumed no harm in any way. After all, he was my friend, so I excitedly said, "Of course."

Then he turned to me and asked me to close my eyes and open my mouth. After following his instructions, I felt a white dandelion enter my mouth, and I began coughing. I opened my eyes to see them laughing and pointing at me. I was so hurt I just ran off sobbing. Young me couldn't understand why he would take such actions. He was my friend I cared about.

This was the first of many times my guy friends started trying to *impress* the girls at my expense. I was his target, but the betrayal of our friendship hurt me deeply. Rather than lashing back at him, already feeling like something was wrong with me, I internalized his actions as justified. "Of course, they would make fun of me. Why wouldn't they?"

It's when I started to feel an even more profound sense of shame about being different.

To think I would develop such shame around my innermost self because of little things like this. Not even because I was gay but because I was gentle. Because I expressed feelings. Because I showed my vulnerable side.

I started to learn not to cry.

So many boys face this in their early lives. All children, including boys, are capable of loving and tender feelings. Still, many don't have families protecting them from the shame perpetuated by our society around our sense of masculinity. Too often, they have just the opposite environments in which they are told to *toughen up*, some forcibly so.

Because this happens to them, they go on to do it to others, creating this terrible cycle of punishment and shame around those softer, honest, and more revealing aspects of who they really are.

I found refuge at home, quietly in our house, separate and away from what happened at school. I'd play with Amy, Melissa, Sarah, and Cait as if nothing had happened. I didn't tell my parents.

Thank God I had an escape.

SERVICE TO OTHERS

While starting to realize I wasn't like other boys my age and being picked on for being different, I would find safety and refuge from my troubles in the seemingly other world of my maternal grandparents, Frank and Shirley, at their home in Albuquerque, New Mexico. They constantly reminded me of what was right and just within the world, even if I didn't fully understand what precisely that meant at the time.

I felt their love deep within my heart and bones.

My parents sent Sarah and me to their house for parts of the summer every year while we were children. Our cousin Scott, from Arizona, and our cousins Veronica and Nathan, who lived in town, often joined us. Since we only got to see them occasionally, being with them was always so special.

My grandparents' home was a four-bedroom house with two full baths, a living room, a fireplace, and a formal dining room complete with a piano. They converted the garage into a den where we would spend most of our time. It had creaky floors and a style reminiscent of the 1970s when it was in vogue. A constant smell of frankincense indicated my grandparents' commitment to their Catholic faith. I have the same incense in my home to this day.

My cousin Scott and I would sleep on two rickety twin beds in the same room my uncles shared as kids, while my sister stayed in another guest bedroom where my mom and aunts slept as children. We'd play ping pong or throw a ball with their two Pekingese dogs, Summer and Chenwa, on their covered back patio, constantly laughing and poking fun at one another, as family does. It was a special way to connect with our cousins and beloved grandparents.

My grandparents helped build our curiosities about the sciences, arts, and deeper truths of the world. They'd often take us to places like the Sandia Mountains, Cliff's Amusement Park, Albuquerque Botanical Gardens, or the New Mexico Museum of Natural History and Sciences. Each place we went to always felt so surreal and special, especially when it was with them. It was their way of helping us appreciate what was possible in life and feel like the world was a vast ocean before us.

Once, we went to an IMAX movie at the Natural History Museum, where we watched a film about the Great Migration in Tanzania. In one scene, a crocodile caught a baby wildebeest. It brought me to tears, and my grandmother had to take me out of the theater.

As I stood there crying, she knelt down with her arms around me and, to comfort me, shared, "It's okay, Ryan. I understand it was difficult to watch. Sometimes the world isn't as big and beautiful as we may believe, and the harder truths are also things we must bear witness to. It is sad, and it's okay to be sad."

And then she gave me a hug. I remember so many warm, tender, and deep hugs from my grandmother, who always comforted me. They were such compassionate people.

As kind and generous as they were to us, their grandchildren, they also exponentially gave that love to the world and everyone they encountered. My grandparents, throughout their lives, were dedicated individuals of service.

We'd constantly meet people throughout the Albuquerque community who held such a deep reverence for my grandparents for what they had given to the local community.

While attending a local cultural festival where my grandmother had a candy-covered booth set up for one of the numerous organizations she volunteered for, several people approached us to heap praise upon her contributions to their lives.

"Shirley!" A man stopped by with arms wide open, giving my grandmother a huge hug.

Kneeling and turning to us with excitement on his face, he shared, "You kids don't know what an amazing person your grandmother is. She has changed people's lives. You should be very proud of her."

His words aligned with my appreciation and understanding of who she was, reinforcing the magnanimous ways I always had seen her. She was a saint in my eyes whom I, fortunately, got to call my grandmother.

This happened over and over again whenever we were with her. In fact, it was often said of my grandmother that she had such a strong and loving network that she could get off a plane in the middle of Russia and know someone, which coincidently, actually happened.

In fact, my grandparents were avid travelers and passionate about global affairs. My grandparents regularly hosted foreign exchange students as a part of their commitment to international peace. It was yet another way they demonstrated their love and kindness toward the youth of tomorrow. We met several of them.

As a proud Irish American, my grandmother served as president of the local chapter of the Irish American Society. To assist with peacebuilding in Ireland during the 1990s, my grandparents hosted one Protestant and one Catholic over a summer to build meaningful relationships among individuals who otherwise might have become bitter enemies. They would share a room, go to the same school, and work together as they explored and discovered life as just two people living in the world.

At the time, Ireland had been in an almost thirty-year fight between Catholics and Protestants in Northern Ireland. Decades of violence had overrun the country as discriminatory practices in housing, employment, and governmental representation pitted Catholics against Protestants (Bardon 2012).

Bearing witness to my grandparents' push for peace left yet another profound impression on us as to how one shows up in the world and the small, incremental ways one can give to the world around them. Their generosity was not only during the later years of their life but had been a staple of their lasting mark on the world.

In the 1960s, my grandparents fostered, over the course of three years, six unaccompanied minors from Cuba, ages five to fourteen, all alongside their own five children. Following the Cuban Revolution, in which Fidel Castro overthrew the democratically elected Baptist government, substantial reforms were set in motion to ensure Cuba became a communist country. Resources were reallocated to the state, including individuals' wealth (Segrera 2011).

Companies suddenly became arms of the government. Universities and places of higher education were shut down, and Cuban citizens were forced to undertake indoctrination programs. The government targeted many upper and middle-class families, and thousands fled the country, particularly to the United States.

As this happened in waves, many families sought to smuggle their children out of the country before they became the *property of the state*, or so rumor had it. As a result, parents had to make the heartbreaking choice of sending their kids ahead to what they felt was a better life without knowing if they would ever see them again.

Through a secret program of the United States government called Operation Peter Pan, in partnership with the Catholic

Church, social service organizations in Florida evacuated numerous unaccompanied minors from Cuba and tried to identify foster homes throughout the country (Conde 1999; Allen 2011).

The six Cuban children my grandparents fostered fled with very little besides a suitcase full of clothes. One little girl, Lourdes, escaped with a teddy bear stuffed with small diamonds inside. They spent two years being cared for by my grandparents as if they were their own children.

When their parents came to retrieve them, their families were forever grateful for the humanity shown to their children. They became like distant relatives who, throughout my life, I would learn more about. This would include over fifty years later when I traveled to Cuba myself for the CODEL. There I saw the abandoned homes many fled and the conditions that led to their escape.

My grandmother, in particular, cared deeply for social justice issues and matters of her faith. She felt such a well of empathy and compassion for all those she came into contact with, especially those who were down on their luck or who, by the accident of birth, faced greater injustices in the world. It emanated from a traumatic past that compelled her to see the world in a much more loving and giving way than most people may have ever presumed about her.

At an early age, her family abandoned her. She was just a few years old when her father dropped her and her younger brother off with a foster family on the South Side of Chicago. Her biological mother, for reasons still unknown to our family, left and was never heard from again, leaving my grandmother's father to care for the children.

As a single father working on the railroads, he felt he had no choice but to leave her with a foster family who could better care for the two children. It was a painful decision. Luckily, he returned a few years later to retrieve them. However, he remarried and had two more children.

My grandmother would tell us stories of having joined a new family and being treated somewhat like Cinderella. She never felt good enough.

Her stepmother never gave her the same attention as her siblings. Instead, she'd beat my grandmother for not cleaning the house, sharing her toys with her siblings, or other seemingly harsh reasons, leaving her covered in bruises she couldn't hide. Finally, it got so bad that she ran away from home at sixteen to live with her best friend's family for her last two years of high school.

She found refuge at school, where her teachers excited her about the world and challenged her to think differently.

Movies also served as an escape. She worked concessions as a part-time job. At that time, movie stars would tour different theaters to promote their films. She was always so enthralled with the escapism movies provided in addition to the glamour Hollywood portrayed as they would come to her theater.

When she was old enough, she stole away from that difficult environment in Illinois to Colorado to become a secretary at a local hospital. While there, she met my grandfather on a hayride put on by the local community while she was on another date.

The two fell in love very quickly. My grandfather often bragged that he stole her away. He often described her mesmerizing beauty and soulful, energetic presence that could captivate anyone.

And wow—was she a stunning woman in that 1950s movie star way, often donning the latest fashions and being the most graceful of women you would have ever met. She was the spitting image of Aubrey Hepburn or Sophia Loren.

Just after her passing, we stumbled upon an album full of the most beautiful black and white photos she had kept. It included several pictures of her with different people, including other men.

My grandfather shared with us someone had proposed and she was previously engaged before but had faced significant hurdles and ended the relationship. Once, she had fallen in love and was engaged to a man of Asian descent, only to have their relationship upended due to the tensions of World War II and the racist treatment of Asian Americans at that time. His parents were survivors of the Japanese internment camps (Brockell 2021). They didn't want him to marry a white woman, fearing further reprisals from a deeply segregated society.

She was a woman who, like me, wore her heart on her sleeve and magnanimously loved wholeheartedly. She believed in love and was likely as brokenhearted over such loss. Nonetheless, she would go on to meet my wonderful and amazing grandfather and fall deeply in love with him too.

During the dust bowl era, my grandfather grew up poor in DeSoto, Missouri, and was the youngest of ten children. They all shared the same bath water. As the youngest, he was always last. Growing up on a farm, his family subsisted on what their farm produced.

In fact, his family often provided food to other families to get by during the economic downturn of the Great Depression when so many other families had gone into poverty. He'd share stories about walking miles to school, uphill both ways, with two hot potatoes in his pockets during the harsh winters—one for him and one for his friends.

As the youngest child, he learned the art of humor to get by. Every dinner or drive into the countryside, he would tell joke after joke after joke. It softened the trials of life and helped their family to persist. During our visits, there was never a moment where we weren't laughing with him.

He was a budding athlete in high school, developing a passion for baseball, even on his way to becoming a semipro. Then, World War II started to pick up, and he had to put down his baseball bat to join the Navy, where he was stationed in Hawaii shortly after the attacks on Pearl Harbor.

After retiring from the Navy, he joined the US Department of Forest Services. During this time, he was in Colorado and met my grandmother at the hayride.

In Colorado, my grandparents had their first three children in a suburb of Denver, including my mom and my uncles David and Keith, before moving to establish a new life in Albuquerque for my grandfather's job. They would later have two more children, my aunts Karen and Mary.

For work, my grandfather often had to be away from home, leaving my grandmother to care for their five children. However, my grandmother found a way to make it all work.

They stayed very active in their church and community. My grandmother often volunteered for political events. She was a "Kennedy Girl" in the late fifties and even served as a delegate for Hubert Humphrey to the 1968 Democratic Convention back in Chicago (History.com Editors 2018).

During the women's liberation movement in the 1960s and 70s, my grandmother went back to school to get her bachelor's in education and library sciences degree while my mom also went to school (Shulman and Moore 2021). She later obtained her master's degree and earned forty-five-degree credits toward her PhD.

She would go on to become a beloved schoolteacher in the Albuquerque school system and often taught in inner-city schools or on nearby Native reservations, continuing to be driven by her faith and belief in serving those most marginalized in society. Upon her retirement, she stayed invested in the school, helping train future teachers.

In their later years, my grandparents loved traveling the world and connecting with people from all walks of life, including visiting their children and grandchildren around the country.

One excursion they talked about all the time was traveling aboard a program called Semester at Sea, which took them to China, Russia, Germany, Egypt, and elsewhere. It was one of the things I loved about them. Their sense of adventure and desire to see the world. They would always send us little trinkets from their travels, which we'd proudly display to all our friends.

I found inspiration, hope, and belief in a much wider world whenever I was with them. I thrived in all the beauty they introduced me to through stories of their travels. These stories taught me different faith traditions and beliefs about the world, influencing aspects of my own spirituality.

My grandfather was a staunch Catholic, often dedicating himself to the service of others. He supported my grandmother in every aspect of their spiritual lives and beloved community.

My grandmother had grown up exploring different religions to find meaning in her life. At one point, she had not been religious at all. Later in life, however, she, too, became a devout Catholic. In many ways, the Catholic faith had offered her a new lease on life.

Her childhood abandonment built within her the desire to support and offer other underserved children the love and kindness she so often ached for in her youth. This extended to her grandchildren. She would rock us to sleep, sing us lullabies, and share numerous children's stories based on the Bible, imparting the same values she worked toward through a higher calling in life.

Through her and reinforced by our parents, we learned the values of doing unto others as you would have done to you, thou shalt not lie, care for the huddled masses, honesty is a virtue, and respect the elderly and those who had come before. Things that, had they come from anyone else, I might have received differently.

In addition to her Catholic faith, she spiritually was not limited to a particular religion. Given her time on Native Reservations, she also imparted other vital lessons from the indigenous peoples she served. Values of honoring the land and being interconnected to all things. Accepting and embracing nature's more profound spiritual energies and how we as human beings have greater strengths within us if we can access these parts of ourselves.

Demonstrative of this, she had eye surgery one summer just before picking up my sister and me from the airport. To be able to do so, she decided to withhold anesthesia for the surgery. She explained that instead, she would draw upon native beliefs around withstanding pain.

She'd often buy us books about Native American culture, social justice issues, plants, animals, and many curiosities about the world. It was one of my favorite gifts she would always send our way. She'd impart her wisdom about the purpose and meaning within our lives, even sharing about guardian angels offering protection to us.

As a birthday gift one year, she brought a guardian angel painting and introduced its meaning to me.

"Ryan, we brought this very special gift for you. Do you know what this is?" My grandmother lovingly presented me with a painting of a guardian angel looking over two children. "This is a guardian angel who is always with you, wherever you may go. You are never alone in this world because she will always be with you."

I always felt a divine spiritual presence when I was with my grandmother. I felt so immersed in love and surrounded by a deep connection and energy. This space often let me forget the trying times back at school whenever we visited over the summer.

One early morning we went on yet another adventure throughout the city that struck me profoundly and heightened my awareness of her spiritual presence within my life. We were in the car. My Grandfather Frank was at the steering wheel, my sister sat in the passenger seat while my cousin Scott and I were in the backseat on either side of my grandmother as she held us both tightly.

She started singing a hymnal from her church choir in a low, quiet voice as she gazed down at us. She sang the song by Jimmie Davis and Charles Mitchell, "You Are My Sunshine" (1940).

As I gazed back up at her calming presence, a glow from the shining sun behind her created what I imagined to be a halo. I could see her outline, and beams of light were shining all around her. I felt this overwhelming sense of calmness. Something that fundamentally shaped me and connected me to all things.

She had such a supreme confidence that would forever imbue itself into my heart as if she was already a guardian for me. Like Albert Einstein's theory of quantum entanglement, she always felt close wherever I was.

My grandparents' lives reflect, to me, the most humbling aspects of the human experience. What they dedicated their lives to, every day, in every action, was a profound reality to consistently bear witness to throughout my young life. It wasn't just what they said or did, but their mere presence and social justice mission was, in totality, who they were.

Their continuous selfless acts of service to others were an immeasurable testament to what they knew to be bigger than themselves. Most importantly, how they loved me, our family members, those in their community, and even complete strangers was so awe-inspiring.

Their everyday example is something I've striven to emulate in my own life and what I have borne witness to in other saintlike figures I would later meet and be drawn to over the years. They instilled in me a moral compass and gave purpose to my life. To give love to others selflessly and without condition.

To see the beauty all around us and to be open to the possibility within others for good. This gave me permission from a young age to ask meaningful questions, dig deeper, and wonder about the world with amazement and curiosity.

It was one thing to have their loving example set such a high bar for how to bring oneself into the world. At the same time, it was another thing to return to the reality of youthful angst and the evolving heaviness of the broader world that would greatly test what they had helped instill within me.

BULLIED AND BROKEN

Before I was allowed to be a kid and figure myself out, I was given an all-consuming message, spoken and unspoken, from many of my peers. You aren't worthy of love. Something is wrong with you. The small but digging messages from my peers about being too sensitive ate away at my sense of self. What made it worse was that I knew I was different and believed I somehow deserved such treatment.

Coming home from summer breaks with my grandparents to the loving home my mom and dad provided, I would return to school where things weren't always as bright.

In fifth grade, my mom got a job at another university, and we moved to a new town, Greeley, thirty minutes away. The rural agricultural and farming town hosted one of the world's largest meatpacking plants and housed many working-class families who worked for the plant or one of the surrounding businesses that serviced the community.

At first, being the new kid in class was a luxury, which gave me a short reprieve from the teasing in my previous school. I didn't get picked on as much. While leaving behind my old friends and ways of life was difficult, I quickly made friends and got involved in various school activities.

To acclimate to my new surroundings, my parents signed me up for a club soccer team, where I discovered a wonderful group of friends who would later become like family to me, similar to the Stills and Samars. The then eighteen-year-old soccer coach, Greg, would become a permanent fixture in my life, like an older brother.

At soccer practices, my teammates and I began to discover our emerging sexualities. We'd talk about sexuality in lighthearted ways, integrated into everything else we discussed. We all bonded and became closer the more we got to know one another.

At school, like most kids, our sexuality was still just that thing that was over there. I had some fear about my sexuality, as I was starting to learn what gay was, but it wasn't something that others seemed to really care about in the fifth grade. I knew little more than I felt close to and drawn to other boys—something I had yet to feel was that different than anyone else. *Doesn't everyone feel this way?* I would think.

I just did what the other kids were doing. I playfully had *crushes* on girls and interacted with my peers as their socialization turned into dating. I befriended a pair of twins in my class, Marie and Jessica. They lived down the block, and we'd find ourselves playing around after school.

One day we were at my house, and to mess with them, I wrote in my journal that I had a crush on Marie and planted it somewhere in my room. I feigned to them that I had a secret in my journal.

She searched for it, found it, and then blushed. We were ten. And she became my first girlfriend.

One night, we were rollerblading outside her house, and our sisters started to egg us on to kiss each other. So, complete with our helmet gear, elbow pads, and knee pads, we briefly kissed. I didn't feel much. Of course, I blushed and then skated home with my sister in tow.

There wasn't much to do about it other than the fleeting moments of playful taunting from other kids while we sat beside each other on the bus. That was the extent of it, like we were playing house. It was what you were supposed to do. Ultimately, we broke up after a few weeks of dating.

At the same time, I had another set of friends in a nearby neighborhood I got to know—two boys who went to another school. We became close and often played sports together, like roller hockey or basketball. We'd go on adventures climbing piles of dirt at new construction sites or have sleepovers at one another's houses.

Once, at a sleepover, we played truth or dare, daring each other to get naked and other stuff. Frankly, typical kid stuff. But rather than just being another thing kids did, unlike my kiss with Marie, I couldn't stop thinking about it days later.

It both exhilarated and frightened me—something I'm sure nearly every person experienced in their own way at that stage in their lives.

Back at school, kids would continue to play at dating. All my soccer teammates seemed to have girlfriends. One teammate, Jon, broke every girl's heart.

From movies to TV shows and songs, as well as stories passed down through families, the whole world was set up for how one was supposed to go through this part of life. It was an openly accepted way of the world surrounding us. My heterosexual peers continued going through the motions of discovering this part of themselves, not having to question it at all.

Not for me. I had many questions as I continued to think about the sleepover at my friend's house.

Later that year, as our sexual urges and other changes in our bodies started to rage, our fifth-grade classes were separated by boys and girls so our teachers could show us a sex-specific film around puberty and then give us a pamphlet to give to our parents.

Looking back, it's almost comical how uncomfortable everyone was, especially the teachers. At the end of the video, the male instructors asked if we had any questions. Not one fifth-grade boy raised their hand or made eye contact with another person in the class. We left having a new appreciation for our male bodies and still a limited understanding of female anatomy.

And oh, did I experience puberty. So did all my classmates and teammates.

The following year, we took a giant leap forward in our development, not only physically, but as we moved up to middle school.

Suddenly, relationships between boys, girls, and boys and girls seemed to become more explicitly defined. You were supposed to be friends with those of the same sex, and you were supposed to date those of the opposite sex.

People clearly had urges they were experiencing, but it's what we learned those urges meant and what we were supposed to do with them that they instilled. Societal pressures felt far more focused on what not to do than what we could now do, furthering the shame and stigma around sexuality all of us developed at some intrinsic level.

So many new rules and ways of being moved us farther away from the childlike innocence we were coming from. We went from one class to several classes with different teachers across different periods. We faced more complex issues, including gang violence among some of our new peers, teenage pregnancies, drug experimentation, and a general pent-up teenage angst. Yes, in sixth and seventh grade.

Frankly, kids were just meaner and more judgmental then.

With the surge of hormones, and the discomfort of our changing bodies, including our cracking voices and unexpected urges occurring at the most inopportune times, kids often took out their stress on each other, just out of sight from the watchful eyes of their adult teachers and parents.

As I entered this world, an even harsher reality than I had known before confronted me. My difference became much harder to hide. It was a scarring time in my life and, as I would later learn, is daunting for many kids at that age.

If you put a timelapse video above the schoolyard during my sixth-grade year, I started at the center of the group of boys and slowly migrated outside the group before primarily hanging out with my female friends.

The boys would rough house and often talk about their relationships with girls. Their ideas of masculinity were based on some false notion of being a man. When I didn't have much to say, or my answers to their prying questions seemed suspect, they started to catch on that I wasn't exactly like them. When they would ask which girls I liked, I deflected, saying I was busy focusing on soccer.

With the typical stereotypes we all held, they started feeling discomforted, believing something was perverse to my nature and questioning my sexuality.

That innate part of me, held deep inside, suddenly seemed to become more obtuse and visible to the outside world. But the hardest part was that it was true. I was gay. A kid's intuition is often spot on. Yet at the same time, I didn't want to accept it about myself, at least not the cruel things said about people like me.

It wasn't something I looked deeply into, let alone knew my feelings about, especially as it pertained to my identity. It frightened me and made my future seem so uncertain.

Some friends, especially my guy friends, didn't want to associate with me anymore. After all, what would people think if they were friends with the gay kid? Did it make them look gay too? I became an embarrassment to many of the guys I thought had been my friends. They started to tease me as the other boys did.

This reality ate away at me. I internalized their negative ideas and became even more full of self-doubt and uncertainty about how I was supposed to live, especially if my mere presence was something to be ashamed of.

Their teasing began to have a greater frequency.

This joking behavior was all very much a part of the adolescent experience. Everyone at some level experienced some form of bullying. A part of me knows that I engaged in some of it myself.

When I joined the female group more and more, it wasn't that they didn't ask me the same intrusive questions or prod here and there. It's more that I wasn't as harassed for it. Instead, I was embraced for the kinder, more caring qualities I revered within myself because my family instilled them in me. This offered safe passage in a dark time of my life.

While we were all learning about ourselves and beginning to understand how we related to each other within the world, homosexuality or its connotations wasn't something fully formed yet in our minds. The judgments from my peers weren't necessarily because I was gay, given I had never disclosed my inward feelings to a single soul, but rather, they were reacting to the common stereotypes and prejudices they had picked up elsewhere and how they likely applied to me.

And it was no wonder. At a societal level, conversations around homosexuality in the mid-nineties largely revolved around the HIV/AIDS epidemic in the US, which had eviscerated entire networks of gay men and had been ongoing since the late seventies and early eighties (Halkitis 2012). The media constantly reported on gay men dying of the virus. There were many homophobic responses to those in the community, fearful the *gay plague* would somehow harm our wider society. Simultaneously, the gay liberation movement was gaining ground.

It was especially difficult as the religious right took hold in American society with constant bombardments of intolerance toward the LGBTI community. From Senator Jesse Helms' rhetoric that homosexuals were degenerates and morally weak wretches; to Anita Bryant's efforts to "Save our children," which remained a favorite taboo of the right that gays would recruit children; to Jerry Falwell's attempts to say there was a cure for homosexuality and believed it to be a false choice. All had broader consequences within our society (Fitzsimons 2018).

On TV, there were few representations of LGBTI people themselves. Some movies had background characters that hinted at the character's sexuality. Famous talk shows like the Phil Donohue Show or Jerry Springer would invite LGBTI guests but often treated them like a circus sideshow, a spectacle for outsiders to observe. Even Disney villains had a hint of flair, sway, a high-pitched voice, or meager body—gay tropes—that would make their villains that much more dangerous (Ryan 2015).

As a youth, my peers and I were a part of that culture, fueling how we treated each other.

Of course, we all got the message that to be gay was not just something you were but was something perverted, obscene, deviant, morally depraved, and sinful. These negative mindsets were all around me everywhere I went. My peers thought that to be weak or vulnerable was gay. That to express emotion was gay. To be interested in girly things was gay. It then figured to mean that you were those perverse things. Heck, the phrase "that's so gay" was at the height of its popularity.

Boys were to be strong and only girls were weak. Boys could be friends, but not too close of friends. But then again, what is too close? It was all just so fucked up when you actually think about it.

I had to toughen up. I didn't cry as much as I had in elementary and learned to turn my feelings inward. I was still a softy and just floated between groups. But the teasing continued. A comment was made in my direction nearly every day. If it wasn't to my face, I would hear about it later from friends.

What was once something I just knew I was grew to be something I was deeply ashamed of. When the teasing from my peers turned into rumors and then outright insults, I slowly retreated within myself. My peers started calling me *faggot*, not even knowing what the word fully meant other than it was derogatory.

"Hey, faggot," would be whispered in my direction under a person's breath as I passed them in the school hallway. I'd hear faggot shouted at me from across the playground. I would often be taunted or shoved by some of my peers while waiting for the bus to go home.

I couldn't fight back when asked smugly to play smear-the-queer by a group of boys I barely knew. Rumors swirled around the middle school about my sexuality. "He's gay!" I would hear.

I knew they were right, even though I didn't want to acknowledge those things within myself. I had no place to hide.

Like my grandmother in her previous life, I found refuge in my classes with my teachers. There I could focus on being a student. I would quickly walk between each class, hoping to avoid being called faggot in the hallway.

Soon, the bullying that started on the playground and in the hallways between classes moved to the classroom itself.

My friend Jason, whom I'd played basketball with after school in front of my house, went from being a close friend to taunting me. One day, in my language arts class, I was going to sit down, and he pulled the chair out from under me. I fell to the floor. The whole class pointed and laughed. I felt the blood rushing to my cheeks with embarrassment.

My classroom was no longer safe. My school was not safe. People I thought were my friends came to find my friendship a liability.

Another time, he stopped me in the hall, put his arm around my head and hand on my lips, and then kissed his hand, making it appear as if we had kissed.

"Do you like that, faggot?" He laughed alongside his other friends, who evidently bet him to do so.

While I chuffed it up to regular hazing that friends did with each other, inside it ate away at me.

I would play basketball with him later that day.

On the outside, most people saw me as going with the flow, a relaxed kid, and someone to joke with. Just a sweet, kind, and caring person who happened to be a little soft and loved the girls since I always hung out with them, as some adults would chuckle. I got by.

However, I continued to inwardly see myself in darker and darker ways. I saw myself as a social pariah and strived to create separate worlds I could escape to.

I'd often seek refuge in places that reminded me of when I was with my grandparents or immediate family, where I didn't have to focus so acutely on this part of myself I wanted to hide.

We'd celebrate birthdays with the Stills and Samars, go on outings and hikes to the nearby mountains and take family trips together. They always were welcome reprieves from constantly feeling like I had this massive thing on my nose that everyone could see.

Being with them reminded me of my joyful youth and helped me to ignore all that was happening at school. They still didn't know about me, but they always loved me for me. All the parents just assumed I would marry one of the girls one day, and we would all be one big happy family. It felt, to them, like the natural progression of how things would turn out.

Every day after school, I also looked forward to soccer practice with my team. I was one of the better players. There I didn't get called *fag*.

It was an environment where we were there to do one thing, play soccer. I had a bit more control over life and where I could turn my focus. I was just another one of the guys.

I grew very close over the years to that group of young men and our soccer coach, Greg. I cherished my time with them. Many had no idea how much the razzing was impacting me.

We would travel throughout the state together for games, participate in tournaments out of town, and bond during the in-between spaces we shared. My family had a van with a TV, a VCR, and a Super Nintendo. Naturally, most of the guys wanted to travel with us. We spent hours playing Mortal Combat as we drove to various cities around Colorado.

We'd play in all sorts of weather conditions—from rain to snow, at night and in the middle of a hot day. We won a few tournaments and lost others, always celebrating with our families at a local restaurant after a game.

We'd have team get-togethers at one another's houses, including mine. At one teammate's home, they made huge bonfires in their backyard, and we'd all sleep over. We got so close.

One year, just like they had done with my dad's basketball teams, my parents took us to an overnight retreat and coordinated several team-building exercises. We did everything from a mini-ropes course to trust exercises and team strategy meetings. All the boys slept in a big cabin together. We all had a blast. They even elected me as their team captain. With them, I felt safe.

However, my separate worlds weren't always separate. One year, we enrolled in a city-wide youth lock-in night at the local recreation center for New Year's, where they had a tournament for youth sports clubs.

We partnered with a girls' team our age, many of whom were my friends, and competed in a series of athletic and intellectual challenges. There were dozens of activities. Combinations of small teams would accumulate points toward the final team score to determine the winner. Each team required an equal number of boys and girls.

I played in 3 vs 3 basketball, 3 vs 3 soccer, and joined the debate team. Throughout the long night, we dominated in all the games. We were having the time of our lives, and then suddenly, as we were preparing for our next basketball game, in front of my teammates, a kid from my middle school, whom I didn't even know, came up to me and started angrily calling me a faggot. I wasn't one to fight back and just stood there going numb.

My teammate Josh, from another school, stood up for me and told the kid to leave me alone. I hadn't experienced that before, someone standing up for me. I'd usually internalize such sentiments and feel like a burden to others around me after such incidents. I was so grateful.

At the same time, it made me even more acutely aware that my separate worlds were moving closer together. I became more paranoid. I wondered what would happen if people found out about me, including my parents.

"What if I lose every person I have ever loved because of this part of myself?"

I'm not sure where, but I learned parents often abandoned their gay kids. Their parents had been so disgusted they'd rather see them dead than have a gay child. Kids were being thrown out of their homes and left to fend for themselves on the streets, disgracing their families.

I knew, like me, parents also got messages from the world around them that they were to be disgusted with their children if they were gay. They needed to ward off such obscenity and question whether their children may have been recruited or harmed in one way or another. After all, gay men were considered predators seeking to convert children into their so-called lifestyle.

Even worse, parents were told if their child was gay, they had failed as parents. Men weren't teaching their boys to be manly enough and failed as fathers. Mothers were clearly too overbearing on their sons.

I took to heart all these messages. The thought of being abandoned by them became one of my greatest fears. I became paranoid about bringing such shame to my family, particularly my father.

My parents were such good people. I didn't want others to blame them for me being gay. I didn't want them to think my dad had failed in his duties as a father and wasn't tough enough on me. He was an incredible father, and that was the last thing I would want to befall upon him.

Later that year, my family and I went to see a movie. We got in a long line outside the theater, just a few people behind a group of girls from my school who all suspected I was gay. I briefly nodded toward them but was terrified they might call me faggot. After that, I stopped wanting to go out in public with my family. I'd just stay home when they went to the movies or the mall.

My fear of my parents finding out about me only grew when we would attend church together on Sundays. The same kids who called me faggot in school and their families sat in the pews right in front of us.

In those tense moments, as I kneeled next to my father, mother, and sister in prayer, I just waited for them to turn around and call me a fag. Channeling my grandmother, I asked myself, "How would an all-loving God only want their parishioners to be good one day of the week? Wouldn't He/She/It want them to be good in every moment of their lives? Why only in this place and not everywhere? "

I squirmed in my seat, nervous about saying anything that might draw attention to myself. The church no longer *was* a safe space for me.

As rumors continued to spread around my school about me the more, I began to feel like an outcast. I began to begrudgingly accept that I ultimately was what the bullies and society at large had labeled as perverse. I emotionally distanced myself from those I loved, including my parents, in preparation for the blunt force trauma of their ultimate abandonment. Who would I be without my family? Without those who were like my family?

Of course, this was illogical if I had thought about it deeply. As a student administrator, my mom had overseen several student clubs at her university, including the gay-straight alliance. She prominently displayed an "Ally of the Year" award she had received from them the previous year alongside all her other awards and accolades. Likewise, my dad consistently demonstrated tolerance and open-mindedness through his upstanding character. I never once heard him say a derogatory term toward another person in my life. But I entrapped myself too much in my own thoughts to realize it.

I found myself isolating, alone in my room, listening to music or watching movies hiding from the world. I'd watch from my window upstairs in jealousy as my sister continued to make friends with the neighborhood kids. She would constantly be shuffling from one friend's house, in and out, and off to another friend's house. I constantly ached to have that. Just one person who knew the real me and wouldn't be scared of who I was. I was afraid of myself. My inner and outer worlds were in conflict.

At the end of middle school, at the seventh-grade awards ceremony, I was surprised to learn I had won my teachers' Student of the Year award. My teachers recognized me as being a kind, caring, and resilient kid. In a way, it felt like a small valve release on the mounting internal struggles ongoing within me.

At least I had something to show those kids.

A CLIMATE OF FEAR

—

Why continue living when the world tells you everything about you, the things that make you you, are somehow sick, perverted, or gross? When trapped within yourself, questioning your mere existence, you can't help but wonder—why am I here at all?

I had so many questions about my existence and things I had to reconcile. I sat in my room alone and wondered about my purpose through the internal turmoil constantly troubling me.

By eighth grade, we had moved from our middle school to junior high school, where I learned to live with the constant questioning of my sexuality and the reality of my peers continuing to discover themselves.

Our sexualities evolved during junior high. I developed a more profound curiosity and attraction to some of the boys around me. I remember feeling physical sensations in my body I had never known before that would creep up at the most inopportune time—like when I wore tight jeans to class and would start thinking about someone I liked in that way. Even the slightest peak at someone's bare thighs or a guy with his shirt off would excite me. After the brief elation, I immediately felt shame, curious if anyone had noticed.

I particularly had trouble when it came to changing in the locker room. Just the thought of somehow being turned on in any way in such a setting frightened me to death. I was so scared one of the boys would think I was looking at them. So going to PE, my favorite class, soon became a nightmare.

I began overcorrecting myself, aware of every movement I made to ensure no one thought I was staring at them. I often avoided any situation that would put me in such a position at all costs. Even if my knee touched a friend's or my arm briefly grazed another boy's arm, I would cajole backward like I'd committed the most heinous crime. I couldn't even hug my friends. Would they think I was hitting on them?

I strived to maintain a low profile. I considered myself a floater who hung out with different groups of people. It was a way of never being too scrutinized or in the space of being able to be figured out. I generally hung out with a group of girls who had journeyed with me from elementary and middle grades to junior high and who had been in the orchestra with me.

As my girlfriends shared their crushes, I would secretly agree with them to myself. I learned to speak in code, interchanging gender pronouns of *he* for *she* so I could be a part of the conversation in broad brushstrokes, expressing my feelings without too much suspicion. In our heteronormative world, it was a way to fit in. It was also a matter of survival.

I tended to focus more on soccer to turn my mind away from the near-daily stressors of my hidden truths. It was a way to avoid answering questions about who I was dating or interested in. After-school practices with my teammates were my escape.

As life became busier, shuffling around my sister and me to our various afterschool activities, my parents decided they needed help as they worked late into the evenings. So, they asked my soccer coach, Greg, to watch us. This was a godsend.

He would stop by after school and hang out with my sister and me. He and I spent almost every day playing soccer late into the evening in our backyard when we weren't at one of our practices. My dad built us a mini-soccer goal out of PVC pipe and an old soccer net from his high school.

We'd play different soccer games in my garage or basement in the wintertime. When we could have the whole team over, we'd sneak onto the golf course and play some more.

Greg drove us around and treated us all like his kid brothers. I inherited some of his old T-shirts and soccer shorts, some of which I still have. As a coach, he further developed my passion, skills, and talents for soccer. He offered me brotherly love and advice as I faced the cruel world, even though he didn't know the full extent of my experiences then.

As I transitioned into ninth grade, I reluctantly accepted a few people would pick on me. I embraced my reality as being that awkward, strange kid in everyone's eyes. I still wore the heavy crown of having to live in shame about who I was. I found my way to make it through the day by scurrying from classroom to classroom, getting along with my teachers, and avoiding tough subjects while in conversation.

I maintained a duality in my life, ignoring those parts of me I understood to be what gay was. I continued to stay involved in extracurricular activities and leaned into my athletic abilities, hoping to play soccer in college someday or even go pro. It was far easier to hold onto these ideals than to dive more deeply into the realities of who I actually was.

After making the high school JV soccer team, I tried out for the first-year basketball team, given the lifelong love of the sport my dad had instilled in me. But the tryouts were incredibly intimidating.

At the tryouts, a number of the kids who had called me fag were among the kids also trying out. While I had almost come to an unspoken understanding with those same kids not to call me fag anymore, the residual harm from the previous three years remained. Every time I saw one of them, I silently shuddered. Wearing worn-out basketball shoes slipping and sliding during sprints, I competed alongside them and did pretty well. Leaving the tryouts, I just assumed I hadn't made the team. Even though I loved playing basketball, a part of me was relieved I didn't have to play with them once tryouts were over.

A few days later, I was in my next class shortly after the bell and heard my name just outside the classroom door. From the chatter, I learned I had made the team. In a way, it was a sweet surprise. It was just as surprising to the others who had made the team and others in my school who assumed I wouldn't make it because of my soft nature.

While I sat there with a slight smirk, knowing the bullies who taunted me had been wrong in their assumptions, my joy would be temporary. It started to set in that I would be spending more time with the same kids who bullied me, including in the locker room, where I assumed they would continue their taunting.

Later that day, I told the coach I no longer wanted to play. She was taken aback but very kind and spent some time trying to convince me to play still. She gave me a day to think about my decision. She also called my dad the coach. My idol. The person I strove to emulate in all I did.

He was just as surprised as she had been that I suddenly didn't want to play. He couldn't fathom why his son, who played hoops in the front yard every day, loved basketball, and was a chip off the old block, an all-star basketball player himself, was claiming he didn't want to play after making the team. He knew I wasn't telling the whole truth.

That night he drove me around in his car, pressing me repeatedly to explain. I couldn't tell him. I was too terrified to tell him my *why*—that I was intimidated by the bullies who had also made the team. That I was terrified of losing him and our whole family and all our friends.

"I'm not interested in being a benchwarmer," I told him. "I didn't make the starting five."

He knew I wasn't telling him the whole truth. Finally, after an hour of driving around and trying to convince me to change my mind, he reluctantly gave in and accepted I wouldn't play without fully understanding why.

However, the interesting thing about making the team was its great equalizing power among my school peers. Not that suspicions about my sexuality dissipated, but suddenly their awareness of my athletic prowess demanded a certain level of respect. I still hid who I was, but it was no longer a primary focus of my concentration. Sports were.

I started to ask more of myself. Was I a good person? Was I indeed less than? I tried and tried and tried again to be a good person, and I did everything I had been told I was supposed to do. Why were the same kids who had been so hurtful to me suddenly being so nice? What exactly had changed, other than them seeing this other part of me? Would I ever be truly known? Would I ever have friends who genuinely knew all of who I was? What future was before me?

While things appeared to be getting better at school, the growing hatred in the country would become even more palpable and hit closer to home, making all too real the hatred I had experienced over the years before.

Two major earth-shattering events happened in towns only an hour from where I lived: the heinous murder of University of Wyoming student Matthew Shepard simply because he was gay and the Columbine Massacre, where two gunmen killed fourteen of their classmates after facing years of unrelenting bullying, the first of what would become a growing trend of mass shootings in the country up to this day.

For those unaware of the story, Matthew Wayne Shepard was a student at the University of Wyoming who was beaten, tortured, and left to die near Laramie, Wyoming, on the night of October 6, 1998, because he was gay (Shepard 2010). A jogger eventually discovered him, initially thinking they had seen a scarecrow. The jogger only recognized he was a person when he had seen where Matthew's tears had left streaks down his cheeks on his otherwise blood-covered face.

The first officer on the scene approached his seemingly lifeless body. He was unconscious. She quickly untied him and began providing CPR to stabilize him. Matt was then rushed to Poudre Valley Hospital in Fort Collins, Colorado—ironically, where my sister and I were born.

His parents, Judy and Dennis Shepard, rushed home from Saudi Arabia, where they had been living at the time to be by his side. He was in a coma and died six days later from severe head injuries.

He had been at a local bar, the Fireside Lounge in Laramie, where he ran into two men, Aaron McKinney and Russel Henderson. They started a conversation with Matt and, after a while, offered to drive him home. They put him in the middle seat of their truck and drove off. Once outside the city limits, they began robbing him while brandishing a gun, taunting him because of his sexuality. He tried to fight back but was unsuccessful.

They ultimately reached a clearing near a wooden fence out in the prairie, forcing Matt out of the car and tying him up as he begged and pleaded for his life. They hit him several times with the butt of their gun, causing Matt to bleed heavily from his head.

They then cruelly removed his shoes to prevent him from walking back into town, should he escape, and drove off, leaving him to suffer throughout the cold, dark night.

Evidence from the bar and crime scene led to their arrests. The prosecutors determined the two plotted to target Matt because of his sexuality. The defense tried to add a twist to the story, suggesting Matt had somehow hit on them, which caused Aaron and Russel to react in a blind rage, forcing them to beat and ultimately murder him. They coined it the *gay panic* defense as if Matt had caused their actions.

They were found guilty and sentenced to life in prison.

Numerous news reports shared stories for the American public during the event, including Matt's funeral. One interview was with his parents, Judy and Dennis, standing in the rain before the funeral with protestors from the Right-Wing Westboro Baptist church shouting and holding signs that read, "God Hates Fags" and "Matt is Rotting in Hell" (Sheerin 2018).

Cameras were rolling as his parents asked the press for peace and respect for their privacy. Dennis stood there reading their prepared remarks while Judy tearfully couldn't bring herself to say anything. Instead, she stared off into the distance while resting her sorrowful head on her husband's shoulder.

As his mother would later describe, Matt was murdered simply for being who he was. She described him as a spirited young man with an infectious enthusiasm for life. He was carefree and independent, despite all that was on his shoulders. He had hopes and dreams of working in an international field where he could address the hatred and discrimination others faced. All those around him deeply loved and cherished him, including his family and closest friends.

His death served as a national rallying cry against the hatred millions of gay men faced around the country, just like Matt.

There were vigils throughout the US in his honor, as many saw a young kid just like them facing such brutal acts of violence. It also reminded them of some of the daily violence they faced too.

I didn't have a direct correlation to the incident at the time, but I sure do remember the feeling of knowing someone was killed because they were gay just a few hours from where I lived. That being gay was dangerous. That people would hate you. Even kill you.

As I continued learning about myself, asking meaningful questions, and dealing with the almost daily hypocrisies of the world around me, this event stayed in the back of my mind as something very real and very close to my home that could happen to me if I were to ever disclose to anyone who I was, at any moment. I continued my life, trying to stay low, out of sight, and with as little fanfare as possible.

In April of that year, I came home from school one day, turned on the news, and saw images of a young man with a bloodied foot crawling out of a shattered window into the safety of heavily armed police officers rescuing him from his high school. The Columbine Massacre happened just an hour south of where I lived and was the first time a school shooting shocked the entire nation. Like earlier that year, after Matthew Shepard's murder, fear for my physical safety crept in again.

On April 20, 1999, Eric Harris and Dylan Klebold murdered twelve students and one teacher. They had secretly plotted to attack their fellow students with AK47s and had even planted pipe bombs that, fortunately, had not detonated (Goldstein 2019). They, too, had faced extreme forms of bullying in their school. The taunting and teasing tormented them in their early adolescence. Their friendship turned to darkness as they carefully plotted how they would seek revenge on their classmates who had made them feel worthless.

Watching these horrors through the lens of the small TV on our kitchen counter, I was in shock. It would become the beginning of a decades-long epidemic of gun violence that few could escape. Now, even elementary school kids go through drills in case it happens to them.

Everything we could discern, we had never seen before. I was the same age as many of the victims at Columbine. The school environment became different that day. School safety suddenly became a big issue, and for the first time, we had to consider what if that happened here. Metal detectors became the norm in our schools, and there was a higher presence of conduct officers patrolling the grounds. It set in that such violence was possible, even to tender youth like us.

These profound historical events caused deep existential questions within me. Why would someone be murdered just because they are gay? How could kids be so hurtful to one another? Turning back to my school, I wondered how safe I was. So many of my experiences had already frightened me into being a fraction of who I was. What would happen when I grew into the wider world? What kind of future was before someone like me?

A NEW BEGINNING, A SECOND CHANCE

The world outside crept closer and closer. With the murder of Matthew Shepard and the Columbine Massacre less than an hour away in either direction, many existential questions arose about what life ought to be.

By tenth grade, I started to find a new stride to my step, but I still struggled to know my place in the universe and what my future held, especially when it came to love.

Externally, I started overcoming the barriers my peers had placed before me. I would walk down the halls of my high school, saying hi to everyone. I'd raise my hand in classes and ask a million questions about what the world outside looked like and began delving into the social issues of our time.

During soccer practice, I'd score goal after goal and began being noticed by the head coach of the high school team. That fall, I made the varsity soccer team as a lead defender.

I wouldn't say I was the most popular kid. Not at all! But it felt as if I got along with just about everyone. Externally, things appeared better than ever while my inner world remained in doubt.

My silent suffering continued to grow as I became more aware of who I was, aching to free myself of such pain. It felt like I was lying every day to my friends and family. The emotional labor of hiding who I was, who I loved, and who I wanted to be was exhausting. In my newfound confidence and budding friendships, I questioned every action, every connection, and every situation I was in.

I continued to fear I could lose it all in a matter of moments. Being unable to be my most authentic self still left so much doubt within me. Of course, it didn't help that hints of the homophobia I experienced in middle school and junior high would continue to rear their ugly heads here and there.

In one of my leadership classes, we gave a presentation on people who had inspired us in our lives. So, I decided to pull together a presentation on the inspiring women in my life. I shared more about my grandmother, mom, and aunts and their powerful journeys as exemplary women within their communities. Several of the guys chuckled throughout my presentation. One said under his breath. "Gayyyy."

Another time I was cheering my dad's basketball team on at his high school as I had done since I was a little boy. His players were now all my same age. I noticed the student section from his school was looking at me, pointing and laughing. At first, I didn't pay any attention to it. In fact, when I was little, this same laughter was at the entertainment I provided as a cute kid rooting for his dad's team. However, a young woman came over at halftime and bluntly asked me, "Are you gay?"

I suddenly froze, dreading I had somehow been found out. Before I could respond, she laughed and called me a "faggot" and walked away. A complete stranger. I was filled with fear, as if someone had found me out, and I became afraid in a place that had always been a home to me.

These small moments continued to fuel doubt with me and many *what-ifs*.

I continued to grapple with my sexuality and the dominant gendered norms that pigeonholed me into being an extreme other. As my friends were coupling up and going through the experience of falling in love for the first time, I grappled with whether love was even possible for someone like me. Like them, I, too, had received messages from movies, songs, and books about a destined love I would find one day.

Many of my favorite books, films, and songs posited the possibility of finding a deep connection with someone you were meant to discover and be with. I'd take a movie's heterosexual storyline and the underlying love story and imagine it as my own. I did the same with books and music. It was always about the more profound sentiment expressed I related to, regardless of the gender or sexuality defined within it—something universal to me.

When we read *Romeo and Juliet* for class, I wondered about love that existed where people couldn't be together, and they'd rather die than live apart. I found it fascinating that in the original play, Juliet was played by a man because women weren't allowed to perform back then.

Popular movies like *Before Sunrise* or *Truth About Cats and Dogs* explored themes like finding one's soulmate and examined the true nature of love. I so profoundly ached to find someone who would love me for me.

And, of course, all the love songs. Music was a true escape for me. All the expressions spoke to what I had been experiencing in my loneliness and the hope I held for something different. I always deeply felt every single song, like "It's your love," "My Best Friend," or "One of These Days" by Tim McGraw and Faith Hill, imagining my crushing loneliness finally dissipating. Etta James's "At Last" reminded me of when I might finally meet someone to take away all my pain and let go of the mounting weight I carried.

I so ached to discover love—a love I had been made to feel such shame around.

Love showed up in many forms for me. The relationships between my parents, grandparents, and family friends expressed different forms of what I thought a profound love ought to be like. I saw them show up for each other and find the best in one another. In my loneliness, I just wanted to find someone like me and to have what I thought my parents had, so I wouldn't be as alone in the world.

Yet with childhood dreams of finding a soulmate and spending the rest of my life with someone, I asked, would someone like me ever find love? Would I feel alone forever? What did it mean for me? This all mixed with my feelings of self-doubt, "How could anyone ever love me? I scare everyone away. They would be ashamed to be with me if they ever knew the real me."

I developed deeper crushes on some of the boys I interacted with, struggling to know what to do with my feelings. Just as my earlier feelings of finding a few boys attractive in middle school were simultaneously met with fear of reprisal, the emerging feelings of love and connection I felt with a few of my close friends were even more prohibitive. It's almost as if love itself was the root of my deepest pain and the cause of my greatest anguish—so desperately wanting to unearth the deeper connections I felt while becoming terrified at losing the slightest taste of it and, in turn, those who might finally see who I was.

Having been a massive part of my life, I naturally was first inclined toward the soccer teammates I had grown up with. They had been my closest friends, people I had come to deeply love and care for, including their entire families. We were even fortunate enough to do a soccer tournament in Sweden together the prior summer. When I thought about love, it was natural I thought of the friendships I formed with them and the layers within them as people. There wasn't one specific person on our team. Still, with those guys, I felt the greatest affinity and connection, the people I wanted to spend the most time with, and thought, *Wouldn't it be nice if someone was gay too?*

A few times, some of them might do something generically gay, and I would think, are they? Maybe? I'd go for days trying to piece together all the signs that maybe, just maybe, one of them might be like me too. Wishing it was true so I wouldn't be alone anymore.

By that time, I had learned enough that if I dared get too close, I would be chided or corrected in one form or another. This juxtaposition between my external and inner worlds continued to build and felt more obtuse than ever.

The loving and tender feelings I felt became experiences of pain, even shame, rather than the joy they ought to have elicited. The loneliness of holding onto and keeping all of it to myself seemed insurmountable. Not only my physical attractions but the loving connections I couldn't dare express for fear of being abandoned altogether.

The pain seemed so unbearable. It was the first time I seriously started not wanting to wake up in the mornings. To no longer live in a world where I couldn't envision a future for someone like me. How could love be such a painful thing?

To numb the bourgeoning pain, and due to the advent of the internet, which was still in its relative infancy in 1999, I started to explore more online about what gay meant and how to find other gay men like me.

I snuck into adult sites like Gay.com, where I secretly chatted with other men. Like Grindr, it was a place where most people went to find hookups. There weren't many resources at the time to help young people find their way.

I was fifteen, going on sixteen. Nonetheless, I began conversing with others like me, wanting to learn more and explore my sexuality further. At that point, I even dared on my family's landline phone to call someone and talk to them when no one was home. Even picking up the phone and dialing someone was so terrifying to me. Once I heard a voice on the other end, I suddenly felt a huge surge of relief, only to be cut short by hearing my parents' arrival home.

The gay men I met online at that time were also mostly hiding. It was still taboo to be gay, so finding others in our small town was difficult. Everyone I interacted with seemed to carry this weight of shame around who they were. Given my age, it's not like a lot of other teens were exploring the interwebs. I'd talk to people but wouldn't act.

At one point, comically, my dad discovered *someone* in our family was going to the website gay.com. Unbeknownst to me, the cookies on our family computer had logged the sites I had visited. My dad asked both Sarah and me about it.

"Kids, I see someone has been visiting gay.com on our computer. Have either of you been to this site?" he asked.

I immediately responded, even before he could finish, "Of course, it wasn't me, Dad! It was probably Sarah! You know, girls get into that these days," certain my answer had satisfied his questions.

Meanwhile, my younger sister just stood there, stunned, not even knowing what gay even was.

If the immediate world around me wasn't in some shape or form colliding with my reality, the broader culture of America was also going through a transformation. Emerging in popular songs, shows, and the national conversation was a more positive representation of queer life. While still taboo, I began to better understand, or so I thought, what gay meant.

I'd stay up late in my room, secretly watching a midnight show on our local PBS channel featuring news stories produced by the regional LGBTI community. The mere fact there was a show in the town just thirty minutes away engrossed me. I wasn't alone? As shows like *Will and Grace*, *Ellen*, and others started to appear on TV, the conversation and subsequent national discourse became more open. It also created conversations in small towns like mine, making it all the more present in my life.

Yet I remained terrified and lonely. I didn't feel the characters or stories represented someone like me. Instead, they were representations of stories far and away from the life I had known. With the greater visibility of being gay, the part of myself I was avoiding became even harder to hide from.

That summer, though, on *MTV's Real World New Orleans*, I finally saw someone I felt was like me on TV (Johnston 2000). Danny Roberts came onto the show as the third-ever *out* cast member in the series' history. I immediately fell in love with him.

He was a handsome young man with a slight Southern drawl who hailed from Georgia. He had just barely come out himself and, through his presence on the show and everyday life, encountered many realities faced by other gay men. In particular, the struggles of living in a homophobic world and navigating relationships with family and friends.

Almost religiously, I watched the show, following Danny's evolving storyline as it unfolded over that season. He navigated some painful and awkward moments with his cast mates, making coming out in the world even more possible for someone like me. I felt a little less alone then in that small country town in Northern Colorado.

Somehow, it gave me hope. Maybe I'd meet someone like Danny someday. I dreamed of escaping to a bigger city like Boulder,

Denver, Seattle, or San Francisco, where I would finally find others like him and like me.

That summer, my parents sat my sister and me down to share that we would be moving. My mom had gotten a job as dean of students in Spokane, Washington, at the prestigious Gonzaga University. It was a private catholic school known around the country for its Cinderella basketball team, which had beaten all the odds to make it to the NCAA tournament the previous year.

I'd never heard of it. It was a phenomenal opportunity for her, yet I was devastated.

I was just becoming more liked by my peers, getting by in school, and even being scouted for college soccer teams. I thought I'd finally made it, and now I had to leave after all I had overcome. Despite dreaming of other worlds, the idea of moving terrified me. However, as a family, we all supported this incredible opportunity with her job.

By the end of the school year, we started packing our belongings and saying our goodbyes to our friends and extended family.

My high school soccer coach unexpectedly stopped by while we were packing boxes to wish us his best. He shared how he had hoped to make me team captain the following year. To my younger self, this was the highest honor.

We had a goodbye party with my original soccer team, their families, and of course, Greg. There was cake and a few parting gifts. Standing up in front of the whole team, I gave a tearful goodbye speech about how much they had all meant to me.

"I love each and every one of you. You were my best friends and made me a better person. You are the closest people to me, and I want the best for you all." It was difficult to imagine anything better in whatever might come next.

On my last day, I planned to go to lunch with a close friend from school to say my goodbyes as I had done during the previous weeks with other friends. We met at the door to the restaurant, and as she and I walked in, I was surprised by the presence of about twelve of my closest friends from school. I started to bawl. I never expected to be surprised in such a way.

So much of my self-doubt and fear of my own shadow made it impossible for me to believe how much my friends had, all along, truly cared for me. Only realizing it at that moment made leaving that much harder.

We took one last look back at our house. Then we set off in a moving van toward Spokane, Washington, about a thousand miles northwest of Colorado, where we would begin our new lives.

As we rolled into town, the second largest city in Washington State, a place we had never been to before, I first noticed its industrial feel. Several large, abandoned grain silos and dated train tracks were at the city center. In the city's prime, it had been a major hauling center for grain, steel, and aluminum shipped throughout the country. Now the same buildings were just abandoned and covered in dirt. The highway we came in on created an overpass that stretched from one end of the city to the other with graffiti-covered walls as long as we could see.

For this small-town kid, it was an intimidating sight.

We lived on the Gonzaga campus during our first year in Spokane because we were selling our house back in Colorado. We found a three-bedroom home just off the main road leading to the university. Several college students had previously rented it. The walls were very thin, the appliances were old, and the beds supplied to us by the university still had plastic wrapped around them.

Several people experiencing homelessness walked the nearby streets and often slept under the overpasses. We encountered several as they dug through the community dumpsters behind our new home at all hours of the day. Every time we let out our family dog, we first had to ensure there wasn't anyone sleeping on our stoop. It felt big and scary.

In an effort to continue building out my budding soccer career, one of the first things my family did when we arrived that summer was to look for another competitive traveling soccer team I could join.

I needed to continue playing soccer as college scouts knocked on our door, figuratively speaking. We found a team, and I attended one of their practices as an informal tryout. I fit in well with the players and was on par, if not better than most. In that first scrimmage during practice, I scored several goals, impressing the coach. I was invited to join the team and started regularly attending practices and games.

However, I soon learned my new coach had a militant style and prioritized the kids already on the team, given the pivotal time for college recruitment. Despite being one of the better players, the coach told me I would sit on the bench.

Having started on most of my teams, sitting on the bench for most of the game was difficult. Though, at the same time, being a team player, I accepted this role. However, I noticed the coach wasn't putting me in the game beyond not starting. The coach seemed to have developed some sort of antagonism toward me.

At one game, our team had just scored a goal, and I started cheering from the sidelines in excitement for the team, but the coach scolded me for being too excited. After that, I fell back into my shell. My enthusiasm and cheering from the bench had angered him for some reason. There was something about me he couldn't quite figure out but sensed he didn't like.

The following weekend we had a game four hours away in Seattle, where we needed to spend the night. My parents couldn't go, so the coach agreed to take me with another kid in a van he had borrowed from the parents.

On that day, I started hanging out with my new teammates and connecting with them more meaningfully. We had gone on an unplanned hike in the nearby woods and then kicked a soccer ball around in the hotel parking lot—just like I had done in my backyard with Greg and my old soccer teammates. We all had dinner and then retired to our hotel rooms to prepare for the next day's game.

I shared a room with the coach and the other kid on my team we had driven with. Since I was new, they each had one of the beds while I slept on the ground with a towel and a pillow. After turning in for the night, our coach left, and we quickly fell asleep.

A few hours later, we were awoken by our coach stumbling into our room and turning on the lights. He was heavily inebriated. He started loudly bragging about having had sex with a random woman in the back of the van we had driven.

He made lots of noise as he moved throughout the room. I was terrified and tried to pretend I was still asleep.

He stumbled over to where I was lying at the far end of the room, hovering over me. Then he suddenly lurched down on top of me, holding his body just above mine and leaning no more than six inches above the back of my head. He started to shout at me at the top of his lungs.

"You little faggot! You are a pussy. You are scared of me, aren't you? You worthless piece of shit. Fagggoooooooottt! You Faggot!" He then angrily punched the ground just next to my face. And then got up and fell onto the bed next to us, I presume passing out.

I didn't move, trying not to wince. I just lay there in silence and utter shock. I didn't cry. I was sixteen. I had no idea what I had done or why I received such abuse. But it was terrifying.

After all the subtle and not-so-subtle times I had been bullied in one way or another up until that point, his words surged across my mind every other time I felt so unsafe.

The next day the team played our game, drove home, and spoke nothing of the night before. I went to a few more practices before finally telling my beloved father, the coach, about what had happened.

With surgical precision, I detailed to him how my coach had drunkenly come into the room, bragging about hooking up with a random woman in the van and accosted me, claiming I didn't like him. I made no mention of being called faggot.

My dad comforted me and told me he was sorry I had to experience that and then told me it was no problem if I quit the team. I then withdrew from the team with his full support. I had yet to finish a summer in Spokane or even start school, but I had already joined and left a soccer team.

After all the joy I had experienced with my previous club team and all I had anticipated going on to achieve by possibly playing soccer in college someday, not being able to play was a big blow to my sense of self. I didn't know if I would ever play soccer again. And further, I wasn't sure what the rest of my time in my new city of Spokane would turn into.

If I couldn't play soccer, how would I avoid the thing I was running away from? It certainly made me even more apprehensive about starting school in just a few weeks.

NEW SCHOOL, NEW REALITY

I found myself sitting just outside the roof door of my new school on the first day, sobbing into my lunch. I felt so out of place.

Making new friends, trying to understand my new environment, and not knowing what was next overwhelmed me. I was the small-town kid suddenly going to school in this big city. Nothing felt familiar. I was nervous and unsure of how to navigate this new chapter in my life.

Our new school, Lewis and Clark High School, was being renovated. For my junior year, a downtown office building was converted into temporary classrooms a few blocks away.

As the first few weeks passed, I made a few friends and started easing into my classes.

I noticed slight differences between my new school and my previous one. Coming from a conventionally small town, everyone seemed so well-dressed. Despite being in eastern Washington, there was a greater diversity, for which I was grateful. There was even a gay-straight alliance.

While it was only a small group, the fact there was a gay-straight alliance both terrified me and gave me a strange comfort. It satiated those dueling parts of me that I both ached for and silently feared. But that it was even there was inspiring.

The group leader was a skinny, seemingly nerdy kid with blue hair. His confidence in being himself subconsciously spoke to me as a closeted kid that the school was a safe place. Unfortunately, we never became friends, but I will always admire him.

Late that fall, I joined an indoor soccer league with a few kids I met from the club team the previous summer who also played on the high school team.

The team's energy and tone were far friendlier and more welcoming. No coach was telling us what to do. We were just a bunch of ragtag high school kids who loved playing the sport. I showcased my skills and gained acceptance from my peers. I also learned to stand firm in myself in my new environment.

During one game where we were at a tie with just a few minutes on the clock, I was on the field, and the star forward of the team yelled at me from the bench.

"Ryan, quick, let me in so I can score a winning goal!"

I was immediately frustrated he thought that, of all the players, I needed to leave so he could score. Was he underestimating me like everyone else had throughout my life? It rubbed me the wrong way, but as the new kid, I decided to acquiesce to his demand.

As I started heading to the bench, I unexpectedly got the ball. In my frustration, I squared up, and scored a goal in the upper corner, winning the game. I sharply glanced up at him, and he became quiet. I felt a strange sense of power at that moment.

While on this team, I met a new friend, Ben, who was also in my advanced placement classes. He was one of the most intelligent kids in every class, and he knew it. He would chime in answers to questions before teachers even had time to ask. He was cocky yet had a charm about him that everyone loved. He loved soccer too, just like me. We had become fast friends, and playing on the indoor soccer team that winter solidified our friendship.

We hung out more. He invited me in the dead of winter to pick-up soccer games after school he and others would organize under the overpass, which passed right in front of our high school. I would put on a thousand layers of clothes, and we would kick a ball around for a few hours using abandoned tires as our goals. It was typically dark that time of year when we would play in the bitter cold, sometimes until midnight.

I had found my people.

Tryouts for the high school team took place that January, and I quickly made the varsity squad. Ben, I, and other teammates would start spending time together after school at practices and even outside of training.

At school, I became more involved than ever as a student leader in my community. With my mom's encouragement and in the spirit of my grandparents, I became the president of our student volunteer club, Key Club, where I helped organize service events for my peers. Volunteering was something I never would have done at my previous school but had always yearned to do.

By the end of the year, I felt like I fit in.

I had gone from rising in popularity back in Greeley to finally finding my stride and comfort in a new school setting. I was starting to feel a joy I hadn't really felt before. I didn't have the baggage of carrying the years of rumors about my sexuality that had once plagued me. I was freer to be me.

Given that it was our junior and senior year of high school, mixed with the diversity of our school, my sexual identity wasn't as big of a deal to most folks. Most people were just trying to figure out where they would go to college in the next few years. So, I didn't have to worry as much about it.

That summer, we moved from our on-campus house to our new home in the hills just outside Spokane. Our house back in Colorado had finally sold. Moving out of the on-campus house to our beautiful and spacious home made our move to Spokane feel more permanent. Our family got to let down our hair and spread out.

We had our family dining room table back, where we started to cook meals again and spend night after night together as a family. It was often the case that after a long day of work, my dad would sit on one end of a rectangular table after making us dinner, and my mom would sit opposite him. My sister and I would sit on either side while we all laughed and carried on about our days. It became a special time in which we would bond during that final year when we all lived together under the same roof.

I'd spend part of the summer with friends I had made at school. I spent most days with Ben.

It felt like we were always doing something together—going to the movies, playing soccer, and hanging out at friends' houses. We'd film ourselves doing soccer tricks like in the famous Nike soccer commercials. He was one of the first friends in my life who always invited me wherever he went. I started to feel less alone in the world because I had someone who seemed to always want to be around me like I wanted to be around them. I wasn't the monster to him. I had always felt such warmth around him.

Our high school finally completed its renovation, so we spent our senior year going to school in this spectacularly beautiful building in the heart of downtown Spokane. There wasn't an established ranking system among my peers at school. Everyone seemed to get along, especially those in my senior class, no matter what social group they belonged to.

This was especially true when we all woke up to the attacks on the Twin Towers in New York City on 9/11. It was a tragedy felt all around the world, even in Spokane. Yet the tragic events brought many of us together and shaped how we brought ourselves into the world during our last year in high school. It made us realize the finite nature of our lives and the temporary reality of it all. It also reminded me of the other tragedies in the past few years that had held a similar weight.

During that year, I joined our student council, where the high school soccer coach, Kenny, was also in charge. He reminded me of my old coach, Greg, and was someone I really came to care for. I also continued serving as the president of the Key Club. Again, I found new ways of building excitement around my peers' sense of social responsibility, something my grandmother was very proud of.

We organized a day of service cleaning up the neighborhood around our school. We had a friendly competition with our rival, Ferris High School, to see who could collect the most amount of canned food for our local food bank—which we won. We even had a drive to collect coats for kids, sponsored by the local news station, which got us a feature story on their nightly broadcast. Of the dozen or so high schools in Spokane, we had collected the most winter coats for those in need.

We became one of the most popular clubs in the school. We were even awarded a spoof award, a can of spam, at an all-school pep rally to honor all we had done to contribute to our local community. It was something I was incredibly proud of. School felt like a place of belonging to me in many ways—finally.

My sexuality wasn't something people asked about. I never was called faggot by my peers. I just got to exist. For what felt like the first time in my life, I had a group of friends I got to hang out with, just to hang out with.

Of course, this was primarily because of Ben. Still, it felt so surreal to have a group of people who actually wanted to hang out with me without needing a base reason or organized activity to come around. It felt, for all intents and purposes, *normal*, and I was indeed a part of something. It was all I had ever wanted when I was lonely, hiding from my own shadow in my room back in Greeley. It was also something I gave myself permission to finally feel and accept.

Over the course of that year, the closeness I felt with Ben only grew. It was a friendship I had never known before. We did everything together.

One day at six in the morning, I woke up with him to go play basketball at our high school before school started in the dead of winter.

He would always come to my place, and we would play ping pong, watch movies, and rewatch old soccer matches. He spent the night several times, including when we stayed up late watching the world cup in South Korea and Japan. He became an intensely close part of my life, and I considered him my best friend.

As happy as I was to have finally felt like I had a community, it's almost as if I dreaded my own happiness. I felt such joy and acceptance from my peers and gratitude for my deep connection with Ben. Yet that joy also felt extremely painful.

It was the same sentiments I had fought against before but grew with the authentic experiences of joy I was feeling.

My friendship with Ben became particularly difficult to manage. The reality was he didn't know I was gay.

I started to feel so terrified of losing him. I had wanted a connection like I had with Ben forever, yet I couldn't fully trust it. All I wanted to do was to let down all my walls and let him in. To tell him exactly who I was in hopes he wouldn't push me away.

The unbearable idea of losing him left me feeling empty inside when I was alone with my thoughts. If I wanted these true friendships, if I could trust Ben was the best friend I thought he was, wouldn't I ultimately have to disclose my honest truths?

Such thoughts led to more existential questions. Despite my greater happiness, the looming dread of being discovered made all of it feel fraudulent and temporary. When I let my mind ruminate for too long, I would again wish for death to wash over me. To not wake from my slumber.

Soon, Thanksgiving was approaching, and I invited Ben to join my family for the celebration. He accepted the invitation, and I was elated to celebrate the holiday with him and my family—something that had become one of my favorite traditions over the years.

However, Ben couldn't come at the last minute for whatever reason. I still don't know why, but this broke my heart. I became distraught. Not only at him not being there but the suffering I was enduring in hiding who I was. His absence sparked a spiral of doom within me, where all the questions I would constantly ask myself overwhelmed me.

I feared maybe he started to become suspicious of me and no longer liked me. My fear of being abandoned for who I was began to peak. Would I experience this loneliness forever? Would I ever be loved for who I am? The cyclical questions just reeled and reeled in my head.

My mom and I were alone the day after, sitting at our family dining room table. As my mom and I talked, it was apparent to her something was off.

"Yesterday's Thanksgiving was great. Wasn't it?" she remarked.

"Yup."

"Didn't you like that casserole?"

"Yup."

"Didn't you say your friend Ben would join us? Whatever happened to him?"

"Oh, I guess he just got caught up with his own family. I don't really know." Trying to deter further questioning.

My eyes welled up with tears.

She saw the gloom in my eyes and wanted to understand what was wrong.

She kept prodding. "It's completely understandable that someone might not make it. So why is it upsetting you so much? What's wrong, Ryan?"

No longer able to contain the pain bursting within me and feeling the weight of it all raining down on me, I finally sobbed back, "I'm gay." Then, I started to sob uncontrollably, apologizing to her repeatedly.

"I can't help it. I'm sorry! I don't want to bring shame to you and our family, but I'm just so sad. I'm so sorry!"

Caught off guard, my mom hadn't expected I would tell her I was gay. As I sobbed to her over those thirty minutes, she immediately did everything within her power to soothe and comfort me in the best ways she knew how.

I began to tell her the story of having hidden from her and everyone for years. Her immediate response was to both listen and give whatever advice she could as her worry for my safety also set in.

"Don't let anyone hurt you."

"Please protect yourself if you decide to have sex."

"Ultimately, please know how very much I love you."

I'd like to think while I had years to turn over and better understand that I was gay and what it meant to me, she was just learning a whole new conception of who she once understood me to be. Her understanding of our past experiences and the future she had once dreamt of for my life started to disentangle and reconfigure. It was only the beginning of her journey.

Above all, my mom was an immovable rock who offered me the space and comfort to share with her what I had hidden from the world. Immediately, the profound pressures and immense pain of feeling so outside and different began dissipating.

Even in that fleeting moment, I felt such a sigh of relief. All my tears, snot, and ugly cries let out years of stress and loneliness that are hard to describe fully. I was finally able to cry again.

I pulled myself together, and we continued to talk. At the end of our conversation, she asked if it would be okay to share this information with my dad.

My immediate response was no. I still had this strange shame and fear around my dad, my hero, finding out and thinking he had done something wrong. I wasn't yet ready to face what I believed would be *hurt* that he might endure because of what I was.

Intuitively, I knew he would be just fine. But I wasn't ready to give up wanting to be the *good* son he could be proud of. I was also so overwhelmed. I had no plan. No pathway forward. No understanding of what I was supposed to do next or how to do it.

So much of what came out of me at that moment was not hopeful or forward-looking. It was the opposite. It was a reluctance, an acquiescence to what was the inevitable.

That following week my mom and I began the process of rediscovering each other.

My mom brought me home several resources from a colleague on homosexuality, the gay community, and other articles she thought might be helpful. This would turn out to be an incredible spark for me.

I started to devour them. Reading about lesbian, gay, bisexual, transgender, and intersex people (LGBTI) throughout history, movements led by advocates around the country, and the latest research on human sexuality, gender, and more. Did you know that Michelangelo and Joan of Arc were gay?

I remember one article highlighting the history of the word faggot. It was the word used for the sticks that would make up the bonfires used to burn alive heretics back in the dark ages, particularly those accused of having dark powers like witches.

These individuals were often accused of being witches simply because they were different or fell outside of the norms of society, particularly as they pertained to gender and sexuality. "You are a woman and don't want to take a husband? How dare you! You must be a witch!" The absurdity.

Even though the word was so offensive, I had never understood its root meaning. When I learned what it meant, memories of the taunting I previously faced felt even more guttural. *They wanted to burn me alive? They wanted me dead?* I thought.

These resources ignited my ceaseless passion for unearthing the greater truths about human gender and sexual diversity. There was so much I had never known, but such knowledge started to provide me with the comfort I desperately needed. That a whole history of people like me was out of sight and away from places where I might know where to have looked. I hadn't actually been alone—like, the whole time?

There were others just like me who had experienced the sorrows I had only known up until that moment, but who could relate to me? Heroes? People who had changed history? Who contributed to their communities? Who were leaders? Why had I never known?

That Christmas, my grandparents visited, and we spent quality time with them for the holiday. At one moment, I was sitting in our study on the computer and had been down. Even though I had started to come out, I still had a long way to go to find peace within myself. My grandmother noticed and asked, "What's wrong? I notice you are quiet?" I couldn't muster the courage to tell her. But the fact that she noticed and asked meant the world to me.

It would be the last time I saw her. She would pass away later that spring. She had given all she could to the world but left such beauty and grace behind. The lessons she had imparted to me I was forever grateful for. Despite her physical absence, I've felt her spirit with me ever since, guiding me along my journey. As she was in real life, so too in her death, she was my guardian angel.

I continued to hang out with Ben daily and experienced our friendship more profoundly and meaningfully. I spent that New Year with him and our mutual friends on a hill in the frigid cold, seeing our breath in the air as we overlooked our city and rang in the year ahead. I felt so at peace. I had found a friendship that meant everything to me. While I still hadn't come out to Ben, my feelings of safety and comfort were the highest they had ever been.

Later that year, our soccer team would win our division and play in the State Championship game. While we ultimately lost to the fourth-ranked team in the nation, it was an achievement I had dreamt of since watching my dad win the state championships with his girls' basketball teams back in Colorado. We ranked twelfth in the nation, and three players, along with our coach, were named to the All-State team, including me.

I ended my senior year on a high. I had a great group of friends and felt loved by my classmates and teachers. I received numerous awards for my commitment to community service and all I achieved during my short time there. Soon, we'd all part ways as we entered a new phase of our lives. University.

That summer, Ben's mom stopped by my house to give me a gift from him as he had already moved away for college—at least one she claimed was from him. She expressed gratitude for the friendship between him and me and how much I had meant to him. Words I know he couldn't fully articulate, but a sentiment I knew only a mother's love would be able to recognize and name. Inside the bag was a framed photo of him and me. It meant the world to me and is a photo I still cherish.

While I certainly was sad about having to part ways with Ben because everyone was going off in a thousand directions at the time, I didn't anticipate nor expect things to be too different between us, other than him living far away.

I was already excited and nervous about my college experience at Gonzaga in the fall. But as many of my friendships did during that time of great transition, our friendship faded into the background. I am forever grateful. Our friendship is a time I will always fondly look back upon. He's the reason I came out.

Coming out to my mom was a huge step in my life. With the release of all that silent suffering, I started feeling even more comfortable in my own skin.

I've learned over the years that coming out is not just one step. It's a lifetime of having to share with the world your innermost self. Sometimes, it is made more difficult, depending on those encounters. And there are other moments where one has to come out to themselves to realize, even years later, that there is still so much to unlearn from what one had been taught to believe about themselves.

In preparing to go off to college, I still had a lot to work through to unpack and better understand the internal battle of deeply wanting the world to see me for me without a clear pathway. I still knew very few queer people, and there were no immediate examples around me of where I was supposed to go or what I was supposed to do now that I had shed an old skin.

I still had a long way to go to discover myself. What would be next for me?

ACT TWO

GATES

Hate is a learned behavior; we can unlearn that behavior. We can live our lives in love if we make that choice.
—JUDY SHEPARD

I always look at the optimistic side of life, but I am realistic enough to know that life is a complex matter.
—WALT DISNEY

If you are not personally free to be yourself in that most important of all human activities—the expression of love—then life itself loses its meaning.
—HARVEY MILK

A GATE OPENS

With a whole world before me, I had the chance to discover new horizons and pass through new gates of life that would forever nudge me toward the person I was meant to be and, indeed, who I've always been.

While high school was certainly a time of growth, and I was sad to say goodbye to friends like Ben, I was also grateful to celebrate with those friends who had been there all along.

Just before I started college, our family and the Stills and Samars took a vacation to Puerto Vallarta, Mexico, in honor of my graduation. It was one of my first international trips ever. We got a penthouse suite overlooking the Pacific Ocean with enough space for each family. It was one of the best weeks of my life.

We spent days on the beach, went on a catamaran where we swam with tropical fish, and ate shish kabobs in a local village. We toured the town, stopping at a few restaurants to enjoy the local cuisine. Being reunited with childhood friends with whom I had felt such authentic joy was so special. I hadn't told anyone I was gay just yet but enjoyed spending quality time with friends who wouldn't have cared anyway.

In the evenings, Sarah, Melissa, Amy, Cait, and I strolled along the beach, collecting shells and dried-up starfish. We'd gaze at the stars and talk about our lives. Most importantly, we'd laugh hysterically. Typically, my sister would spark most of the jokes, something she picked up a knack for from our grandfather. As we had experienced since childhood, we were deeply connected and continued the explorations that started years prior on the pond behind our houses.

One evening, Melissa and I decided to sleep outside on the lounge chairs of our deck. It was a clear sky where you could see all the stars. We stayed up late into the evening, chatting nonstop. The temperature was a breezy seventy-five degrees, and you could smell the ocean air as we fell asleep in the bright moonlight.

That trip was one for the books. I relished simply existing and being alongside my chosen family, the emotional place I always returned to whenever I felt at odds with the world.

That fall, I started at Gonzaga University, where my mom worked and where we lived when we first moved. I was drawn to its purpose-driven focus to educate the whole person and inspired by the messages of humanity, justice, and leading a purpose-driven life espoused by the then president, Jesuit Father Spitzer. It aligned with the values exemplified by my grandparents throughout their lives and instilled within me by my parents.

Having my mom on campus as dean of students was an amazing feeling. She was a deeply loved administrator, and many students appreciated how she brought her whole self into the world.

The campus was straight out of a postcard. It had sprawling green spaces and beautiful buildings spread out across the quad. The administration building looked like the streets of some English city covered in green vines and copper roofs.

As the school year was about to start, I joined a preorientation program called Reality Camp to meet my fellow first-year students.

Approximately twenty incoming students came together for a week, sleeping in the basement of a church and conducting various acts of service in the broader Spokane community.

I couldn't have thought of a better way to jump-start the social justice mindset that would stay with me for the rest of my life. At night we offered peanut butter and jelly sandwiches to people experiencing homelessness, cleaned a battered women's shelter, spent a day getting to know individuals with physical and intellectual disabilities, cleaned up a neighborhood, spent time at an elderly home, and spoke with delinquent youth—all within a week and under the spiritual guidance of service to others.

On the last day, they led us on a scavenger hunt throughout Spokane Riverside Park, tasked with finding clues in search of the *meaning of life*. Once we got to the final clue, our guides directed us toward a fifteen-foot-tall statue and told us to climb to the top, where we would find the secret.

When we got to the top, we were supposed to read the engraving silently. The engraving read, "Transcend the Bullshit." At the time, we all laughed coyly at the seemingly silly message. I would only learn the power behind its profound meaning later at Gonzaga.

As freshmen in college, we entered an uncharted aspect of our lives. A few of us elected to live on campus in a living-learning community dedicated to abstaining from drugs and alcohol. I soon found a community of friends eager to create new adventures that didn't require always partying.

I lived in a suite with five other future campus leaders. It was quite the eclectic mix of individuals who eventually led or were part of clubs and student programs like the Kennel Club, the ROTC, The Knights and Setons, College Republicans, and our Black Student Union. Yet it worked! We had several amazing dorm mates in the suite next to us and found friends on the boy's, girls', and engineering floors just below ours.

Living alongside one another as you do when you are thrown into a new life-changing experience far and away from everything you had ever known brought us all together. Everyone quickly became close friends. We each came from distinct backgrounds that colored and shaped who we were at that moment. They even elected me president of our hall council—something my mom and my dad had done in their college years. A few years later, my sister would also become the hall council president of the same dorm.

While we were still getting to know people, I made a few activity friends, including a guy named James, with whom I would regularly play racquetball. He was the cute guy on the first floor of my building I happened to notice. Then we started to connect and eventually became friends. It was the start of what would become a long friendship throughout college. But we will get to that.

With the fresh start of college, I progressively opened up to my new friends about my sexuality. I wasn't yet at the point of pronouncing it to the whole world, but I found strength grew with each person I came out to. At the same time, it was something I was no longer hiding.

Initially, I felt a very strong sense of acceptance from everyone. There were very few out individuals on our campus. To come out was still a big deal.

As those first few months pressed on, my dorm mates and I formed quite a powerful bond. On my birthday, they surprised me with a cake in my favorite park in Spokane, Manito, and we rented a fancy room at The Davenport Hotel downtown, where we continued our celebrations.

In such a short time, especially being my first foray into living my life more honestly as an out gay man, I was grateful to find such a close group of new friends. I felt like I had finally arrived at something I'd been waiting for forever.

Though my journey in living openly was just beginning.

In my classes, I had the chance to connect with peers from across the wider Gonzaga community. Courses ranging from philosophy, critical thinking, religion, sociology, and literature, offered me thought-provoking paradigms with which to view the world. As a part of a Jesuit education, students explored topics of existential purpose and meaning about the seemingly mundane and trivial pursuits within life—all toward educating the whole person.

The Jesuits are also known for their social justice mantras and align their values to Catholic teachings that emphasize service to others and our interconnected ways of being—a divine and undeniable existential purpose within everyone, everywhere—that we somehow connect to.

We began conversing about our existential realities, exploring the consequences of our individual and collective actions and their impact within the wider world. What did it mean to be a giving and loving person? What truly was *social justice*? What was our responsibility to one another as human beings?

Until then, my consciousness of the wider world had been limited to my immediate surroundings. Mostly about what was happening at school among my peers. Rarely were there discussions or debates about one's purpose and meaning in this world. Let alone LGBTI rights.

In my desire to be more involved in the campus community and to meet others like me, I attended a meeting of the gay-straight alliance on campus, HERO or Helping Educate Regarding Orientation.

It formed initially as a private group the Jesuits helped to organize and was meant to assist those struggling to overcome their homosexual desires through the power of prayer to cure them of their sins. However, due to some rabble-rousing students years before my time, the club eventually transitioned to a gay-straight alliance, more affirming students' gender and sexual identities. Something pretty powerful for a private Catholic school in the late nineties. They couldn't *advocate* but rather could *educate*.

When I went to my first meeting, it was hidden away in the back of our student union. I entered the room, and only about five people were there. Most were sullen and shy.

It was a low-energy space with some sharing of personal updates on small activities they were organizing. The group had a hushed tone. I got the sense being gay was still somewhat shameful and meant to be kept quiet, even to those in the group.

A part of me was glad to be there, but I didn't feel as much of an affinity with those in the club. They were good people, but we held different interests. My outgoing, bubbly personality contrasted with their own.

I was still evolving as well. I barely interacted with the gay community until then and still had so much self-doubt and internalized homophobia I needed to work through. I still held many stereotypes about being gay, ones I adopted in my youth. I didn't want to be like "those people over there."

I was afraid to come off as too feminine or to express myself and my thoughts that might stand out or draw too much attention. I was even afraid to be near children since people labeled gays as pedophiles. Those middle school bullies trained me well. I knew somewhat about the overt sexual behaviors people described as perverse. I learned a little about HIV/AIDS. I was even still fearful of my own sexual desires, not knowing what I truly wanted.

There was no composite of what kind of life I could live. I didn't expect much, nor did I put a lot of forethought into who I wanted to be. Coming out was like restarting my life. I had never met a loving gay couple. I had never been to a gay bar. There wasn't another person who was also gay in my life that I considered a close friend—at least that I knew of. Nothing was set out before me.

I was also unaware of the broader cultural movements taking place or the homophobic backlash still facing LGBTI people throughout the country. I didn't know about the existing legal barriers that did nothing to prevent discrimination in housing, education, or employment based on sexual orientation. If you were gay and in the military under the "Don't Ask, Don't Tell" policy, you had to stay closeted. If they discovered you, you would receive a dishonorable discharge. In some states, being gay was still criminalized (Raghavan 2021).

Marriage wasn't even a thought or consideration as an institutional reality. The Defense of Marriage Act, or DOMA, still prescribed marriage solely between a man and a woman and was passed in many states. The president at the time, George Bush, had even actively campaigned to add a constitutional amendment to limit marriage to couples of the opposite sex (Stout 2004). So, as I dreamt of maybe meeting someone someday to quell my loneliness, I didn't even equate that it was still forbidden or legally obscure. There was no *how*. I just had to exist.

While I grew up in the Catholic tradition, I was not made aware of its negative beliefs toward individuals who were gay coming into college. Unlike today, homosexuality wasn't openly condemned from the pulpits of the churches I visited with my family.

Given the doctrine of the church to love and care for one another, I naively assumed I would be one of those individuals loved and cared for, especially as the university president and Jesuit priest had espoused in our opening day lectures. Instead, I would go on to learn of the church's teachings throughout my time in college, perspectives that I would argue are still obscure and antithetical to other church doctrines. But I digress.

As a result of my ongoing evolution, I still led somewhat of a double life. Away from my new friends and college classmates, I started to experiment more. I would meet up with guys to have some fun. In certain ways, it was liberating to experience these new aspects of myself I couldn't explore before.

Gay adult dating websites became a go-to place to meet up with other guys in the city. However, it wasn't as I expected. I had thought I would meet sage guides, people who might take me under their wings, individuals who would know what I had been through and empathize with the pain and suffering I once knew.

Instead, I began to feel commodified. It was all fun and adventurous at first, but I would walk away feeling as though the individuals I'd met only wanted one thing from me. And frankly, maybe I was doing the same. They didn't want to know my story, who I was, or anything I had aspired to. I began to learn about the community-wide hurdles yet to be overcome. There were still so many closeted individuals fighting their internal sense of shame too.

I met my first boyfriend after we met up through one of the websites. I felt connected to him based on our mutual passion for soccer. It was exciting to meet someone with whom I had something in common. He was beautiful. He also loved the music I loved. We sometimes cuddled in my car parked outside my old high school and listened to Coldplay.

While it was a nice feeling, dating itself was also unconventional and somewhat uninspired. Yet it was what you were supposed to do. Going out to dinner in public was still a scary thought. Society had yet to reach a point where my boyfriend and I could publicly hold hands without fear of harassment.

During that time, I also came out to my sister, then a junior in high school. I had been visiting home one evening for dinner, and she noticed I was in the study on the computer talking to someone on AOL chat—my boyfriend.

When she entered the room, I suddenly shifted as if I was talking to someone special. She asked, "Ohhhh, who is Shibydude1510?"—his AOL screen name.

Caught but no longer bound by the closet, I decided to tell her. "Sarah, I'm gay. This is the guy I'm dating."

Being my sister, my lifelong best friend, and someone who knew me better than just about anyone but also likely fumbling with the right words to respond, she blurted out, "I'll carry your child for you if you and your boyfriend need me to. I saw on TV how sometimes women carry their friend or family member's babies for them through invitro fertilization if they can't have their own children. Or at least, that's what Phoebe did for her brother and his wife on the TV show *Friends*."

"Wow, umm, thank you. We aren't that serious yet, and I'm still figuring myself out. But I appreciate it," I replied in shock.

It was the most beautiful and accepting thing she could say and was full of profound love and wisdom for where she was at in that moment of her life. She was the quickest to adapt to accepting that I was gay. I even asked her later that semester to go to the movies with my boyfriend to get to know him.

My explorations of this aspect of myself weren't like what all my heterosexual peers had been able to do when we were in middle school and junior high. Still drawing on some heteronormative paradigm, I had a boyfriend because that's what you were supposed to do when you liked someone. It was like going through the motions, in the same vein as I had dated my first girlfriend, Marie, back in fifth grade.

Starting to come out was more complex than I had imagined. There wasn't this flip of the switch when my inner world suddenly became my outer world. Instead, I started to reflect more deeply on my true purpose, who I was as a person, as a being roaming this great earth. Despite the excitement of starting a new school, making new friends, and even being well-liked by my peers, my doubts, fears, and hesitations did not necessarily subside.

It didn't help that after the initial joy of making new friends in my dorm, some of my peers, who at first had seemed so open, were, in their own subtle ways, not as accepting as I had thought. As time passed, I realized their acceptance of my sexuality was more complex and conditional.

They would sometimes dismiss or outright ignore the budding reality that I was gay. I was embraced, but not fully. We would hang out together, gossip, and spend time in one another's rooms. Yet when my sexuality came up, or I expressed myself in that way—say, liking a boy—it was ignored or not discussed. There became an unspoken conditionality to our interactions to not talk about that thing I was.

Once, I had just returned to my dorm with one of my new friends and remarked that I felt a guy we met that evening at a social gathering was pretty cute. She turned to me, put her hand on my shoulder, and in a soft, caring voice said, "But, Ryan, you're not really gay." I was befuddled and just left it at that. I wasn't yet used to the subtle ways people would accept me, but not all of me. Not wanting to make much of it, we continued our friendship.

Later, I was taking out the trash when suddenly I felt a wisp of air go by my head. A tennis ball bounced on the concrete in front of me. I turned around to see where it was coming from, and my College Republican roommate was standing there laughing with his buddy. I suddenly knew that it was no accident. They had thrown the tennis ball at me.

A part of my loneliness started to creep back in.

In a world where I wasn't fully embraced for who I was, I started questioning where I was supposed to go with my life now that I was out. I started to question what being gay really meant. It wasn't providing me with the happiness and joy I had assumed it would before coming out. What was love, and what might marriage look like for someone like me? Romantically, I didn't know what to do or where to start.

All I really wanted was to recreate the love between my parents I had witnessed throughout my life. I thought about my greatest states of happiness, my greatest memories of when I felt most safe, and the most authentic space I had known up until that point. Then, I started to think about our chosen family and closest friends, the Stills and Samars.

The caring way I felt about them was the most profound feeling I knew of what love and happiness ought to be. I could think of no other happier times in my life or where I felt most alive than when I was with them. All the bellyaching laughs and the sacred bond shared among our families. Isn't that what love should ultimately be?

I so profoundly ached to find that somehow, someway.

At the end of the fall semester, my parents decided to renew their vows on their twenty-fifth wedding anniversary to honor their love. For many, twenty-five years of marriage is a long journey—something worth celebrating.

My mom rented out one of the cherished homes owned by the university, the Bozarth Mansion. It was situated among a forest of pine trees just outside town and had over fifteen rooms, a massive great room, a large kitchen and dining room, a library, beautiful English Gardens, and more.

My parents invited family, friends, and special guests to bear witness to their vow renewal ceremony. As a representative of our SOS crew, Melissa would also be coming to celebrate with us.

Having struggled with fully understanding what it meant to be a gay man, to imagine a future where I fit in, and desperately wanting to have a future life that resembled the peace and warm-heartedness of my own family, I thought in anticipating her arrival, *What if I actually did marry Melissa?*

After all, does marriage necessitate a physical manifestation of some kind? Is love really all about sex, or can it be more than that? Could I be content marrying a woman but just not having physical relations with her? Even having some understanding—especially if we truly loved each other at the end of the day.

The younger, more naïve part of myself thought, well, of course. I should dedicate myself to Melissa. After all, our parents had always hinted this was inevitable. So, just like some of my other hair-brained youthful ideas, I decided to give Melissa a promise ring when she came and tell her I thought we should get married one day. We could be married and just not have sex, I thought. I'd rather be happy with her than be with a guy and not feel the same happiness I had already experienced with her and our SOS families. After all, she was one of my best friends in the whole world, and aren't you supposed to marry your best friend?

As the event grew nearer, I contemplated what I would say to her when she arrived. I had racing thoughts about everything I truly wanted to express. At the same time, because Melissa was my best friend, someone I wholeheartedly respected, it was of utmost importance to me to ensure she knew about my sexuality. I had to be honest with her. I wanted her to be equally as happy. I didn't want such a thing if she, too, didn't want it! I was, after all, a feminist, just like my mom.

For some reason, I thought Melissa would see what I had seen. It seemed so apparent.

We were so excited to be together when the guests arrived, including Melissa. My paternal grandma and my maternal grandfather were there. My aunts and uncles were there—so many people who had reminded me of what love was all about throughout my life.

After the commitment ceremony was over, at the reception dinner, we all had the chance to offer expressions of gratitude to my parents. It was truly an evening of love and celebration. My parents' love for each other inspired me. They both cried as they danced to their favorite John Denver song in front of everyone.

We spent that weekend at the Mansion. Melissa, my sister, and I had so much fun and laughed like we did when we were kids. We played games, sat by the fire, and watched the snow fall outside.

As we settled in for the evening, Melissa and I shared a room, each of us in our own twin bed with the bright moonlight filtering off the white snow outside. We chatted late into the evening like we always did. I kept thinking about what I wanted to say to her, with my whole plan in mind. But most importantly, I had to tell her I was gay.

I somehow ended up blurting out, "Melissa, I have something to tell you. I'm gay!"

I was so nervous about possibly losing her friendship I don't remember the exact conversation that ensued, what I said, or how I said it. But what I remember most was the warmth and profound intelligence she responded with—even at our tender ages.

"Ryan, I'm so happy for you. I hope you find a guy who makes you feel special and loved someday," she said.

It was a blur to me because I was caught off guard, expecting her to either hate me or go along with my plan. I didn't even get to tell her about the idea of us being together. Those were the only two options I presumed were possible. It was outside of my mental construct at the time that she would say what she said.

Of course, I immediately became embarrassed. I realized how ridiculous my idea had been on so many levels. To think it would work out. To even conjure up something like that. While my intent was undoubtedly beautiful, it was almost like a last-minute attempt to escape my reality.

However, I revel in its extreme awkwardness because of how transformative that tiny little gesture was. Within the blink of an eye, my entire personhood felt like it had changed.

I suddenly started to get what it meant to be gay in a way I hadn't contemplated before. To love another man. A guy. A dude. To love them. To truly, unmistakably love them. Like I loved and cared for Melissa and Amy, the whole SOS crew in that chosen family way? But in an even deeper, more complex way. Something I intuitively knew was possible, but until that moment had not given myself permission to feel or to even connect between all the different aching parts of my heart.

A certain set of conditions allowed me to hear this information I couldn't have imagined otherwise. My childhood best friend, someone I sincerely cared for, at my parents' twenty-fifty wedding anniversary, said it with the genuine love and tenderness a true friend ought to say. Because it was Melissa who had opened that gate, because it was about love, I heard it differently than I had considered it before.

She permitted me to imagine that possibility for myself and my life. As my friend and someone who cared for me, she saw me at that moment of vulnerability and recognized who I was capable of becoming. Something I couldn't see in myself.

I felt awake in a whole new way. My entire world changed thereafter. My dueling worlds started to come closer together.

But where would I go from there to figure it out?

A WORLD TOO PERFECT

Would I ever find my own Prince Charming?

While forever changed in thinking differently about myself after Melissa opened that gate for me, I had yet to put myself in an environment where I could fully live out loud as the person I was or now knew I could become. All that was about to change.

Coming off the fall semester of my freshman year, I decided to spend the spring interning at Walt Disney World.

I discovered their Walt Disney World College Program at my mother's suggestion and interviewed with a recruiter who had come to our campus that previous October on the off chance they might accept me. I even wore a special Mickey tie my dad had given me for the interview.

The program intrigued me because you worked at the parks full time while attending business courses, learning about the company, and earning college credits. I expected to have fun and learn a lot in this program, but I had no idea just how much I'd discover about myself and the power of finding an accepting community.

My new friends at Gonzaga had a send-off party for me. There were many tearful goodbyes for the close friendships we had already made in that short span of time. A part of me was really sad to leave all of them while I was also nervous about the opportunity ahead. My parents and sister were also sad to see me go so far away for so long. We were grateful my Aunt Karen lived in the area.

I packed a suitcase full of my belongings, shipped my desktop computer from my local post office, and hopped on a nine-hour flight across the country. My aunt picked me up from the airport and helped move me into the Chatham housing complex provided by the Disney Company for those on the program. She even stocked my fridge and pantry with a few weeks' worth of groceries to help me get by.

Thousands of us came from all over the world to work at the parks in various roles. We were greeters and hotel concierges, food and beverage staff, custodians, ride operators, and some even played world-famous Disney characters. We weren't just employees at a company but cast members performing on a stage and providing world-class customer services for our guests.

During the first week, they onboarded us, starting with the Disney Traditions class. It helped us gain an even deeper appreciation for the company, its history, and its world-class guest service experience. The ultimate aim of any cast member was to provide a top-notch once-in-a-lifetime experience for all who came to Disney. Some families saved for years to come to the parks just once in their entire life, and it was our job to give them the best experience possible.

Each program participant was assigned a particular area to work in for the duration of their eight-month internship. It felt like the sorting hat in Harry Potter. You weren't sure of your exact role until you arrived on the first day of your internship. I was overjoyed to learn I was assigned to serve as a world-famous skipper at the Jungle Cruise, something I had only dreamed of when we had visited Disneyland with our chosen family a few summers before.

The next day we started on-the-job training. I was issued the traditional khaki shirt and matching shorts, a Crocodile Dundee hat complete with a leopard print bandana around the center, and a Disneyworld name tag with a red ribbon that said Skipper in Training. About thirty of us started as skippers at the Jungle Cruise from my program. Little did I know that many of them would become lifelong friends.

I met my trainer, and we went through the routine tasks of learning my new role. We went over our rotations from loading to unloading to spieling and would shadow a fellow skipper for a day or two before giving it a go ourselves. We had to learn all the jokes and went through a series of tests, being closely observed by our trainers and then being given the mic on our own.

I was trepidatious at first. I would forget a joke, too nervous trying to avoid messing up. I was monotonous in my delivery. But, with time, I overcame my initial hesitations and started to get the hang of something I wasn't sure at first that I could do. It reminded me of when I was the Nutcracker in elementary. I loved being in front of an audience and making them laugh.

Soon, I was integrated into the regular shifts and would deliver twenty to thirty spiels daily while on an eight- to ten-hour rotation.

"Hello, folks, my name is Ryan, and I'll be your jungle cruise skipper today. I'll also be your alligator wrestler and, quite possibly, your swimming instructor. Welcome to today's cruise, where we'll be sailing across four of the world's most famous rivers," while gesturing with five fingers. I eventually got so good at it and had so much fun I started using an accent.

Like at Gonzaga, my most immediate colleagues became my closest friends. Through happenstance, and like the people you meet on a plane, we all ended up in the Walt Disney World College Program at that time and place and discovered in one another a vibrancy only found among fellow Jungle Cruise Skippers.

The recruiters tended to select individuals they had met along the way with great pizazz and energy to serve in that role and had clearly seen something in all of us that we would later discover in ourselves. Plus, something about making a fool out of yourself for days on end brings out a jovial side to life. My grandfather would have loved it.

We all became fast friends, spending days, nights, weekends, and holidays alongside each other, interacting with guests from around the world who came to the parks with a wide range of circumstances, personalities, and needs themselves. I often marveled at the diversity of people I got to interact with on a daily basis.

I quickly realized the program was full of other people who were gay too. Everywhere I went, I met someone else who was also gay. People were so open with their lives and expressed themselves in ways I hadn't experienced before.

Back home, I felt like I was the only gay in the village. Here you couldn't walk ten feet without running into someone who was. I went from feeling like I had something on my nose and everyone was looking at me to being just one of the crowds, and I reveled in it. It was an entirely new normal.

Talking of cute guys, relationships, or even just expressing one's feelings and emotions more openly was an established reality. Many were already well out of the closet and living out loud in all they did. It was just a fact of life, which led many more to come out throughout the duration of my program. People could be themselves and exist to the point where it was just seen as another aspect of the great diversity existing throughout the parks.

We were everywhere you turned, some with larger-than-life personalities while others simply faded into the background. I was so normal, I was boring! I no longer stuck out as I seemed to do for as far back as I could remember.

It was the first time I was open about myself unapologetically while also existing in a place where I didn't have to constantly wonder if people would like me if they only knew who I really was. I was free in a way I had never been before, except maybe in early childhood when I didn't know better.

While there, I decided it was finally time to come out to my dad. So I wrote him a long letter about how much he had meant to me and how it had been difficult to come out to him because of my love and respect for him. I told him I didn't want to disappoint him or for him to think he wasn't the best possible father out there.

I gave the letter to my mom and asked her to give it to him and discuss it. Of course, as with any revelation, there was a deal of anxiety around finally telling him.

My fears soon subsided when I received a beautiful letter back from him.

"First, foremost, and always, I love you. Thank you for letting me into your world," he said. "I'm so sorry for all the pain you've endured and for the cold world I know you will face. But I'm always here for you."

He, too, had to reconceive a future for me. But his letter to me will forever remain engrained in my heart because of the beautiful acceptance he showed me. It gave me even more space to be me, which only helped enhance my time at Disney with the weight lifted.

At the Jungle Cruise alone, there were several other gay skippers. One of them was so full of pizazz and energy, Christopher. He completely inspired me with his outgoingness and his way of just being himself in every aspect of his personhood. Every single boat he took out returned in hysterics with how funny he had been. His aliveness was infectious and made individuals come out of their shells with how he could create a mastery of his role as skipper.

While there, I joined the company's version of a gay-straight alliance, their LGBTI employee resource group. There I met with a crisscross of people from throughout the company who were doing incredible things with their careers. From imagineers to corporate executives, movie and television producers, and others working in the parks like me, it was far more than a social club. It helped Disney to think through how it might reach untapped markets that LGBTI people made up.

It sparked in me a passion for diversity and inclusion and how such efforts might bring more equity to even more places like my home back in Spokane and at Gonzaga. I even was asked to serve in our Adventure Land area diversity council—all in my short time there as an intern.

After work, my fellow skippers would often hang out at a local restaurant, ironically jungle themed, and we found further merriment in one another's company. The playfulness of working at the Jungle Cruise spilled over into our relationships with one another. There was nonstop laughter and jokes all the time. Something about laughter just brings out a vulnerable state within a person.

Within a few short months, I felt like I had made lifelong friends and individuals who liked and cared for me, despite all my imperfections. Something about being able to joke around and let loose in a nontraditional manner allowed different sides of me to come out.

With such a cast of characters from all walks of life, gay and straight, men and women of all racial and ethnic backgrounds, and from throughout the world, I developed deep friendships with my colleagues. Friends who didn't judge me and were fully aware of who I was from the beginning. I didn't have to constantly second guess this time; if they only knew who I really was, would they still like me? It was such a profound experience of self-discovery.

The exaggeration of being a Walt Disney World cast member, especially a comedic Jungle Cruise Skipper, enabled me to be more carefree and energetic about life. Not only was it a part of the persona, but it was how many people felt getting to work in the happiest place on earth.

We relived aspects of our childhoods or the ones we never had. As a result, I could let go of some of those self-protective aspects of my personality that helped me survive middle school, like hiding parts of myself or keeping quiet about things that mattered most to me. For gosh sake, I could even say out loud that I thought someone was cute and not fear being called faggot for saying it.

While on the program, I dated a few people too. It was fun exploring this aspect of myself so openly, where my simple crushes and romances were just as real and nuanced to my peers as any of their heterosexual ones. Unlike back in Spokane, where there was still so much of a hushed, even shameful aspect of meeting people in our somewhat conservative town, on the program, I could meet people in real life whom I was actually attracted to, go up to them in a bar and strike up a conversation.

I even briefly had the chance to date a guy who played Prince Charming, Aladdin, and Prince Eric. He was some white boy from Wisconsin. It was a fleeting romance, maybe a month-long, but it was the first time I could date someone I was genuinely attracted to. I was so into him and felt like I tripped over myself whenever I spoke to him.

Outside of my personal journey, the program allowed me to connect more deeply with and open up to others from all over the world from an authentic space within me. While not everyone knew I was gay, including the countless teenage girls who would get on my boat and snap a photo every time I turned around or giggle at the most innocuous things I'd say, I got to meaningfully connect with thousands of guests.

There were so many little interactions with guests that made me so happy. Making people's experiences, bringing them a little hope and joy, especially cultivating core memories, inspired me every day I came to work. I developed a passion for seeing people smile or feeling moved in one way or another.

I learned how to interact with guests with disabilities, those from diverse backgrounds and cultures, those who didn't speak English, and others. I interacted daily with guests of all ages, from small children to the elderly.

I especially loved returning to my childhood and just being a kid again. It was all in the character of a Jungle Cruise Skipper—from small jokes with kids and pretending to have sword fights with pirates dressed as tiny children to enjoying the wonder in the eyes of the kiddos on my boat. To me, the ride offered a safe way, especially for children, to develop a sense of adventure in exploring the world around them while having the comfort of their parents along the way.

As guests waited in line, we played small games with the kids and interacted in ways that excited everyone for the ride. One little girl I realized didn't speak English, so I learned I could interact with her in different ways—motioning with my hands for her to step forward, then back, then forward again and back again before we both smiled and laughed as she realized I was messing with her, even without having to speak a word.

Outside of taking shifts on the ride, we also supported events like setting up parades or working crowd control for the evening fireworks. I always loved these moments because I would interact and play with many guests who lined up early to snag a good spot to watch their favorite character atop a parade float.

In one such instance, I met an incredibly polite young boy. He responded, yessir, to every single thing I said. I asked him to help with something, and he was extremely kind. He clearly was a military kid and just such a good little guy.

Remembering a time in my life when I was also a good little guy and did as my parents asked me to but was later bullied for it, I wanted to do something to make sure he knew how special he was and how important it was to value and honor the kindness he had shown.

I approached one of our area managers and asked for a *No Strings Attached* pass. Disney offered this to its cast members for those small moments of guest recovery where a kid lost a balloon or ice cream to assist them in getting a new one at no additional cost. They also offered these passes in rare instances to guests who had issues with a ride, such as a ride unexpectedly shutting down. It allowed them to go to the front of the line of another attraction.

I wrote him a No Strings Attached to go to the front of any five rides with him and his family. I wanted his kindness and curiosity to be rewarded and reinforced, as I didn't feel like kids were raised to appreciate these qualities within themselves in those days. He was so grateful. He showed his parents, who were beaming with pride.

The next day they returned to the Magic Kingdom, and all stopped by the Jungle Cruise to express their thanks again. "Mr. Ryan, Mr. Ryan!" I heard him shout. They even got to ride in my boat to listen to my spiel.

I let him steer and wear my jungle cruise hat. The whole family was covered head to toe in Disney merchandise and having the best day. They all thanked me and, most importantly, told me they were having a great time. Seeing the smiles on their faces and the pride in his parents' eyes taught me how important it was to make someone's day with the smallest of acts.

One of my favorite experiences working at Walt Disney World had little to do with the cast of characters or the rides themselves.

Rather it was the faith in humanity behind the guest experience and the unique role I played in cultivating impactful moments for folks who sometimes saved their entire lives just to attend one day at the parks.

Disney World had a unique program that revolved around a concept called Give Kids the World, in which terminally ill children would come and spend some of their last days on earth celebrating with their families at the parks (Szostak 2022).

One night at the Jungle Cruise, one of these Give Kids the World children came to my boat with an hour until closing. No one was there except them. She, her little brother, and their parents had gotten the boat all to themselves.

The little girl and her brother were like any other children, laughing and playing, and when I would tell jokes and poke fun at them, they were just as interactive as any other children. You wouldn't even know they were with the program except for the big blue Give Kids the World button pinned on her shirt.

But there was a stark contrast in her parents' demeanor, sitting in the dimly lit back of the boat who seemed to know what was coming. They had blank faces, just watching their daughter.

A third of the way through the trip, though, I noticed they were beginning to open up. My jokes were making them laugh. They were enjoying themselves. And by the end of the tour, we were all cackling. And in that tiny little moment, I realized my impact on their lives. It was one more moment, one more memory, they could hold onto when they were at peace and in joy with their little girl and as a family—something to remember.

My time at Disney World was far more than just the happenstance of a make-believe world. The castle, the fireworks, the childhood characters, and the nostalgia was all surreal to be a part of, but it wasn't what ultimately moved me. Instead, it clarified for me what was possible when you give people a North Star, an ideal world for which to strive. When you offer something to aspire to beyond oneself, a state of being and consciousness in which something brings us all together to enjoy the tiniest moments in life and to never take them for granted.

Those eight months brought me such joy in what felt like a lifetime. I made the most incredible friends. I had gay colleagues, mentors, friends, and people I loved who were just like me. I got to be a part of something much bigger than myself, all as myself. I felt free and happy and was able to live. It set a North Star for me of what a perfect world might look like and what happiness I might achieve someday. A beloved community. Acceptance and belonging when I had previously only grown to accept betrayal and loneliness.

When the program neared its inevitable end, I struggled to decide whether to convert my internship into a full-time Disney Cast Member role or return home to my private Catholic school to finish my degree. Many of my peers had decided to do just that, stay and work in the parks and continue their magical experiences as full-time cast members.

The decision, in one respect, was relatively easy. Coming from a family where higher education was the expectation, not an option, it was evident I needed to complete my education. But having started the journey of discovering my most authentic self and finally being in a place where I could thrive, it became difficult to leave what seemed like the perfect world.

While I wanted to stay, I also recognized the imperfection of this perfect world. It was essentially a bubble in which people from all walks of life came to escape the realities of their world. I didn't want to do that. I couldn't. I needed to feel connected to the bigger world out there and, hopefully, be able to use my powers for good in ways I couldn't do for the guests at the parks.

So, I decided to return to Gonzaga that fall.

BECOMING AN ACCIDENTAL ACTIVIST

Coming home from Disney, I never would have guessed that the authentic joy I discovered in finally being myself would cause any type of controversy. Why would my happiness cause harm to anyone?

As I would reluctantly learn, to hold onto that happiness, I had to make a choice—to be myself.

I returned to Gonzaga for my sophomore year of college, naively expecting things to be how they were just before I left. I'd go to school, become more involved on campus, have the same friends, and continue my life as a student.

I'd grown through my experience at Disney World in ways I hadn't even put words to yet. So many things we go through in life we don't even realize their impact upon us until we've had time for reflection.

My newfound self entered the realities of the world outside of that protective bubble.

I gladly returned to the same suite set up as my first year, a mix of student leaders from different backgrounds and belief systems alongside my old dormmates.

My friends asked a ton of questions about my time at Disney. I would gather them in a circle of chairs and take them on an imaginary Jungle Cruise ride. Using our imaginations, I'd point to elephants, crocodiles, and hippos on the banks of an imaginary river while delivering my spiel in an Australian accent.

I told them about my time making such close friends and interacting with guests from around the world. I excitedly shared about my life, dating Prince Charming, and discovering myself and who I was.

While I hadn't fully grasped how much had changed within me, my friends had definitely noticed. My newfound confidence in who I was, particularly my sexual identity, was obscure to them, even off-putting.

While they all knew I was gay our first year, it was that quiet thing kept tucked away from the everyday discourse and saintly expression they all held themselves to. If the gay thing came up, they would casually dismiss it and wouldn't want me to go further.

"Let's go do something," they might interrupt as I spoke about one of my experiences.

"Anyway..." as another might roll their eyes to change the subject.

Before Disney, I accepted this as the way things were, but now I couldn't help but notice this conditionality. Even saying I was gay held some friction in and of itself.

One day an event came up that I thought one of my roommates Nick would want to attend. I thought he'd like to join me, given that we used to go to various events together before my departure. He was the first straight guy I had ever come out to, and I felt deeply connected to him, given the kindness he showed.

I casually went to his room and asked if he wanted to come. Not looking up from his desk, he said no. His response seemed unusual and cold, so I asked, "Why not?"

He looked up and blurted out, "You're different now. You are so much gayer than you were before. I have a responsibility to help you." Implying he thought I needed to overcome my homosexuality.

Given our past, it caught me off guard and underscored that while he had been kind to me and even cared for me, he felt something was wrong with me. The old "hate the sin, not the sinner" adage.

Suddenly, my walls came back up. This perspective doubted the worthiness of my humanity and would be something I'd repeatedly hear over the years in condescending ways. There was a weariness and distrust of me as if I had done something wrong by being me.

It deeply saddened me. I thought he knew me better than that.

My other friends seemed to carry a similar perspective. I cared deeply for them but knew the fixing wasn't within me. I struggled with reconciling my genuine care for them while also living aside their implicit disapproval. Always under the surface, never outright.

As anyone can attest, it's often that first core group of friends in college who become such an important aspect of your campus experience. It was no different for me.

Back on campus, my sexuality was something I was far more open about.

I had to talk about it in certain ways as debates took place throughout the nation and across my campus around the decriminalization of same-sex sexual activities, gays in the military, marriage equality, LGBTI rights in education, etc. In addition, as a Jesuit University, the topical intersection with the Catholic Church was regularly debated.

While my deeply conservative dormmates preferred not to talk about sex at all, others on campus felt just fine asking me the most invasive questions about my sexuality, despite my then-prudish ways. As my fellow students began to dabble and explore their sexualities, my own became a sideshow curiosity. Many still held taboos around homosexuality that hypersexualized the experiences of gay men and women. In certain ways, the reverse stereotype of me as a gay man being so open to all forms of sex was slightly insulting. Heck, I was such a prude, given the great anxieties I had developed around my own sexual feelings. But I had to talk about it.

However, I eventually came to appreciate the liberating aspects of transcending a number of the taboos surrounding sex and sexuality. While forced into the discomfort, I also found relief. Many, in return, started sharing with me the most intimate details of their own lives, often unprompted.

Having such difficult and uncomfortable conversations became commonplace for me. This led to many different conversations with people of all sexual orientations and gender identities.

In ways, it helped shape even deeper bonds with the people I would meet. "Ryan, I've never told this to anyone, even people I've known my entire life." I'd regularly hear. Such vulnerability created pathways to profound conversations and connections.

I began to feel more comfortable dabbling in my own sexual explorations and liberating myself from some of the shame I had previously felt around my desires and the sensations of my own body. Finally, I'd have a little fun and learn to let go of the tensions that once frightened me so much. I realized this liberation was not just my burden to shed but a burden many still carried that ought to be lifted. So much of it fueled the homophobia and harmful gender norms that undergirded so many of the oppressive arguments used to suppress sexuality in our culture, including for my heterosexual peers.

From witch burnings of the past to rigid controls over what could and could not be discussed in polite conversation to proselytizing religious dogma to save our souls—there were so many hang-ups around sexuality that many faced, not just me. It was simultaneously embedded within our culture through various sexual expressions across numerous mediums—from movies, song lyrics, and TV ads—both in romantic love and pure unadulterated graphic depictions of sex everywhere you went. Yet I was the problem?

National debates around homosexuality, campus-wide controversies, and deeply personal disclosures around sex and sexuality became something I couldn't avoid as an out student on campus. I was like a beacon for many who ached to free themselves of carrying such burdens. The freeing space of disclosure opened doors to many with whom I interacted. This safe space found its way into my more formal roles on campus.

On campus, I got a job coordinating student programming around issues of diversity and inclusion out of the student activities office. Given my prior involvement at Disney World as a representative for my area on the diversity council, I gained a level of understanding I could build into my new role. I was excited to offer my fellow students programming that could inform their worldviews and expand their perspectives regarding our complex world.

A small part of me also hoped in doing so, I might also be able to convince my friends in my residence hall I wasn't as awful as they may have presumed.

In that role, I hosted listening sessions, brought in speakers, and devised creative ways to explore the world of diversity and inclusion throughout my sophomore year. The events would take place in our student union, challenging the student body to think more about what it meant to coexist in the world with people from a multitude of backgrounds, identities, and perspectives and to push beyond the borders of our limited purviews especially when it came to controversial issues of homophobia, sexism, racism, and more.

To commemorate the fiftieth anniversary of Brown versus the Board of Education, I pulled together an event I modeled after the brown-eyed blue-eyed experiment my mother had shown my sister and me when we were kids (Ott 2005; Elliot 2016). I decided to spend a day in a simulation where we would segregate students who entered the student union by their hair color.

Volunteers helped to *police* the union, and those with blond hair could only sit in certain areas and were limited in what services they could access. Some respectfully went along while others tearfully pleaded and questioned the volunteers. Some students avoided the union that day altogether.

The program stirred a lot of discussion on campus. "Wow, they are segregating the student union. It's so unfair. How could anyone be treated that way? Why would they do an event like that?" I heard as I was sitting in class.

I couldn't help but smirk. It was illuminating and caused further interrogation of the way we move and operate within the world and what we allow and disallow within our societies, particularly around racism.

For World AIDS Day, I brought twelve AIDS Memorial Quilts to campus, which we hung just off our student union (National AIDS Memorial). These were huge, twelve feet by twelve feet quilts, each featuring several individual panels, three feet by six feet to roughly symbolize the size of an average grave of a person who had passed away during the ongoing AIDS Epidemic. Families, chosen or otherwise, would create these panels to memorialize their deceased loved one.

The quilt served as a reminder of the hidden disease that had taken a toll on countless Americans.

The quilts initially grew from just a few hundred to thousands upon thousands. At one point, the quilt was laid out across the entire National Mall in Washington, DC, when HIV/AIDS activists had had enough of the government ignoring their pleas for help. While President Regan had largely ignored and even mocked AIDS activists in the 1980s when the quilt was first displayed, President Clinton and Hillary Clinton set a different tone as they walked among the quilts on the National Mall in the nineties, which had metastasized in size (Carey-Mahoney 2006).

As we hung the quilts, I'll never forget one very special moment I shared with my grandfather. He had been visiting for the Thanksgiving holiday and offered to help me put up the panels in preparation for the event.

He and I never had a direct conversation about my sexuality. However, he demonstrated his support for me in how he chose to show up for me. Throughout that afternoon, he spent time helping me lay out each of the massive blankets. One by one, we removed them from the giant shipping boxes they came in, carefully laid them across a raised table so as not to tear at their fragile fabric, and then, standing on a step stool, hung each one for display. In his own way, it was a tiny gesture of his acceptance of me, something my grandmother would have helped with, too, had she still been alive.

Students would come into the room, observe the quilts, and silently reflect. In addition, we held an event on World AIDS Day itself, featuring college-aged persons living with HIV to spread awareness about the lived experiences they faced to combat the stigma that still surrounded HIV.

Near the beginning of that year, away from my role doing diversity programming on campus, I rejoined our campus gay-straight alliance. As I attended and was one of just a handful of members, they asked if I wanted to join their leadership team, so I acquiesced. But we soon found ourselves butting heads.

Having just come from an incredibly accepting experience in Florida where I could be all of me, I struggled with why the group had remained so discrete. I knew many others on campus would benefit from participating in such a group. As debates would air among TV commentators about whether gays should have their rights protected in the nation, often by individuals who weren't openly gay themselves, I wanted there to be more visibility and engagement on the broader campus.

We couldn't ignore it, and I no longer wanted to bear the burden of carrying around the shame of others by quieting my drive. There always seemed to be internal pushback among the group whenever there was greater visibility around LGBTI rights on our campus. There was this hesitation of being too much, too out there, and an underlying fear of what could result, a fear I no longer held.

Meanwhile, other campus leaders were also making their mark on our campus. Bryce Hughes was a campus leader from years past who fought to establish an LGBTI resource center to offer students a safe space to learn more about who they were. There were also leaders in our Gonzaga Student Body Association, upper-level students who had sought through their visibility to respond to rhetoric around LGBTI Rights. There were also numerous staff and faculty, including Jesuits and people like my mom, who were extremely supportive of LGBTI students—things I would learn as I progressed in my journey there. We all wanted to see change on our campus.

That fall, during National Coming Out month, the Student Activities office decided to put on a Coming Out barbecue. They wanted to go all out in a show of support for LGBTI students. So, they bought a ton of burgers and hotdogs, rented a grill, and sent out advertisements throughout campus for the Friday afternoon event.

They printed colorful T-shirts with "1 in 10" on the front, referencing Alfred Kinsey's famous experiment determining at least one in ten adult Americans had some level of same-sex sexual attraction (Kinsey 1948). Further, that sexuality is not just gay or straight but falls along a continuum and may shift throughout a person's lifetime. Collectively, the T-shirts made up the rainbow colors and were offered to students to wear throughout campus. Many people participated. After all, it was a free T-shirt!

The event caused quite a brouhaha on our campus among college conservatives, many of whom happened to live in my residence hall. They were outraged the campus would *promote* such demonic behavior and shunned the student activities office for promoting evil.

They called into question the use of the "1 in 10" on the shirts for not providing "adequate citation," suggesting it was not a fact but a misrepresentation to the student body of the plausible prevalence of homosexuality. Students had discussions, engaged in classroom debates, and wrote many angry articles in the student newspaper.

The struggle within HERO continued. While my fellow leaders, too, were appalled by the rhetoric and vileness toward gays on campus, they continued to be of the ilk who felt that it might all go away with time. They wanted to remain silent. However, as the campus conversation grew, I uncovered a particular strength within me I hadn't known before. I couldn't stay silent.

I decided to write a few articles, often deemed controversial in our student newspaper, offering my take on the lack of support and hostility toward LGBTI students. In particular, I pointed out to my fellow students the hypocrisy with which their rhetoric lay. I detested the intolerance and condescension they would display at the mere existence of LGBTI students and how superior they behaved in all they did, contrasting with their professed Christian beliefs from the classroom to campus life, to even in our dormitory.

In one article published in the *Gonzaga Bulletin* in 2004, I fathomed how those with the same beliefs as me could carry such hatred toward that which they made no effort to understand (Olson). How could my peers have such "drawn out misinterpretations" of LGBTI students on campus and lack critical thinking to realize that there existed out in the wide expanse of the world people like us? If they believed Jesus had walked on water, why couldn't they believe me when I told them I was gay?

After writing the article, I soon found myself on the outs with the leadership of HERO.

At our follow-up meeting, the four other leaders turned to me and told me they no longer wanted me to participate in the organization. At one point, they cited the article and intimated I had narcissistically compared myself to Jesus. They had assumed the worst of me. I left the room and sobbed in the office of my closest advisor. It was a shocking blow.

To this day, I still don't fully understand their apprehension. What I sense is that they were at different points in their own journey of self-acceptance. They still saw my visibility, enthusiasm for life, and unapologetic nature as threatening, far and away from who they were at that time. Their internalized shame weighed heavily on them, and my drawing further attention to it only exacerbated it. I was the problem. Not their evolving senses of themselves.

A short while later, the former president of HERO asked me if I would be willing to take over the group's leadership. Unfortunately, after I had gone, the group turned inward on itself and didn't want to partake anymore, either with each other or the broader campus climate that was creeping in on them.

The former president, who was finishing up his time in seminary, had seen my potential and what I might be able to do with a soon-to-become defunct group. My building rage and discomfort at the distortions of LGBTI life led me to want to do more. And I accepted that role.

I began organizing weekly meetings for HERO members as the year ran on. We moved from the hidden back room at the far corner of our student union to our new LGBTI resource center in our multicultural center, Unity House.

We had a creative agenda each week and began opening the club to a broader group of students. I'd often tout we had four different types of constituents in our club. Those wanting to be more politically active on social justice issues. Those needing a social space to gather and just have fun. Those still exploring who they were or emerging in their understanding of themselves. And the fourth was just as important. Because of our visibility, those still hidden among the student body who would see our advertisements, walk by our events, or engage with our members and also needed our support.

We began more actively supporting events and gaining visibility across the campus. I created meeting advertisements based on acceptance and inclusion. Each had a different message for supporting LGBTI students, especially those still closeted. On one flyer, I painted a black sheep pink and used the flyer to announce our next club meeting. After that, I would advertise each meeting with a new creative flyer.

Later that spring, we hosted another barbecue with the Gonzaga Student Body Association. We had themed it after Mr. Roger's song "Won't You Be My Neighbor?" This time, rather than the barbecue being on a Friday afternoon, we held it in the middle of the week at lunch on a Wednesday. We had a line backed up for fifteen minutes as students waited for their hotdogs or hamburgers.

It was incredible to have all these people suddenly, in their own ways supporting the LGBTI community.

While I'm sure many just wanted free food, by attending a barbecue and interacting with LGBTI students, we broke down some barriers among our peers, enabling them to see us as fellow human beings.

However, with the increased visibility, there was also additional controversy.

At one point, the College Republicans, closely affiliated with the conservative Christian groups, decided to hold a pledge drive against same-sex marriage on our campus. It emanated from a national debate about whether the government should ban same-sex marriage within our federal constitution.

Outraged but inspired, I banded together with the Young Democrats and the feminist organization on campus in front of the student union to host a counter-pledge sponsored by the national LGBTI organization, the Human Rights Campaign.

Our competing tables were set up side by side, and one by one, students came to our tables. By the end of the day, our pledge sign-up sheet had garnered double that of the College Republican pledge (Dreyer 2004). The tides favored gay rights on our campus. Throughout the country, more and more individuals started to come forward with their support and love for the LGBTI community. They'd speak out as allies in their local newspapers, media, and community centers supporting gay rights.

Though we had succeeded that day, the deep divisions on our campus and echoing throughout the nation were only growing.

Pondering ways to help alleviate this growing tension, and in my role back in student activities as the diversity program coordinator, I decided to organize the most prominent event I would pull off that year. Working with multiple departments, raising a large sum of money, and reserving the world-famous Gonzaga

Kennel, where our Cinderella basketball team sold out game after game, we decided to bring in the mother of the hate-crime victim, Matthew Shepard, Judy Shepard.

It was a surreal experience. I had initially thought of bringing Judy after my mom heard her speak at a national conference for higher education professionals. She suggested I might have her talk at Gonzaga. Matthew Shepard's story deeply touched me while I was in junior high, and as a budding young LGBTI leader, I knew what a powerful impact the Shepard's story had on the rest of the country.

Knowing all she had been through in losing her son to such a horrendous act of violence, I wanted to make her trip as special as possible. So, I booked her a room at the nicest downtown hotel, The Davenport. An ex-fling I knew worked at the front desk and could upgrade her to a suite.

I drove to the airport in my 1998 purple Honda Accord. Exiting the terminal, she had her carry-on bag with a thousand luggage tags, slightly worn out from her flights that day.

I awkwardly greeted her with flowers as I introduced myself. Then I drove her to her hotel. On the way, we briefly struck up a conversation about the music I had been playing from a CD I had recently made. We connected when Sting's "Desert Rose" came on and both agreed we enjoyed the song. Finally, we got to The Davenport, and I walked her in to pass her off to my friend at the front desk. I was so excited to have her speak the following evening.

On the day of her event, I picked her up for an early dinner with student leaders. I'd arranged a special meal at a top-notch restaurant in town overlooking Spokane Falls so we could have more of an intimate experience with her before her speech.

There, we discussed in broad brush strokes the campus climate we had experienced and the controversies surrounding diversity.

She was engaged and learned more about what we had endured over the course of that year and what we continued to face.

We left the dinner and drove to the famed Gonzaga Kennel. Some of Gonzaga's most historic moments were in that room, including what would be Judy's speech.

We sold over one thousand tickets to students, staff, faculty, and those in the wider Spokane community. We set up a stage at the center of the basketball court facing half of the stands in an auditorium style. A large projector screen shined onto the back of the stage, and a spotlight was fixed on the podium in the otherwise darkened room. Looking into the crowd and seeing the entire stands filled to the rafters was incredible.

I had the fortune of introducing Judy. With the bright light of the spotlight blinding me, I read my written remarks in which I called on those in attendance and the broader campus community to consider "where hate could lead," the same title I had given Judy's talk (Laughlin 2004).

I asked attendees to consider the importance of empathy, compassion, and understanding as we worked toward a more just society in our everyday lives. Next, I played a short video Judy provided that shared more of Matt's story and welcomed her to the stage, giving her a brief hug and taking my seat in the audience.

Her speech was profoundly compelling as she recounted her family's loss of their eldest son and his struggles to find self-acceptance and love in his life. Five years after the tragic events that took his life, there was still a moment in which she briefly broke down in front of the audience as she detailed his heinous murder and the aftermath of hate her family received because they loved their gay son. By the end of her speech, there wasn't a dry eye in the audience. It was such a powerful reminder of what was truly at stake.

After the event, we hosted a small reception for Judy, where more community members had the chance to connect with her. We had punch and cookies, just like my parents had done for my dad's girls' basketball teams after a game. Many shared with Judy how her speech impacted them.

People walked away from the event with greater hope of getting to the root causes of such hatred that would push someone to take another person's life with such cruelty. The event with Judy would be discussed for years and led to many classroom conversations emphasizing our need to come together and "transcend the bullshit," if you will.

I drove her to her hotel and the airport the next day. As she departed, she expressed her gratitude for bringing her in and my efforts as our gay-straight alliance's new president. She knew how difficult it had been for me and seemed to sense something important within me—a potential I couldn't even see in myself.

"Thank you, Ryan, for all you have done to make my trip so wonderful. I see a lot in you. I'd like to stay in contact. Let me know if I can do anything for you," she said as we parted ways.

We had formed a powerful connection while she was there, but I couldn't have foreseen what an important role she and her whole family would play in my life in the decades to come.

It's still hard to believe of all her interactions with thousands of young queer people throughout the country, just like me, we found that spark together. In certain ways, and as a spiritual person, I couldn't help but feel some level of divine intervention in our paths crossing. Her family's story deeply moved me and further compelled me into action.

By the end of that year, our efforts to help make our campus more tolerant of others, more inclusive of those with differences, and more affirming and loving toward LGBTI students started to take shape.

In one respect, I began to gain respect and notoriety among peers for my contributions, including staff and students, and even some of the former HERO leadership who once wanted me gone. Yet at the same time, I also faced a greater sense of alienation from others who were unfavorable to my work.

None of it had been in my life plans, nor had I anticipated all I would face. But in doing so, through a series of different experiences on campus, both in public and private life, including small moments that made me feel alive and gave justification and purpose to me, I found myself becoming an accidental activist.

FIGHTING DRAGONS

Underlying my accidental activism was a profound spiritual awakening that gave me new paradigms of my own worth and showed me a window into my capacity for love. Something worth fighting for.

As I was fighting for gay rights on campus, in my private world, I started to fall in love for the first time and truly questioned what it meant to care for someone so deeply. Through that love, I began to see the world in new and magnanimous ways, which fueled my ongoing campus activism.

Teaching to the whole person was a huge reason why I chose Gonzaga in the first place and what drew me most to the university. In our classes, we'd ask what love is. How does it show up in our lives? How do we give it to others? Indeed, many of these fundamental questions caused me to think of my grandmother and all that drove her to care for those less fortunate, give of herself to others, and live as best she could in honor of a greater spirit within us.

In one of my philosophy courses, I had a phenomenal professor, Dr. Bowman, who believed in the Socratic teaching method. Each class period, we'd turn our desks toward each other in a circle and reflect upon the readings he had given us the week before.

We explored topics of resilience, gratitude, happiness, joy, death, despair, love, and relationship. In one class, he stated on the board, "We could all be... blank," and had us debate the ascribed meanings within our lives. We even responded to, we could all be Mother Teresas, and we could all be Hitlers. It was a fascinating discussion.

One of my favorite stories he proffered was the story of a ragged little girl living in filth in the streets.

There was once a little girl living in filth on the streets, begging for food. A man walked by, saw this, and then turned to God and shouted, "This is absurd! How can you let this happen?" and no one answered.

Again, the man walked by the next day and saw the little girl begging again, but this time it was raining, and she was shivering. So, the man shouted at God again, "Why on earth are you letting this happen? Do something!" but he received no response.

For the third time, this time in the middle of winter, the man walked by the alley again and saw the little girl living in filth, shivering with snow coming down all around her, and the man turned to God and shouted, "How can you let this happen? Why haven't you done anything?" And still waiting for a reply. The man felt disappointed and bemoaned how dark and dreary this world was. Was there even such a God?

Later that evening, in his sleep, God finally answered him. "I certainly did do something. I created you."

This left an indelible impression on me and my belief in our capacities to do something to better our world and to carry forth a light within us that enables us to do profound things simply by taking action. It became a core construct of how and why I chose to work toward a just society in small and big ways.

For another assignment, we read Viktor Frankel's *Man's Search for Meaning* (Frankel 1959), which documented how he survived the Nazi concentration camps. The book detailed the horrors and atrocities of that time in our world's history and all that undid him, but also what he overcame when many others could no longer persevere. What struck me most about his account was his optimism and profound belief in love.

At one point, he described how he and his wife, of some thirty years, had been separated in the camps. He had no idea where she was, what had happened to her, or even if she was still alive. As the days turned into weeks and weeks turned into months, he saw the barbaric reality before him. Yet his hope to one day reunite with her was unwavering and kept him moving forward.

This story so deeply moved me as it forced me to reflect upon the very essence of love itself. What was it? Why did human beings harp on it so much, and what did it reveal about our true human nature?

It reminded me of my favorite movie in high school, *What Dreams May Come* with Robin Williams and Cuba Gooding Jr., which I repeatedly watched with anyone who would watch it with me (Ward 1998). Many saw it as a dark and dreary film, as the story reveals a profound sense of loss and hopelessness.

First, a couple's children die in a terrible accident, and they are distraught. Then, Robin William's character, the husband, is killed in a car accident, leaving his wife behind. It depicts him going to heaven but looking down on his widowed wife, where he discovers the darkness she has entered following his passing. Then, as the story continues, she too dies by suicide after the overwhelming loss she experienced from losing her children and her husband. Her suicide was considered an unforgivable sin, for which she went to hell.

The movie concludes by dramatizing his profound love for her and all he goes through, including journeying through hell itself, just to rescue her because she is his true soulmate. The only thing that could save her was his willingness, as her soulmate, to join her—to feel deeply and profoundly her deepest truths. To become one.

Both *Man's Search for Meaning* and *What Dreams May Come* offered me a profound examination of love and how it might appear in our lives. As someone who was still struggling to define, for me, what love meant, especially as a person classified as a deviant for having feelings toward the same sex, I had so many questions about what it was but also what it could be.

As I did in my youth, I ached for love and mourned the idea that I might never find it. Nor did I want to settle for any old love, but I knew deep, prevailing love was possible. That which I had seen in movies, heard in music and observed within my parents' relationship. Or at least what I had thought it was supposed to be. Melissa had opened that gate for me that fateful night of my parents' twenty-fifth wedding anniversary, but I had yet to walk through.

While emerging as an accidental activist, I started to feel those things and that deeper meaning with my friend James. We grew close by playing racquetball together during my first semester of college. We'd have playful conversations about life. He sometimes joked with me, and we laughed at mundane things. He shared about his time back home, attending a private Catholic high school and growing up on a farm outside a major city in Idaho. He seemed curious about me and gave equally as a friend. We had once even considered becoming roommates as I contemplated who I would live with when I returned from Disney.

While my friendships shifted and shaped from when I first started school to when I returned from Disney, so did the one between James and me. As our sophomore year went on, we grew closer and closer. He was no longer just that handsome guy down the hall but had become a close friend.

In our sophomore year, we shared mutual friends and lived right next door to one another, just on the other side of the wall. As we grew closer, our bond only strengthened. We'd naturally always find ways to see each other.

I'd have an excuse to go next door to ask for something, say a pencil or a piece of paper. He would do the same. We were constantly interacting. Even in the privacy of our rooms, we would continue our conversations in our AOL chatrooms, sometimes hours into the night. I'd receive a random message from him that would then turn into hours of debate and sharing more of our lived experiences with each other. He held an intellect within him and a desire to reveal more of himself to the wider world, something his strict upbringing on a farm didn't necessarily allow for.

We developed a mutual love of games and would play Command and Conquer with each other. He'd come over to watch movies and just hang out. Here and there, we'd find an excuse to wrestle and roll around in our common area, playfully grabbing at each other's waists. We'd sit close to each other during movie nights with our friends. Even our racquetball games seemed to become more intimate as we'd constantly fall into each other and find one another with our hands behind or in front of us as we tussled for the ball.

With him, I experienced feelings I had never known before, unlike the previous guys I had developed close friendships with, from the boys in elementary to my senior year of high school with Ben. With James, I started to feel something much deeper—a certain level of closeness I had always ached for but had never known firsthand. A profound sense of connection and belonging. Dare I say, love?

The deep love I was experiencing with him was teaching me I was capable of beautiful things. It helped me to grow more comfortable in my own skin. I felt such peace and serenity. I began accepting my sexuality as not perverse, but quite contrary, something made up of the beautiful butterflies he would give me whenever we were around each other.

I felt so overwhelmed by the emotions of it all. It was so profound to me, even otherworldly. My black-and-white world was starting to turn technicolor. Not only did I feel these things toward James, but suddenly oceans within me began to open up as I realized I was capable of loving the whole world that much more. I had been so afraid of this feeling, but now I was ready to receive it in all its glory.

This capacity within me was so powerful. It started to refract onto all other relationships within my life, areas in which I could love even more deeply than I had ever permitted myself to feel before. I felt like I loved my parents more, my sister more, friends more, even complete strangers more—because I knew I was capable of something so much deeper. All thanks to the love I started to feel for James.

As time passed, he and I continued connecting in everyday ways. However, while I felt more alive and whole, my status as an out gay man on campus became somewhat challenging for him, creating an undue burden on our relationship. It started to make him nervous about being around me.

James started to get razzed by his buddies for being my friend. I was a burden that drew undue attention to something he didn't want to face fully. It brought me right back to middle school.

He started feeling ashamed of his friendship with me. Our relationship waxed and waned. We'd have a wonderful time together, but then I wouldn't hear from him for a few days. It became confusing. While we had nothing but a profound and wonderful connection behind closed doors, our friendship became more muted in the company of others or in public spaces. Almost like it was our little secret.

It also became something I started to protect far and away from campus life. Another duality within my life where in one instance, I was this activist people prominently knew. On the other, I melted into all the stolen moments when James and I could connect in such spaces of vulnerability, even if just behind closed doors or through a computer screen.

We'd have brief moments around campus when we'd run into each other and give a silent but knowing look at one another from across the student union. Suddenly no one else was in the room. For Valentine's Day that year, I left a single carnation in his mailbox without my name. He returned to our dorm with a smile on his face and said, "I know it was you," in a gentle, tender voice. It felt so much like our intuitions just sensed and understood one another in this profound way.

But by the end of our sophomore year, I started developing deep anxiety about our relationship. I felt so connected to him. At the same time, his back and forth of being close to me and keeping me at a distance created uncertainty about what he wanted from me. It was also beyond sexual at this point, but a deep emotional entanglement.

As with all change, I was afraid the end of the year might bring an end to our friendship. I was so terrified of losing him. And what made it worse was my growing feelings for him that were beyond just close friendship but were of a deeper kind, one of love, romance, and intimacy.

I didn't want such deep sentiments to scare him away, yet I felt if he didn't know how I felt, how could I have faith and trust in our friendship if I was withholding such an important part of myself from him?

I took the time to write him a long letter, expressing what his friendship had meant to me and how much I had developed a profound love and respect for his personhood. I sat down at my school-provided desk, staring at my screen and contemplating all the ways in which I had discovered new aspects of myself through his love. As I began writing, I heard his laughter coming from the other side of the wall beside my room. Writing the letter riddled me with fear.

Whereas in a movie, the protagonist may work to win over the heart of their muse, I couldn't throw rocks at James's window and beg him to come on an adventure with me. We were still confined to the heteronormative, homophobic grip of our time. I couldn't ask his parents for his hand. I couldn't fight off the dragons guarding him in a high tower. To say I like you in that way, or to express such feelings, let alone to take such bold actions as asking him out on a date, might invoke further shame, ridicule, or even violent response.

I was so scared, yet all I could do was just tell him how I felt.

In a certain regard, I accepted our fate was written in stone. While I could no longer bear the burden of hiding my love for him, I also expected the inevitability that he would be frightened away.

At the end of the year, I handed him my letter, unsure if he would ever talk to me again.

To my surprise, rather than rejecting me, my letter opened a whole new portal into the depths of our relationship.

He began to open up even more to me. We continued our hours-long conversations while we were away for the summer. A tone in his voice just came through in every conversation that was even more warm and intimate than I had expected, as if he cooed when we talked to each other, kind of like a cat purrs. "Hi, guy," he'd always tenderly say, melting my heart.

At one point, we even met up while I was visiting different friends in Idaho. We hung out for a day. As I was leaving, we hugged each other, and I whispered, "I love you." To which he responded, "I love you too." Finally, we could express externally what had so clearly been felt internally and had gone unnamed. I wasn't as shocked by his utterance so much as I felt calmly affirmed in what I had already known. It became our regular cadence every time we'd say goodbye to each other.

For our junior year, I moved into an apartment with one of our mutual friends, Madison. I had met him through James after one of their business classes together. He soon became a close friend. James would always come over to hang out. While he likely told his friends he was coming to see Madison, he would also often come to see me. It was a way where our relationship could be protected.

I wish I could describe all the subtle ways I knew he loved me. His warmth toward me whenever we were around one another and our mutual playfulness was so calming I had never had that with another person. And when we were in spaces where we could exist, it was the strongest bond I had known up until that point. Even more remarkable than some of the people I had known my entire life.

This profound feeling opened my world up in ways beyond what I can describe here. It was as if my senses were going off all at once. I felt like I saw the totality of who James was: his past, his present, and his future, all at the same time. I felt for his earlier childhood pains he would share with me from his youth. I valued who he was when I was with him, both in private and among our friends. And I saw all I thought he could become if he ever wanted to. All with a grandiosity that was almost overwhelming to me, but I sincerely felt like I was looking into the sun.

That level of love I also felt reciprocated by him. And knowing that I, as a human being, and he, as a human being, held this capacity within ourselves allowed me to be open to those same fundamental human qualities within all others. Something we all deserved and ached for. Connection. Being seen. Feeling understood and embraced for all we are.

It catalyzed me to better understand my own humanity within the wider world. It proved to me being gay was something not to be ashamed of but worth fighting for and sacrificing one's life. I had finally started walking through that gate Melissa had opened to me. James would forever serve as my muse. The baseline by which I believed in my fundamental humanity, that of others, and what was possible within us all. If I was capable of this profound feeling, didn't that mean others were also capable of such love? And as this love had changed and inspired me to care for others, didn't that mean it needed to be shared with the world? Might it solve our joint problems and help shed light on our mutual gifts? Isn't this something to evangelize for?

I would continue to seek out that meaning and fight against such dragons that would dare try to oppress such profound beauty.

DEEP SECRETS
AND HOMOPHOBIC
REALITIES

The unrelenting scrutiny of being an out-figure on campus often took its toll, including on my relationship with James, my muse, and in part, the causality for my activism.

In my newfound sense of self, I started to recognize the power of bearing witness to something greater than oneself. The love I developed with James became the fire by which I could stand my ground as an activist within an all too hostile world.

Behind closed doors and through our AOL instant messenger, we'd continue spending hours upon hours talking about all sorts of innocuous things. He'd come over and hang out. We'd watch my favorite TV show, and when I'd choke up, he'd place his hand on my shoulder to comfort me.

The closer James and I got, the more foreboding it felt for him.

James would open up to me about his background and who he was. He shared with me that I was one of the few people in the world to express so openly an unconditional love for him, even using the words "I love you." Something he shared even his parents rarely used, if at all. His parents were older and of a more stoic generation.

He described the family life where he came from as one in which strict rules were in place. Back on his farm in Idaho, any backtalk received a quick smack across the face. As the man of the family, even at eight, he needed to be toughened up and carry his fair share. He disclosed that growing up, he was a bit effeminate, which others considered a negative attribute, so his parents would push him into more masculine things.

He once told me of a time when a baby goat became sick and needed to be put down. At the tender age of eleven, his father took James, the baby goat, and a knife out to the barn, where he had to slit the goat's throat.

At school, he was made fun of by his peers as well. They all thought he and his childhood friends were likely gay as they didn't demonstrate typical "boyish" behavior. He was a huge nerd, so he enjoyed primarily playing board games with his close friends.

When he came to Gonzaga, he wanted to enter the humanities as either a psychologist or a social worker. However, his parents felt such roles wouldn't help him succeed later in life. It was too soft. They insisted that he get a business degree. Things to *toughen* him up and prepare him for the *real world*.

On campus, James continued oscillating between being my closest friend and staying at a distance, even going so far as to downplay or denigrate me to his friends. He appeared to struggle deeply with his feelings for me. The closer we got, the harder he seemed to push back, which would continue for years.

What was also of particular consideration was that he identified as straight and still does to this day. Something I deeply strived to respect and honor throughout our relationship.

Not once had he and I engaged in any sexual activity, yet we developed this profound love for each other. What I knew concretely at that moment was that love existed. What I learned about love and how I grew with James was through what we ultimately experienced together and the reciprocity between us.

I couldn't feel such a level of depth or feeling without having experienced a similar level of depth and feeling coming from him. The more we bonded, the deeper our connection grew. Like many who experience love for another person, it was all so fresh and new to both of us.

We both stumbled our way through feelings we had never felt before—feelings that made us feel alive in new ways while also entering uncharted territory—experiencing the realities of those feelings in the world we occupied.

As such, we both navigated our friendship in different ways and struggled with how to place what we were experiencing into a context that we could both appreciate. Because I had grown so close to him and didn't want to lose the incredible beauty between us, I would often get caught up in his experiences of self-exploration and self-doubt.

Even identifying as a straight man, he still had to contend with the fact he deeply felt love and affinity with another man, who was an out gay man.

While these feelings existed, we both dated other people. He had a girlfriend he'd had since high school. I started to explore my sexuality more with other men as I became more comfortable in my skin, including a few sophomoric romances. Unfortunately, they seemed more like my childhood games of *house* when compared to my profound loving connection with James.

Among our closest friends, it became clear I had developed profound feelings for him. I openly discussed how much of a close friend he had become, striving not to expose his own sentiments for me in any way. As an out gay man, I learned even to say a kind thing about him, to suggest I cared about him, in itself became slanderous as it provoked suspicion of his sexuality. Anyone I liked, even admired, was scrutinized by my peers under a microscope because what could that mean? As heterosexuals, if they wanted someone, it would be fun banter. If I liked someone, it risked outing someone to the world, which for some could be devastating.

They always razzed him for the fact that the gay guy liked him. Out of his own sense of shame, I guess, he would go along with their jokes, sometimes putting me down as an act of self-preservation. They had no idea I wasn't just the gay guy hitting on the straight guy, but there was a mutuality to it all.

He just had the upper hand because no one assumed he, too, might have similar feelings.

Honestly, I sometimes struggled with understanding where James was coming from. I felt this profound love coming from him toward me in many respects. We'd always look yearningly at each other as if there was no one else in the room, and the moment felt as if it was forever before, suddenly, we would look away. He'd call me in the middle of the night, and we'd stay up talking for hours and hours.

There was such warmth between us. All I completely respect should and does exist between men, including between two straight men, and can and should also be able to exist between two gay men and a gay man and a straight man. At the same time, this also felt different.

Over one winter break, he asked me to look after his pet fish while he went back home to Idaho. So, he came over, and it was just the two of us in my apartment.

We talked for a bit and then started to say our goodbyes. He looked deeply into my eyes and began to move his face toward mine as if to kiss me. Then, at the very last second, his head rolled to my shoulder, and we embraced in a deep, long hug.

I sensed a deep urge in him to kiss me, but then he prevented himself from doing so. We said I love you and then he quickly left. Thinking we were just friends and trying to be a good friend to him, I stood there puzzled.

Countless moments couldn't be couched as exclusively straight to me. Instead, it left me confused and wondering where to place my feelings.

Young people these days wouldn't even have to ponder these questions. In fact, as of 2021, one in five young adults in the US identified as not exclusively heterosexual but somewhere on the sexuality continuum (Moreau 2021). Had James and I grown up in today's era, what might we have become if this was even a possibility?

As time passed, I deeply struggled with wanting to dive into our friendship and love out loud in whatever manifestation we were meant to experience our connection. As friends. As lovers. As soulmates or whatever we were supposed to be.

I would think we were just friends and try to be the very best friend I could be. Then he would do something more intimate and queer, and I'd adjust accordingly. One time he sent me a shirtless photo of himself and told me no one else had seen it but me.

What was I supposed to do with that when he said he only wanted to be friends?

One evening I had invited him to go to a movie with my sister and a friend. He declined but agreed to come with us to my house after so we could all do laundry and enjoy my family's hot tub.

When I picked him up with my sister and our friend in the backseat, he nervously handed me a CD as he got into my car.

"Here, I made this for you."

Surprised but not thinking much of it. I said, "Thank you," and began playing the CD. They were all great songs, but he kept having me quickly scan through each song, seemingly embarrassed. By the time we got to my house, we hadn't fully listened to one, but I thought nothing of it. I was oblivious.

We had a fun time at my house. The hot tub was great. Our laundry got done. And then my sister drove us back with James and me in the back seat with piles of folded laundry on top of us. This time I started to hear some of the songs. They began to make me think.

The songs held these beautiful messages of revealing one's love to someone or struggling with accepting the world's limitations. In the short, fifteen-minute drive, there wasn't much time to listen to the whole CD, but I became intrigued. So, when we returned to our respective apartments, I decided to listen to the entire CD he had made for me.

Almost as if crafted in perfect order, the songs deeply touched me. Seal's song "Love's Divine" with a message of having a revelation of deep love. Pussycat Doll's song "Stick Witchu" is about facing life's hurdles together. Jem's song "They" expressed remorse for society's social constructions that hold people back. Fleetwood Mac's song "Everywhere" talks about the idea of falling in love. Roxette's song "Listen to Your Heart" shares how one should follow their heart before it's too late. Anastasia's song "Sick and Tired" where she talks about the unfair world in which someone dared to love when people were afraid to love. Annie Lennox's song "Why" apologizes for the hurtful ways of the past, done out of fear or shame. Carly Simon's song "Coming Around Again" where she talks about love finding a way. Jon Secada's song "Just Another Day" is about not wanting another day to pass without someone's love. Meat Loaf's song "I Would Do Anything for Love" expresses a fear of love. And finally, Melanie C's song "Never Be the Same

Again" talks about forbidden love and friendships taking the next step of intimacy.

At the end of listening over and over again to the CD, I lay there in shock and confusion.

Were they some coded message he was trying to say to me? They certainly aligned with all I had been curious about after all that time we had been together and things I intuitively suspected. I even recalled an earlier conversation where he mentioned in passing he made CDs for people he was interested in to share how he truly felt.

Yet I couldn't bring it up because I had to wait for him to say it meant something. If I even mentioned it or suggested it might hold a more profound meaning, I feared he might erupt angrily and lash out at me. I might lose him as a friend, this person who had come to mean everything to me and all I had hoped for as a sullen youth.

He never did mention that CD again.

This caused me to have even more existential thoughts and questions. I started to appreciate the unique nature of our relationship more deeply. On the one hand, I wondered if it was possible that he was struggling deeply with his sexual identity and that he just needed time to come to terms with it.

On the other hand, I asked if he genuinely was straight, how might the love we shared evolve to its highest manifestation? What would that look like? Would I be okay with simply being a person on the side who supported him in his life, including potentially a wife and children? To which I started to say, why yes, of course!

As he and I struggled with this duality of our dynamic in our private lives, the space where I felt most free just standing beside him, I also struggled with this duality in my campus life.

The campus culture continued to present both beautiful gifts and darkened realities that I was constantly confronted with.

James's love continued to fuel my desire to better our world so a love like ours might exist in whatever manifestation it would result in.

I might be unable to slay a dragon, but maybe my activism and action in the world might make it safe for someone somewhere out there to one day embrace that which James and I seemed to struggle to reconcile.

As I gained greater visibility on campus through my various roles, I also started to experience a broader reception from my peers and local community members. I continued as the HERO president, garnering greater visibility as time passed alongside the growing leadership of those among our club's membership.

In addition to our weekly meetings, we hosted several events and visibility campaigns, like our annual National Coming Out Day barbecue. We commemorated the annual Day of Silence in which participants took a vow of silence for the entire day, including in their classrooms, to illustrate the ongoing silencing LGBTI individuals had to face in their everyday lives by having to remain closeted.

It became one of my favorite events of the year because, at 5:00 pm, we'd gather on the steps of the student union and "break the silence" by all screaming at the top of our lungs. Several impassioned speeches by my fellow activists, professors, and school administrators, including my mom, would follow.

We threw the first-ever gay dance at a private Jesuit University. While it didn't have the highest attendance, it definitely caused a stir. Behind closed doors, university leaders questioned why on earth the university would be hosting a *gay dance*. My mom quickly reminded them that the other most popular dance for students held on campus was called *the grind*, in which several students showed up intoxicated and danced provocatively with one another.

We were just a few queer kids who wanted to dance.

During our senior year, we published a first-of-its-kind literary magazine that carried numerous short stories, poems, pieces of art, and even short research papers about the queer experience. We called it the *Out of the Shadows* literary magazine. Our primary focus was reaching students, particularly those still grappling with their sexuality, with messages of hope and possibility. Of course, I wrote a hidden poem for James.

Our club had gone from a nascent group of a few students who quietly met in the back of the student union to becoming one of the most popular on campus. Over a quarter of the student body was on our mailing list, and over forty individuals regularly attended our meetings. We developed a beautiful community of peers. Beyond the numbers, what was ultimately most rewarding was watching young people come in as shy first-year students and grow into out and expressive individuals by the end of the year.

What I learned most through my activism was that our ability to love and express ourselves was itself a form of resistance. To simply exist, unapologetically, was half the battle. Openly saying I was gay and living out loud was still such a difficult step for so many. To dare hold hands in public, to ask questions in my classes about queer life, or to even wear a rainbow T-shirt while I was walking across campus. These simple, everyday things some considered radical.

We'd participate in a national kiss-in or challenge students to hold hands with members of the same sex as they walked across campus. We conducted silent pink mafia activities where we would hide rainbow ribbons around campus for people to find. We showed up to popular bars deemed straight by our peers, having fifteen to twenty of us out and proud also there. It was our way of saying we are here. We are queer. Let love in.

But even more profound, an act of resistance I started to learn was the act of love itself. Overriding previous harmful gender norms fed to us that expressing or feeling one's emotions was weak, I felt called to lean into my every moment to break such a harmful tradition, especially given what I now knew.

To tell people I loved and cared for them, freely and uninhibitedly. To genuinely appreciate and value people around me. These, too, were acts of defiance and resistance to the homophobic world in which I had grown up.

In many instances, my fellow LGBTI students started to find a lot of support on campus. While on the other hand, our campus, like many others at that time, experienced a campus climate crisis with many polarized viewpoints and perspectives that made life difficult for nonnormative students or those who existed outside of traditional spaces.

Several students would go out of their way to avoid me. One time I was walking across the quad to enter our academic building. I noticed a group of students who looked at me, pointed in disgust, and crossed the street, as was typical for me.

I started receiving hateful messages and threats to my physical safety from several Spokane community members and angry conservative parents who would call for my expulsion as I continued to make headlines in local newspapers.

Before moving into my new apartment with Madison during my junior year, I briefly sought a roommate to live with. After struggling a bit, one kid reluctantly decided to be my roommate. However, once his parents discovered I was gay, they refused to let him live with me.

In some of my classes, conservative professors would publicly raise issues of the sinfulness of homosexuality and, in front of my fifty classmates or so, try to engage me in debate.

In one of my philosophy classes, a professor started citing Sir Thomas Aquinas and deduced he would have *disagreed* with homosexuality if he had been alive.

"Sir Thomas Aquinas, due to natural law, would not believe in unnatural acts like homosexuality," looking at me with a scowl. Knowing I was in the classroom, he made the point anyway.

Under my breath, I quietly blurted out, "Fuck you,"

"What was that, Ryan?" he asked.

I retorted, "Nothing."

In other classes, the professors would be more overt. In a communications class, one professor asked, "Why is the US government spending so much money on HIV/AIDS research rather than putting it into something more useful like cancer research? After all, it's only homosexuals that are dying from HIV and AIDS while thousands more people die from cancer every year. Make sense of that for me. Why should the US pay for the behavior of homosexuals, Ryan?"

At one point, I was called into the campus police offices. There had been a threat of physical violence toward me, and they wanted me to be more cautious. Unfortunately, they didn't have much information on the incident other than someone reported they overheard at a party a group of young men wanted to teach me a lesson and beat up the *gay guy*.

Their advice? Write fewer articles. Be less visible on campus. Don't be so open, so *out*.

I left their offices stunned. I had never experienced something like that before. All I had known was the experiences of Matthew Shepard and others violently attacked for being who they were. To me, this threat was not a matter of small proportions but indeed called into question the safety of my life.

I couldn't sleep that night and had vivid dreams of what might happen. For the rest of the week, I slept under my bed. I started to reflect on the possible implications of my work and what it might mean for my life.

I had a premonition I likely wouldn't make it to the age of thirty because I thought it was highly likely something would happen to me for the work I was undertaking, and I would ultimately lose my life.

But the love I knew we were all capable of, which I had discovered through James, was nothing to be ashamed of. On the contrary, it was what the world needed most. It needed to be evangelized to all who would listen. It was something worth dying for if it indeed came to that. Frankly, was life even worth living if we didn't have at least that?

My campus visibility not only drew haters but also drew to me individuals struggling with their sexual identity. For some reason, my openness in who I was created safe spaces for individuals to find ways to talk to me.

In certain instances, it perpetuated what has always happened to queer people—individuals looking to meet up to have a little fun but never talk again. But in many cases, it turned out to be individuals needing someone to talk to about their lives, who they were, and what they were going through.

Individuals would find me in all sorts of ways. So many came to me from the most unsuspecting of places. Fraternity brothers, seminarians, athletes, ROTC members, and others. All had something they were hiding about their sexualities and needed somehow to unburden themselves of the pain of carrying such a secret alone. Something I knew all too well.

Some were blunt and would walk up to me in a public space and say we must hang out. I presumed they, too, were out and living full life, only to learn that they were still hiding. In other instances, individuals would become friends with me and hang out, and then I'd learn, not through their words but their behaviors, that they had greater intentions.

In one situation, a young man asked me to meet him in the school's parking lot in the dead of night. With his head covered in a dorm room towel, he had me drive him around town for over an hour before he finally revealed his true self.

All of them, somehow, someway, found a way to reach out to me.

I spent many nights having long, drawn-out conversations with my peers about what it all meant, who they were, and what choices they wanted to make in their lives. Some even asked me to pray with them in church.

I had panicked calls for support as a friend had locked themselves in their room and wouldn't come out, talking about suicidal ideation. In another instance, a friend had lost all their financing for college because their parents found out about them being gay. They had to work with the university to identify alternative resourcing quickly. In other, more harrowing instances, I had individuals disclose their recent HIV diagnosis, of which they felt frightened of what was to come.

As a young person myself, merely twenty-one and still discovering who I was, I found myself in situations where I provided love and comfort to dozens of individuals over the years, many of whom simply wanted to talk and feel comforted by knowing they weren't alone. Many of them were at different stages of their journeys. Some would eventually come out of the closet while others would remain closeted and go on to live heterosexual lives.

It painted a fuller understanding of the world I didn't have before. It also gave me a greater appreciation for the fluidity and expanse of gender and sexuality and its social constructs that were possible throughout our world. Not everyone was always exclusively straight, gay, or anywhere in between. All wanted to be open and honest about their true identities, but like me, they feared rejection and abandonment from those they loved.

Walking across campus, I felt like I saw a whole other world just beneath the surface. I knew dozens of individuals still navigating their identities and who they were. All in all, on a campus with a student population of just over four thousand students, I had over one hundred and fifty individuals come out to me during my time in college. Of course, I was far from perfect in all my efforts, and I am sure I made many mistakes. Nevertheless, it was in part their stories, too, that undergirded the activism I continued on my campus in support of an invisible group of individuals, many of whom I would never meet myself but knew were suffering in silence.

While I faced all of this, I sometimes struggled to know what was happening to me at the moment as a young person too. When I met my own struggles and questions, I didn't have someone to turn to who fully understood what being gay meant, what being an activist on a catholic school campus was like, and other intersections of my identities.

I would try to turn to my close friends at the time and share my experiences, which wasn't always the best choice. When I needed to feel normal or as if everything wasn't moving a thousand miles a minute, I would find solace among my peers from my dormitory. We would hang out. We didn't need to talk about anything but just existed. Or so I thought.

NATIONALLY RECOGNIZED

As I faced continued disapproval and even threats from others while navigating my journey as an out leader on campus, the visibility of our work was becoming noticed on a much larger national stage.

During spring break of my first senior year, the HERO membership decided to organize an alternative spring break to go to Olympia, Washington, the state's capitol, to observe the same-sex marriage proceedings of the State Supreme Court (Kobos 2005; Roesler and Hay 2005). Several brave plaintiffs had sued the State of Washington to strike down the offensive Defense of Marriage Act, which prohibited marriage between same-sex couples.

We wanted to witness history in the making and to understand more deeply the national implications of the State Supreme Court's decisions. We also would leverage the alternative spring break to meet with our elected officials. After submitting our idea to the cable network, MTV decided they wanted to document our experience and sent a few camerapersons to capture our travels.

This, of course, caused yet another brouhaha among our university administrators. Their students would be going to observe same-sex marriage proceedings on television, in direct opposition to the teachings of the Catholic Church?

As the organization's president, I was pulled into an administrator's office just before our journey and asked about the nature and purpose of the trip. This particular administrator was a very close advisor and friend.

Under that auspice, they hinted if I continued with the trip, it could have consequences on my mother's future employment at the university. In addition, they suggested my participation in a nationally televised program might cause embarrassment to the university.

We still went. About fifteen of us, including my amazing sister, who had also decided to go to Gonzaga, camped out in a KOA in small cabins on the outskirts of Olympia. On the first day, we met with our legislative representative for our county. We expressed our support for nullifying the state's Defense of Marriage Act.

That evening we returned to our campsite and prepared for the following day. We made posters expressing how we felt and T-shirts with rainbows on them. We knew there were going to be a lot of people there in opposition to us. One of our members, Amber, had been doing demonstrations since she was fourteen, so we figured she knew what she was doing.

Around the campfire, she shared her perspectives on how we should behave. "Don't back down when you face a mob of people screaming the most horrible things at you. Don't look away. Stand your ground. You've got to prepare for the anger and the frustrations. You hold your poster in their face, don't bow your head, and look at them."

Sure enough, when we arrived the next morning, we saw several dozen state representatives standing on the State Capitol steps offering their opposition to same-sex marriage in front of the media. As if by second nature, Amber headed over, and we followed, standing silently in front of them with our signs declaring our equality and not looking away.

Shortly after, another organizer in support of same-sex marriage approached us and asked us to help create a pathway to the State Supreme Court so that plaintiffs could ascend the steps without harassment from antigay protesters. So, we formed a line, dressed in our rainbow T-shirts, and stood there waiting for the plaintiffs to arrive later that morning along with what we anticipated to be several antigay protestors. My sister and I and our other group members held each other's hands and formed a rainbow wall.

Soon enough, in the morning dew and over the horizon of a grassy knoll, thousands of counter-protestors emerged from a "May Day for Marriage" rally they had just attended. We stood silently as thousands quickly surrounded us. They held terrible signs saying we were going to hell and to read the Bible. Clutching one another's hands, we held the line as the rally-goers pressed closer and closer behind us. The camera crew followed our every move, almost expecting a controversy. Instead, we stood our ground, shoulder to shoulder, as we demonstrated our beliefs in equality and love.

We spent several hours holding the line that day on those steps from the early morning into the afternoon. Pressing up behind us, the May Day for Rally goers would try to goad us into an argument. Instead, we would chant about peace and love, hoping to drown out some of the ugliness we overheard.

I'll never forget when a fellow demonstrator, a woman in her late sixties, befriended me, took me by the hand, and led me through the crowd of the May Day for Marriage rallygoers. Seemingly out of nowhere, she had turned to me and said, "Follow me."

At first, I had been terrified to take such a step, wearing my rainbow shirt among people carrying signs that said I would burn in hell. But as this little old woman tightly held my hand, she turned to look at me and said, "Don't be afraid."

We walked and walked to show our strength. Finally, we emerged unscathed and returned to hold the line with our fellow demonstrators. Hours later, when the proceedings were over, we returned to our KOA campsite and prepared to return to campus the following day, forever changed.

What a powerful experience. We were glad to have it documented and aired nationwide over the following weeks.

On another occasion, when our efforts reached national proportions, we had to respond to an incident during a nationally televised Gonzaga men's basketball game on ESPN (Associated Press 2006).

Our student section, the Kennel Club, had researched a number of the opposition players to chant embarrassing or revealing information about them during the game. The goal was to mess with their head. In this case, they discovered it had been rumored one of the opposing players might be gay. At the same time, the famous movie *Brokeback Mountain* was still in theaters. So, they chanted "Brokeback Mountain" at the player, which garnered national headlines and critiques of their unsportsmanlike behavior.

Breaking national news, several media outlets contacted different people involved for comment, including me as the president of our gay-straight alliance. I was quoted in an AP article, offering my perspective on the incident. Most notably, how unfortunate I felt for the player, but also for all my fellow LGBTI Kennel Club members, who felt alienated and put down by their peers.

For this, I later found myself in a live on-air segment for a little-known political pundit at the time, Tucker Carlson, something I kick myself to this day for (NBC News 2006). I naively accepted the invitation despite the better judgment of some of my peers. Even when he tried to manipulate me, I remained steadfast in towing a middle line. I strived to ensure I represented both LGBTI students, the Kennel Club, and my university in the highest regard by sharing that we had begun the process of healing and moving forward, for which we had.

My former roommate was in the leadership of the Kennel Club. Working together, at the next nationally televised basketball game, we made hundreds of rainbow ribbons and signs that read "Hate has no place here," which we passed out to those in the student section. Then, in a show of solidarity, we all stood together at the game, cheering on our team.

And in the only time I've been arrested, my peers in HERO and I joined a national movement called "Right to Serve," where we sought to point out the hypocrisy of a backward policy in the military that prevented LGBTI people from openly serving, known as "Don't Ask, Don't Tell." Given there were many highly qualified, openly gay individuals willing and able to serve their country, it became absurd when those willing to give their life for their country would have to hide who they really were or receive a dishonorable discharge.

I attended a training in Minnesota with national leaders who taught us how to demonstrate. First, we were to identify a local military recruitment center and seek to apply, with one exception, we weren't willing to serve closeted. Then each of us returned home to our respective locations and began planning.

In our protest, while quite a serious issue, it became somewhat comical as national support for the repeal of Don't Ask, Don't Tell was at an all-time high. Three HERO members, including me, decided we would be willing to be arrested for the cause. The rest would hold signs and silently protest the policy outside. We dressed for church, done up to the nines, and entered one of the local recruitment centers based at an outlet mall.

Only one gentleman was working that day. We approached his desk at the back of the center. As planned, we announced we were there to apply for the military. He gave us details, and then once he said, "Are you interested?" we responded we identified as gay and lesbian and were not willing to serve quietly. He then said, "Well, in that case, I'm sorry, but we can't accept your application."

We responded, "Well, we must protest this unjust and unfair policy," and told him we were conducting a sit-in.

To our surprise, he kindly offered us chairs and told us that he sympathized with our efforts, but he couldn't do anything more due to the policy. He then called the police.

When the police arrived, we anticipated the arrest. However, as I had been trained, we immediately complied when they asked us to leave (Lowry 2006). As we came out, the police officers, too, agreed with our protest. As peaceful protestors, they even asked if we preferred to be handcuffed after issuing us a summons to the court. We were then set free.

The following week, in the courtroom, the presiding judge called us to the front of the room and reviewed our case. Looking at all three of us, with no criminal record and good grades at the university, he too agreed with our protest and, while following the law, dismissed our cases under the auspices that we were not arrested again within a five-year period.

While we had held a relatively peaceful protest, news of our action soon broke out across our campus and throughout the wider Spokane community. Our actions sparked debate and discussion among our peers concerning the legitimacy of such a policy. If anything, the absurdity of our haphazard ordeal of being arrested also pointed directly to the absurdity of such a discriminatory policy. To think of all the armed services personnel whose lives were harmed or whose careers were cut short makes it no laughing matter.

Throughout all that time, since she came to my school during my sophomore year, I also stayed in touch with Judy Shepard, who became an important mentor and guided me as my profile grew both on my campus and in the wider community. When I faced something challenging, she always offered me sage advice and her love and support.

In certain ways, she was one of the few who actually got what I was going through. With all she had experienced in her life and all she had gone on to do after the murder of her son, I felt profoundly blessed even to have met her once. To have her motherly love extended my way became an honor of a lifetime and something I felt forever indebted to.

Following along with my journey, she invited my dad and me during my junior year to their annual "Bear to Make a Difference" gala in Denver, Colorado. Her organization flew us out and put us in a hotel room, and we enjoyed learning more about the Shepard family and their friends. I met her husband, Dennis, and her other son, Logan, whom I quickly bonded with.

I also met others who remained in their orbit, individuals who had been there long before. I met the man who helped devise the angel wings covering the taunts of Westboro Baptist Church members protesting Matt's funeral. I met Matt's childhood friends. I even met one of the responding police officers who had found Matt lying lifeless when tied up to a fence. Suddenly, their story became much more intimate and important to me and my life.

On another trip to Colorado later that year, my dad, sister, and I had planned to attend my old soccer coach, Greg's wedding to his wife, Amanda. Unfortunately, I had dislocated my hip in a soccer game and had been using crutches to get around. While there, we joined Judy and her family on a protest of the Focus on the Family organization in Colorado Springs, the largest organization in the country known for spreading misinformation about LGBTI family life (Ring 2022). My dad pushed me in a wheelchair for a good mile and a half as we protested around the organization's campus alongside the Shepards.

The following year, Judy invited us back to Denver to attend the gala, but this time she honored me with their highest award, the "Making a Difference Award" (Grant 2006). My whole family joined me, including my mom, dad, and sister, which in itself was such a gesture to so many other gay men in the room whose own families had rejected them, along with families who had lost their gay children. They particularly appreciated my dad's unwavering support of me.

The award symbolized Matt's never-ending energy in fighting for what was right and just in the world.

With my proud family in the audience, I accepted and expressed how there weren't enough words to describe my profound love for them. My greatest wish was to know they could feel and sense the depth of love I had for them in their every breath. I emphasized that while the numerous events, awards, and accolades were meaningful to me, what kept me going was my belief in love and the unique journeys I encountered along the way of individuals still struggling to fully accept themselves. I saw the recognition not as an endpoint but as a catalyst to keep going—a call to action.

After that gala in Colorado, we met up with our friends, our chosen family. The Stills and Samars came down to Denver to wish us well and to tell me how proud they were of me. My old soccer coach, Greg, his wife Amanda, and my teammates also came to express their love and support. All of them echoed that which I had been so afraid of losing, the love we all had for one another.

That same year, *Advocate Magazine* recognized me as a Future Gay Hero (Broverman 2005). I was lauded as someone who stood up when it counted and faced adversity with kindness and love. Ironically, a feature story about *Brokeback Mountain* and Heath Ledger was on the cover.

Finally, near the end of my time at Gonzaga, I was recognized as a *twenty-under-thirty young person doing kick-ass work in the Inland Northwest* by a regional magazine, the Inlander (2008). In the feature, they captured my story in a way I felt I couldn't do myself. They highlighted the long journey I had been on and the underlying passions that had guided my path.

This national engagement and notoriety elevated my consciousness and compelled me to move further. I was no longer just a reluctant activist on my college campus. I felt a deep calling within me to keep pushing forward, to continue urging people to transcend their intolerance and to imagine a shared humanity between us all. I wanted to dedicate the rest of my life to it despite the fear and trepidation of not living to see the end results.

Undergirding it all were the profound gifts of love and care I had unearthed with James years before, the never-ending quest to pave a way so that the love I shared with him in another world might thrive and let its light shine to truly change the world.

PRAY THE GAY AWAY

Despite all I'd gone on to do, some still thought there was something wrong with me back in Spokane.

It's one thing for people to think you are evil without having ever met you. It's completely different when those you feel closest to question your character, underlying principles, the defining moments of your life, and the validity of your lived experiences.

That is the true mindfuck of the activism I undertook.

The Spokane Community and my time at Gonzaga offered a profundity like none other, allowing students to explore their existential thoughts and greatest curiosities. But unfortunately, it also left open room for spiritual neglect and abuse.

I had been doing all I knew to do by the university as a social justice champion. Yet some within the Spokane community, different administrators, faculty, and fellow students shunned me in subtle and not-so-subtle ways. Even people I had considered close friends.

From certain members of the Spokane community, I continued to receive condemnation. I remember reading about how sinful I was from community members who would write to the university demanding my expulsion in online public forums or angry emails anonymously sent to my university account.

One time I received a series of vaccines for upcoming travel during the summer following my first senior year. That evening, I started to have extreme contrasts in temperatures. One moment, I was freezing, with my teeth chattering and feeling like death, then minutes later, feeling extreme heat, sweating buckets, and overwhelmed. Finally, I decided it was important to see a doctor.

With my dad, I walked into the clinic, and after describing my symptoms, without having once laid a single hand on me, the doctor told me she suspected I might have HIV. Furthermore, she underscored her authority in the matter, explaining she had seen many cases "just like mine." I was immediately aghast, frightened, and of course, believed her.

She took a swab from the back of my throat. Shortly after, she said she would have the lab run other tests but assumed my positive status. I went to the lab for them to draw my blood and then went home with my dad to await the results a few days later. I was so frightened.

We sat in our family kitchen, partially in shock from the traumatic experience of it all. I turned to my dad, who stood there comforting me, ensuring everything would be all right, no matter the result. His kind eyes and caring heart offered a temporary reprieve from the possible life-changing news from the doctor.

Two days later, a friendly nurse called our house to inform me that my lab tests returned negative for HIV, but the test for strep throat returned positive. She emphasized the yellow fever vaccine I had taken a few days before likely inflamed the strep, and a series of antibiotics would be all I needed to get back on my feet and active. I was relieved and grateful for the news.

However, those positive feelings were short-lived as the doctor called back, negating the test results and insisting I likely had HIV.

"I'm pretty sure you are positive. You will have to wait three months to be tested again. Meanwhile, limit your sexual partners and be careful. As a young Christian man, you should think of your afterlife before engaging in such sinful behaviors."

While I was no longer symptomatic nor felt sick, the doctor's imposing words stayed with me over that semester.

Back on campus, as I leveraged the spiritual teachings I learned in class, I strived to apply the principles of love and nonviolence to my daily life. Apart from being the gay-straight alliance president, I served on the student council as a Senior Class Representative in the Gonzaga Student Body Association. I also coled a volunteer group raising money for St. Jude's Hospital called Up Till Dawn, where we raised tens of thousands of dollars to support kids with cancer in honor of the little girl I took around the Jungle Cruise years before.

I was incredibly active in intramural sports and all aspects of student life. At events like "Take Back the Night," I gave speeches about reproductive freedom and against gender-based violence. I participated in cultural events around campus. For several internships, I volunteered at the Spokane LGBTI Odyssey Youth Center. I lived out and aspired to the example my grandparents had instilled in me since I was little and the ongoing lessons I was taking away from my campus.

I invested my time and talents in numerous ways aligned with my faith's teachings as a Catholic. Yet that which I advocated for, according to some, seemed to be at odds with the university and the church. Certain campus leaders chose not to see my own spiritual journey or an alignment with my faith through my many acts of service. This was reinforced in many ways, where the simplest things we wanted to do faced greater scrutiny.

HERO often jumped across additional hurdles to ensure we weren't offending any who might be offended. The university required us to offer the church's teachings in any of our materials or at the start of any public event, like an opinion article where a person writes at the end their perspectives are solely their own and don't represent the medium upon which they are publishing. It was always subtle but always telling. You are valuable, so long as you stay in line and don't cause too much of a ruckus.

Looking back at what I accomplished during my time there, I often wonder if I advocated for any other cause but achieved the same level of recognition and notoriety, would I have been treated differently?

While the institution regularly played what-about-ism, or both sides are right, I deeply struggled with some of my fellow students. Having others my age and in the same classes espouse such hateful beliefs and attitudes toward me was the most challenging thing. While all in the name of freedom of thought, speech, and religion, this skewed to allow hateful rhetoric to play itself out across our campus.

Events like the Vagina Monologues had to take place off campus, and initiatives to provide condoms and lubricants to students via the university health center, while passing our student senate, were ultimately denied by the university.

Professors were allowed to continuously target students with microaggressions and dismissive, unwelcoming behaviors. Other students had free rein to spout their hateful rhetoric.

Students who supported LGBTI rights on campus far outnumbered those with opposing viewpoints. However, those opposing viewpoints were often given equal weight. As a result, I endured school newspapers, classroom discussions, campus events, and forums in which my very existence seemed up for debate.

The Campus Crusaders for Christ brought a speaker touting the benefits of conversion therapy. They took over an entire lecture hall and offered their baseless claims that individuals suffered from homosexual sin and simply needed to rediscover a heterosexual lifestyle.

Another speaker was brought on campus by the College Republicans to give a talk entitled "The Dangers of Homosex" (Vestal 2005). Most of the audience was made up of silent protestors, including members of the student body association I was a part of. We sat there listening to him ramble on and on in graphic detail about the dangers homosexual sex posed to society, which needed weeding out.

I once went on a spiritual *pilgrimage* through the university ministries, where we took a day-long hike in the mountains. We took turns carrying a large cross at the front of our group. When it became my turn, several students protested under their breath why someone like me was allowed to carry the cross. That evening, we started several campfires at the end. When I joined, the same students rolled their eyes in disgust and left the circle.

Every year there was a new crop of them, spouting the same biblical texts and regurgitating the same talking points the right-wing religious zealots in their hometowns proselyted to them as children. While their numbers slowly dwindled during my time on campus, their hateful rhetoric profoundly impacted my spiritual pathways.

There is something to be said about a group of people who don't even know you, constantly bombarding you with lies, innuendo, and propaganda suggesting you are somehow lying to them, you are a deviant, a pedophile, and not to be trusted. You are someone to be fixed, altered, or redirected, and something is inherently wrong with you that only they know how to fix if only you would follow their ways.

While resilient, these subtle messages can seep their way into your soul and make you question some of the most fundamental aspects of who you are, as they did to me.

And while some of the structural elements of the university and the outright bigotry and hatred of fellow students were difficult, nothing was more painful than the betrayal of what I thought were the confidences of some of my closest friends.

During my senior year of college, as the final months waned for those graduating, I spoke with someone who had been a part of my circle of friends since our first year and asked why it seemed like some of our friends were keeping a distance from me.

Sipping our coffee at a local bakery, throughout that conversation, I learned several of our friends had been praying for my soul every Sunday for nearly four years. They'd pray for my salvation and to rid me of my perverse homosexuality.

I had been to their homes. I had met their parents. I had even been to some of their weddings.

This made me question every aspect of my entire four years of friendship with most of them. The same people I cried with, laughed with, and broke bread with. We had been through so much together.

They broke a sacred bond through such action. Even worse, they believed they were doing what was best for me. In some sick and twisted way, out of what they believed to be love, they thought they were somehow helping me through their *thoughts and prayers*.

This betrayal was more than just on the surface but rather what it meant for the entirety of our friendship. To me, it told me they never saw me. They never fundamentally respected who I was at my core.

After graduation, I never heard from them again.

In hindsight, one of the most challenging aspects of my time in college was the spiritual abuse I suffered. Playing the evil spirit in someone else's mind.

They doubted my worthiness and the sacredness with which I discovered life. And when I shared my good news, particularly that

I was capable of love and light within my life, I was shunned for even mentioning it. Or, as with my dormitory friends, my truths were ignored or cast aside as being misguided and uninformed.

I had to find my own spiritual path in the face of individuals who would doubt and question the sanctity of my life and personal capacities. I learned the hard way that the meaning and purpose of life was indeed to *transcend the bullshit.*

As some say, "Father, forgive them, for they know not what they do."

Life's meaning was not necessarily always found within the four walls of a church or derived from those who proselytized and laid claim to knowing Christianity the best. Those most self-righteous in their proclamation of a religious calling were often the ones who most struggled with their spiritual foundations and belief systems. I had to learn I could trust my gut, and there were far greater truths out there in the world, ones not derived from a single religion or understood by a single person. Indeed, their professed faith proclaimed as much, but they didn't want to hear it.

Just like my time in middle school, after seeing my bullies in the pews next to me and realizing church and spirituality were far grander than they appeared, so were my spiritual awakenings at Gonzaga.

In this sense, I had many profound spiritual explorations far and away from a specific religious grounding or traditional epicenter to which I could apply and live out the spiritual teaching I endured throughout my time there.

In the wider community, I had healers, elders, peers, and those with lived experiences that offered hope and belief in me. I found sage guides, advisors, professors, Jesuits, and others who made up the institution of Gonzaga, who were my greatest allies and offered me profound inspiration and even glimpses of hope.

Dr. Raymond Reyes, the Vice President of Diversity and Inclusion, was this beautiful human being, full of light and love, who constantly inspired everyone around him. He was Native American and repeatedly called forth our energies for good and social justice.

Sue Weitz, the Vice President of Student Life, often consoled me in our private conversations as I navigated everything from falling in love to facing threats of violence.

My professors, like Dr. Andrea Fallenstein, Dr. Michael Jones, and many others, opened my eyes and answered my never-ending curiosities about the world and the subjects they were experts in.

Anna Gonzales supported every one of my ideas for student programming. Even those who seemed to be against my efforts, in other ways, offered me profound thoughts and considerations, like our University President, Dr. Spitzer, who directed us all toward purpose-driven lives, whatever our individual calling.

Another aspect of my spiritual growth and understanding was befriending the Shepard family. Being welcomed into their orbit of friends, family, and all those who once knew Matt was an incredible privilege. Through them, I learned so much about who Matt was and what his life meant to them.

I learned what a strong individual he was and how he could transcend so much in his short life. We had so much in common. I often asked myself questions about his life. If he had a soulmate, who was that person, and were they missing him? What would Matt have gone on to do if he were alive today? To what degree, if you believe in this, is he still an ever-present aspect of all our lives—especially to those who loved him so much? Is he helping us all to grow and evolve in one form or fashion as we keep his spirit alive?

The strength and endurance that the Shepard family has gone on to share with the world and the vulnerability of their tragic loss have taught me so much. To know what they have suffered and to see them continue pressing forward and serving the LGBTI community to the best of their abilities has been deeply inspiring.

I continued my deeply spiritual musings through our university ministries, where I participated in several pilgrimages and led spiritual retreats. One retreat, SEARCH, brought me together with many of my peers as we sought to restore our faith in ourselves and in each other. There was even a point where we were all surprised with dozens of letters from our loved ones and peers back on campus, telling us how much we meant to them. These retreats brought such renewal and a sense of community to me.

Out of the ashes of my lost friend group, I also uncovered friends who didn't let their religious beliefs negate my humanity. Christine and Amanda. Through our friendship, they eventually evolved and grew beyond some of their original beliefs to see the totality within me. They came to know my most authentic spirit and who I was, even offering me support in times of need. We held profound conversations with one another, took trips across the country, attended each other's life events, and found a deep level of love, curiosity, and possibility within our friendships throughout our journey.

For our final spring break, the three of us drove my car 1,230 miles from Gonzaga's campus to Disneyland in Anaheim, California. Along the way, we stopped at the homes of their relatives and found profound joy in one another's company. I enjoyed remaining in touch with some of my friends from Disney and had the good fortune of still being connected to peers working in California. Not only were my Gonzaga friends able to enjoy the park with me, but we got to experience some additional magic along the way. In addition, they got to see me in my happy place.

One of those friends, Christine, even came with me to the doctor's office for my three-month follow-up appointment to test for HIV. Still reliving the moments on the phone a few months prior when the doctor was convinced, I was HIV positive, we went to the hospital for a rapid test. My whole future weighed on my heart as I contemplated the possible results. As I tested and waited to see if I was positive, Christine waited with me in the reception area, holding my hand. I was negative.

And, of course, my experience of uncovering the love and light within me through my experiences of falling in love with James made me feel connected to the wider world in ways that felt like divine intervention.

As our class neared graduation, there was so much anticipation about what would happen next. While I would be staying another year to complete my degree, many of those I started school with would be heading out into the world, including James.

James's departure was the most difficult because there was no promise I would see him again. Just like at the end of our sophomore year, I feared that once he returned home and started his new life, the dynamics of our friendship would shift, as often does, following life transitions.

Overwhelmed with this impending possibility, I wrote him another letter detailing how our relationship had impacted me. I went to his apartment to say my final goodbyes and tearfully sat on his couch as he read my message.

James,

So, as you know, I've been pretty all over the place leading up to the end of an era! Our class graduated and will be moving on with their lives, including you. So, my feelings have wobbled back and forth, wondering what the future holds. And part of that anxiousness is also thinking about the what-ifs.

So, since there is a what-if... I never saw you again, there are a few things I felt like I needed to share with you before you left.

I guess I've always been scared to tell you. I dunno, I just didn't think you'd understand, but nonetheless, there have been some things I've wanted you to know for a while now. I don't know how you'll take it. So I will try to be as clear as I can when it comes to saying what I want you to know... just in case.

All I wanna say is thanks.

Thank you for being you, for letting me love you, for being my friend, and, yes, one of the greatest inspirations in my life. James, you taught me to love myself and someone else, you. And in turn, each and every person that might come into my life. I might even write a book someday.

Because I loved you...

- *I know why couples can get up in the middle of a crowded restaurant and dance to songs that no one gets but them.*
- *I know why Romeo and Juliet cared so much for each other that they ultimately sacrificed themselves because they couldn't bear the thought of living without the other person.*
- *I know what all the love songs, movies, and romance novels are all about... once you know love, they become something so much more like a hidden code unlocking these sacred secrets.*
- *I know what it's like to be willing to go through hell just to be with someone. (Watch* What Dreams May Come.*)*
- *I know why the Mona Lisa Smiles.*
- *I know what it's like to be willing to give my life for someone.*
- *I know a great many secrets of the world as to why people put so much heart and soul into things that they care about.*
- *Believe it or not, I feel closer to God because I loved you. It's weird how loving you has helped me to find a deeper appreciation for their being a greater purpose in our lives.*
- *I know what Jesus, Buddha, Allah, Nature, Life, etc., meant when they said love is the way of life.*

- *I know what built the greatest men of our time, from poets to scientists... the greatest of these beings those that led for others out of love. Martin Luther King, Albert Einstein, Gandhi, Mother Teresa, Jesus, Nelson Mandela, Desmond Tutu.*
- *I know what it's like to care about someone for all of who they are, no matter what.*
- *I know what it's like to see within a person their greatest beauty.*
- *I know what it's like to love selflessly.*
- *I know what it means to have a real friend.*
- *I know why there is no hell, but rather a social creation used to scare us away from this force within us because it is so powerful.*
- *I know why it's worth living every single day of your life to the fullest.*
- *I know why I would face innumerable odds standing up for this belief and this feeling.*
- *I know I am not an evil, immoral person because if what I have felt is at all anything but the most beautiful thing in the world, and it can still be wrong, then I don't believe there can be a real God, a real truth, a real anything.*
- *I know that love isn't just in fairy tales or our dreams, but real and authentic.*
- *I know that love extends itself to our every single action and that once you have loved someone in this way, it spreads itself to each and every part of your life from your closest friends to strangers in the street.*
- *I know what it's like to feel like I have everything in the world.*
- *I know when I die, whether tomorrow or a hundred years from now, I will be able to move on in peace because I will*

have loved in my life, regardless of whether I find it again. I can be happy with my life and who I am.
- *I know what it's like to love someone so much that all you want is their happiness, regardless if that happiness includes you or not. I mean that with all my heart.*
- *I know how we can create peace in the world.*
- *I know what kept my grandparents together for over fifty years until my grandmother passed away.*

And so, James, thank you. I love you so much, buddy. You will forever be someone who reminds me of how beautiful the world is. You were my lighthouse, my north star, and my muse, and it has meant so much to me and my life. You have colored my black-and-white world, and I'm a better person because I have loved you, and I hope you are a better person too.

All the successes of my life that have transpired since I met you have been because I have cared so deeply for who you are as my dearest friend.

So, I love you, James. I always will and will never be ashamed to say that I do. It's not that I don't love you. It's that I love you so much that I just want you to be good. That's all. Your happiness truly is mine.

Love,

Ryan

He wiped a tear from his eye. We hugged each other tightly. We went to lunch, and then he drove off and headed east. And this was how I made space for and reveled in the divine aspects of my story.

Loving James gave me a more nuanced appreciation for and understanding of how love unfolds itself across our lives in a myriad of ways. While he identified as straight and I identified as gay, there wasn't a bone in my body that didn't know how deeply we loved each other.

I had no idea what my next chapter in life would be or what life would hold for me. But what I did know was that despite the questioning, my life had purpose and meaning, and I couldn't let it go to waste.

What would I do with the love I had discovered? How would it play itself out in the world before me?

AN ODE TO FAMILY

Foundational in everything that I accomplished and overcame at Gonzaga was the love and support of my family. My profound love for them seemed unbreakable.

From being a shy, scared little kid afraid of losing his family, I found my love returned tenfold. The same family I feared would abandon me were always my biggest champions.

So much of what I could do was because of my family.

My sister got it right away when I came out to her. From her first response, going out with one of my exes to get to know him; or joining me in Olympia to protest for same-sex marriage—she showed her love for me. She befriended many gay men and supported them over the years. Through her role as a resident advisor, she helped others to come to terms with themselves. She helped to cast her own shadow in advancing and supporting marginalized persons.

My dad, in his own way, showed up for me as best he could as he learned to understand my experience. He embraced me when I came out to him at Disney World over a thousand miles away, sat with me for hours, asked me questions about my experience as a gay man, and stood with me as I awaited my HIV test.

In a show of support for me, he became a club advisor for the gay-straight alliance at the high school where he worked and had me speak to his students. This action meant the world to me, especially given my dad was the head of the boy's basketball team at the time and cast a large shadow on who he was at the school. When I faced times of injustice or difficulty, he was the one to offer guidance, support, and advice on what step I might take next.

One time, he imparted his wisdom to me on how he, as a basketball coach, was not just a coach when his team was in practice or playing a game. But that had he been pulled over by the cops for speeding or made a fool of himself in a public setting, he would still be seen as the coach when his principal or the parents of his players found out.

This lesson influenced my leadership style and cognizance of how I presented myself in the world. As a campus leader, I had to think about how I showed up not just during meetings or when I was at a formal event but in all aspects of my life.

Being the dean of student life long before I arrived on campus, my mom helped pave the way to make Gonzaga a more equitable and fairer campus for all students. She strongly supported diversity and inclusion efforts to ensure students of color, women, LGBTI students, or a combination of them all felt welcomed at the university.

Like a subconscious voice in one's head, my mother's comforting words or sage wisdom always guided many of the decisions I made throughout my collegiate experience. She recommended the Walt Disney World College Program, that I bring Judy Shepard to campus to speak, and to get involved with student activities.

My mom sought to help me see the good in everyone, no matter the circumstance. Even the individuals who perpetuated hateful messages around my sexuality and extolled their superiority of religious knowledge, she still encouraged me to see the best in them.

Behind closed doors among fellow administrators, she sparred and debated with those who thought my presence on campus was a nuisance and felt I should face expulsion for being gay.

There are likely so many more stolen moments where she fought or went to bat for me in ways I will never know. And the same goes for my dad and sister as well. What they have shouldered on my behalf as an act of love toward me has been one of my greatest sources of strength.

My grandparents' spirit, love, and inspiration were also with me the whole time. Their lived example, their commitments to social justice, and the wellspring of love they provided all those around them inspired me. Just like at the county fair in New Mexico, when the man turned to us and told me what a pillar of her community my grandmother was, I too sought to lead by her example.

Through this foundation, I felt like I could face the world, and in many ways, I did. Little did I know how much of the world was still out there.

CIRCUMNAVIGATING THE GLOBE

I always held a sense of something much deeper within me that connected me to a broader spirit I've intuitively known throughout it all.

Enmeshed in near-constant advocacy for LGBTI rights in the US, my awareness of things unearthed through my relationships with those I so deeply loved beat a drum reminding me of an ancient calling I always felt most connected to.

The love of my family, grandparents, chosen family, James, and others were not necessarily opening new doors but pulling back curtains on the things I already felt deep within but was afraid to explore. Their loving inspirations to me throughout my life served as a lighthouse in which to bypass perilous passes and beckon me home.

I would soon validate that deep knowingness in an adventure yet to come.

As my friends graduated from college, I stuck around to undertake a once-in-a-lifetime opportunity.

Just before the end of my first senior year, my mom was selected as Dean of Student Life for a program called Semester at Sea for the spring 2007 voyage, the same program my grandparents raved about from their days of retirement a decade before.

While it would delay my official graduation by a year, my mom felt this was something I couldn't pass up and invited me to tag along, and my dad agreed. It was the greatest gift any parent could give their children.

When my mom approached me, at first, my mind immediately went to my activism. There was still work to do, and I wanted to maintain the momentum of having an impact. With some coaxing, my mom convinced me I had given a lot and this chance might never come again. So, I agreed.

Semester at Sea is officially a multi-country study abroad program on a ship open to all students of all majors, emphasizing global comparative study. In other words, it forever evolved my sense of self and connection to others through an experiential journey like none other while circumnavigating the globe at thirty nautical miles per hour. On board were thirty staff, thirty-three faculty, over seven hundred students, and one hundred plus crew members.

It was a floating university. When we were at sea, we alternated days attending courses related to our individual fields of study and exploring the various nuances of the contexts we visited. When we arrived, we'd then explore the country on curated trips, which included between ten to fifty students, staff, and faculty who took various excursions preplanned for us ahead of our arrival.

Between classes, we'd have our meals in one of the three major dining halls and partake in one of the many activities on board, from social clubs, exercise, or lounging around by the pools.

We set sail from the Bahamas and sailed around the world, stopping in over ten countries, including Puerto Rico, Brazil, South Africa, Mauritius, India, Malaysia, Vietnam, China, and

Japan. We stopped in Hawaii to refuel on our way back across the Pacific Ocean.

Mom and I led different lives on board as we did back at Gonzaga. She dealt with various student-life-related issues while I attended classes and hung out with fellow students. We'd often share meals on board the ship and go on excursions together when we were in a country. We spent late-night hours in her cabin talking about our travels and the lives we missed back home, including my dad and sister.

The ship's first port was Puerto Rico, where we got to do many things, the highlight of which was visiting one of only six bioluminescent bays in the world one evening. When we got there, guides were waiting for us with several kayaks. In pairs, we kayaked down this long stream from the ocean, deep into the mangroves.

Covered by the canopy of the trees in the pitch-black darkness of night, fish jumped in and out of our boats. I would hear a shrill or two from fellow students when a fish smacked across their faces. As the night descended, the water started to glow with every paddle.

Microorganisms in the water were like fireflies, glowing whenever activated. As we made our way down the river and deeper into the mangroves, we saw streams of glowing plankton trailing behind us.

We soon reached a large clearing where our guides explained the science of bioluminescence to us and then told us to get into the water.

The microorganisms attached to our bodies. I could see every inch of myself as I swam. My toes, arms, legs, and fingers lit up as I kicked my legs and moved my arms. Pulling my hands closer to my face, I saw the little microorganisms swarming around. What mysteries the world held!

We made our way back to the busses and then to the ship, where we dressed and got ready to go out later in the evening.

We joined a few local students to go salsa dancing. Getting to know them was a whole other introduction to the island. They were warm, welcoming, and genuinely wanted us to have the best time. We partied late into the early morning until we had to return to the ship to set sail for our next destination, Brazil.

Puerto Rico was just our first stop, but the enjoyment I had hanging out with students our age, dancing, and living our best lives set a strong precedence for the rest of the trip.

We arrived in the town of Salvador, Bahia, a few days later, just in time for Carnival, where the whole country was shut down to release all their *sins* before the fasting season of Lent came around.

As we disembarked that morning from the ship, beautiful Afro Brazilian women in traditional Carnival clothing with colorful swooping dresses and done-up hair offered us colorful Brazilian wish bracelets to give us luck.

For the first half of our stay, I went with a group of students to the southern part of the Bahia State to a small beach community where we learned about endangered sea turtle populations. We celebrated Carnival with the locals, different from mainstream Carnival events in the bigger cities throughout Brazil.

Families brought their children as people dressed up in sheets, aimlessly carrying on in the streets. Young men, painted in black and wearing ghoulish masks, went around playfully, scaring people reflecting the demons meant to be rejected in the months ahead.

The next day, we canoed down the Amazon River. With our packed lunches, we navigated the river terrain. At one point, we carried our canoes through a set of mangroves, where thousands of tiny red crabs scurried out of our way as we passed. Our final destination was a deserted beach. For miles in either direction, no one else was in this pristine place. We enjoyed this incredible setting for the rest of the afternoon before heading back to our lodging.

The next day, we took a brief tour through the Amazon rainforest with a local guide. We saw a wide assortment of animal and bug species, which included monkeys, birds, and sloths. We climbed over logs and crawled under low-hanging branches braving fire ants as they bit into the crevices of our toes. Oh, the pain! We waded through neck-deep murky water, unsure of what lay beneath. All these things I was too intimidated to do in my previous life.

We made our way back to the ship docked in the city of Salvador and discovered another part of Brazil that night in the controlled chaos of Carnival. Everywhere we went felt electric. In the city, we danced down the streets behind drumming bands until dawn. We ate street food and conversed with locals we met along the way.

The next night, we joined millions of people crowded along the sides of these tiny roads as colossal monster trucks carrying massive speakers hosted some of Latin America's most famous singers, like Shakira. Whole caravans of dancing and singing people moved along, sometimes inch by inch. Some floats allowed revelers to hop on and off as they drove through the city. Every thirty minutes, a new truck would roll by with thousands of people in tow, all dressed themed to the float, just wanting to have a good time.

I was knocked in every direction and lost almost all hearing, yet on the way back to the ship, I wore one of the biggest smiles on my face. It seemed as if every person in the city had come out in celebration to drink, dance, and sing together in harmony and spirit.

Brazil had the most exuberant energy and brought out an amazing freedom within me, allowing me to enjoy the country and its people through song and dance.

The next day we set sail for seven days crossing the Atlantic Ocean, bound for Cape Town, South Africa. Spending several days at sea gave us a lot of time to focus on our studies while also enjoying ship life. Finally, we arrived at the beautiful marina with the majestic Table Mountain towering over our ship.

My mom and I joined a four-day, three-night game drive in Pilanesberg National Park. The game lodges sat in a giant U shape, with a large lodge and pool area in the center. Each bungalow came with two king-size beds covered in mosquito netting, a balcony overlooking the park's savannah, and an indoor-outdoor shower area.

Rangers woke us up early, around 5 a.m., piled nine to ten people in an uncovered Jeep, and drove us around to spot game as the animals rose with the sun in their natural habitat. We saw elephant herds crossing the roads and giraffes sticking their long necks into the sky to nibble on a tree's higher leaves. Hippos peered out from under pools of mud. Hundreds of impala, wildebeest, and zebra roamed the savannah as lions and leopards lurked nearby. I had only ever seen such animals in zoos or on TV when I was a kid, never once believing I would ever see them in real life.

South Africa left an indelible impression on me, one I will never forget.

After South Africa, we made our way to India. My mother and I sailed on the Ganges River in Varanasi, stood at the base of the Arulmigu Thiyagarajaswamy Hindu Temple in Chennai, and saw one of the Wonders of the World"—the Taj Mahal in Agra.

The Taj Mahal consisted of the finest marble and ruby red cut stones symbolizing the fifth Mughal emperor, Shah Jahan's eternal love for his wife (Sherriff 2022). A mirror structure in black was meant to sit on the opposite side of the river to commemorate him but was never built.

At sunset, reflecting the moon's light, I couldn't help but think about James as I traced my hands along the marble surrounding the princess's tomb on the inside, considering all one might do for love.

My time in India was different from anything I had known before. It felt as if all my senses experienced something new. Taste, sound, sight, touch, and smell, all of it felt different. I was overwhelmed, yet the journey pushed such spaces I'd never considered. It felt so liberating.

We sailed on to Kuala Lumpur, Malaysia. On our way, our ship's crew had to look out for pirates as we crossed the Bay of Bengal in the northern part of the Indian Ocean.

The region was known for pirates who'd stalked and boarded large ships, holding their crew hostage. However, on the stern of our ship, five water cannons could be used should there be any attack. Our ship was also one of the fastest in the world and could outrun any pirate ship.

When we arrived in Kuala Lumpur, we explored the city for a day before I joined a group of students who flew to Borneo, where we visited an orangutan orphanage. Deforestation devastated the animals' habitats, putting them on the brink of extinction. The orphanage helped to protect the majestic creatures.

From the dense underbrush, the orangutans emerged. From just a dozen feet away, we watched them play and interact with one another. Other monkeys came out to play with our cameras, clothing, and whatever else they could get their hands on.

Malaysia provided me with a connection to a rare part of this Earth and an experience of seeing majestic animals in their natural habitats—something that might not exist for much longer.

We moved on to Vietnam, sailing up the Mekong Delta, where mountains spiked high into the air out of the water forming breathtaking landscapes before us.

I traveled across the border to Siam Reap, Cambodia, where we explored ancient temples, including another wonder of the world, Angkor Wat. Walking among the formerly Hindu, now Buddhist temples in the same places people walked thousands of years before was hard to even wrap my head around. To imagine the labor and effort it took, let alone the spiritual devotion that went into building such a site was beyond my full comprehension. I loved visiting both Vietnam and Cambodia. The two countries offered me a purview into different histories; both plagued with shifting forms of dominance and power they still grapple with today.

We returned to the ship in Ho Chi Min City and traveled the next day to Hong Kong. In contrast, Hong Kong was a modern metropolitan city pressed right up against the Tai Mao Shun Mounds and before the South China Sea. This huge bustling city had skyscrapers that disappeared into the clouds, with dozens of high rises built against the foothills.

My friend and I decided to go to Hong Kong Disneyland to contrast my experiences in Florida. We spent the day figuring out the transportation system to get there, thirty minutes away on the outskirts of the port where we docked. We marveled at how Disney adapted some of its core themes to fit the cultural norms of the people of Hong Kong. Their version of the Jungle Cruise was entirely different while retaining the core principles.

From Hong Kong, a group flew to Beijing, where we spent several days learning about Chinese culture. We visited the Forbidden City and Temple of Heaven. Countless Chinese citizens were out and about with their families. Most families were multigenerational. Teenagers seemed to actually enjoy being with their parents while the elderly cared for the toddlers. It reminded me of my family back home, including my chosen family in Colorado.

The next day, we hiked to the top of the Great Wall. It stretched across the entire horizon. It is the only man-made structure that can be seen with the naked eye from space. We slid down to the base on a metal slide.

That night, a group of students went into the city to hang out with other young people from the Beijing area. We found a spot where we smoked hookah and made friends with locals.

China had a mesmerizing culture and people. I was grateful to reimagine whole communities and individuals I had previously only held tainted ideas about through a Western framework. There was so much still to learn about that country.

The next day we met our ship after traveling North to Qingdao to take us to our final destination, Japan.

Docked in the city of Kobe, my friends and I bought bullet train tickets. We spent each day traveling to different cities like Nagasaki, Hiroshima, Kyoto, Nagoya, Osaka, and Tokyo.

While in Tokyo, I spent two days visiting Tokyo Disney and had the time of my life. The park was all that Walt had imagined but in full size. It was massive. I went to a baseball game in Kobe and visited the famous Buddhist temples in Kyoto while learning more about Japanese culture from local Geishas. It was an incredible experience.

Japan was such a fast-paced society that shifted how I viewed myself in the world. I loved it.

As we wrapped up our last port of call, there was much to reflect upon. Each changed my life. But so, too, was our eleventh port—the ship itself. It's one thing to travel to ten countries. It's another to also see the middle of the Indian, Pacific, or Atlantic Oceans alongside a beautiful group of new friends.

Throughout the Semester at Sea voyage, not only did we have the profound opportunity to circumnavigate the globe, but we got to live on a ship traveling with a bustling community of individuals who started out as strangers but who would become bonded for the rest of our lives.

By the end of the voyage, it felt as if everyone knew each other. So many of us had gone through many life-changing moments together in the countries we visited that led to many late-night conversations exploring the depths of our souls. I even started a secret society with a few friends to debrief each of the countries we explored and how we saw ourselves shifting as people within the world.

In my classes, I sought to explore the notion of queerness throughout the countries we visited and, more broadly, the masculinities in which societies shaped men. I sought to examine the social constructs around manhood and how those shifted from culture to culture, asking what the constants were and where lay the variability.

On the ship, I joined several student groups like I did on my home campus, including the ship's gay-straight alliance, which we lovingly named "Sea Queers and Friends." We primarily formed to support one another in finding a safe space to share our experiences as LGBTI people on the voyage.

Not only did we want to get to know one another, but we wanted to learn more about the lives of queer people in the countries we visited. When we were in each country, we sought to learn as much as we could about the LGBTI experiences people had. In some cases, we were able to meet with local advocates.

We soon realized the unique privilege we had to live so openly as ourselves. We learned over seventy-six countries criminalized homosexuality at the time. Many, including the United States, had no employment, housing, or education discrimination protections. There were countless tales of individuals being ostracized or cut off from their families and communities simply for being who they were, facing extreme forms of violence, torture, or even death.

The group became one of the most supportive and uplifting communities I had ever participated in, reminding me of my fellow skippers at Disney World. I found other queer people with whom I shared such profound moments.

I'll never forget the night we were in Hong Kong and spent the evening trying to find a gay bar in a country where they still criminalized homosexuality. It was all very much underground.

We first went to a karaoke bar on top of a high-rise building. We had a good time and sang a few songs, but noticed the bar was relatively empty, so we decided to move to another bar we had heard about. We crammed into a tiny elevator and began to go down.

Then, one of us accidentally bumped into the buttons, forcing us to stop on nearly every floor. We soon realized most of the other floors were "massage" parlors. When the door opened, a young woman would bow and say, "Leiho."

We laughed at ourselves and moved on to the next bar. As it was hidden, we struggled to find out where it was. We eventually found ourselves in a discreet lobby with no signage other than a small, bland door at the end of the hall. We told the bouncer we were there for a drink, and they let us in.

A reasonably large room lit in pink and blue came into view. Everyone turned and noticed us. It was all men, clearly gay, and unbeknownst to us, the bars at that time were sex segregated.

As only two of us were men out of the eight in our group, the whole bar started shouting, "Nooo, nooo, noo." gesturing for us to go away. We were quickly pushed back, and the door was closed on us.

We were disappointed and started to head home when one of us realized there were actually two bars in the same building on the instructions we had printed on the ship. There were no smartphones back then.

We took the elevator to the other bar on the top floor and Eureka! It was a lesbian bar. While there were two men, we blended enough into the crowd that no one cared. Most in the bar already had short hair or wore masculine clothing, so we only stood out a little.

By the end of the voyage, we all realized that not only our small group was affirming of LGBTI people, but a majority, if not the whole of the ship, was also incredibly supportive. Maybe something about traveling the world together and living on a ship in the middle of the ocean helped people overcome some of their personal prejudices.

As a club, we decided to do a community-wide series of events for Pride month, which was fast approaching. During lunchtime, one of the events asked individuals what their definition of love was.

We wrote down their responses on different colors of construction paper. Then we strung them together into a larger mural we hung in the central atrium of our ship. It formed a rainbow. It showed how diverse the idea of love was and how it manifested itself in many ways. What made it even more touching was how every person on the ship had to pass by it at some point as they went about their day. I even caught the teacher of the children's program sitting all the kids down in front of it to discuss what love meant.

We also sponsored a community-wide drag show, whereby anyone who wanted to participate could do so. We put on a show for the entire community. Coming from Gonzaga, I expected the attendance to be low. But to my delight, the entire theater was packed with our fellow students, professors, staff members, and even their kids.

Even more surprising was the diverse range of performers we had identified.

First, a group of jocks on the ship decided to perform, dressed in their female friends' clothing and makeup. Then, one of my favorite professors and her two daughters performed as drag kings. Our host was one of the most fabulous drag queens I'd met with such beauty and grace, navigating the moving stage as our ship rocked us side to side, passing over waves. And the person who won it all was this beautiful Puerto Rican straight student who was so good at moving his body to Shakira that he had the whole room on their feet chanting his name. He capped off his performance by taking his then-girlfriend, dressed as a drag king, bending her over his knee and smacking a big old kiss on her to underscore his sexuality.

The entire community came together in support of its LGBTI students. It was something so special that added to the weight and impact of the whole voyage and helped me, a young gay rights activist, feel more connected to the lessons learned throughout the trip.

While I could go on and on about the many grand and granular adventures we experienced on our program, we had something even more magnanimous that guided the entire voyage—a wise elder whose sage guidance forever shifted how we knew ourselves as human beings roaming this great Earth.

NDIBONA UBUNTU KUWE

As we learned throughout our voyage about the common human experience we shared with the people we met and interacted with around the world, I began to feel a greater sense of interconnectedness with all those we came across. Of all the people I met on our voyage, I had no better guide toward the drumbeat of our human calling than the presence of an extraordinary guest who joined us for the duration of our hundred-day journey around the globe.

Nobel Laureate, Archbishop of South Africa Desmond Tutu and his wife Leah became huge fans of the program when the ship regularly stopped in the port of South Africa each semester. The archbishop always made a point to spend time with the students when the ship arrived in Cape Town on previous voyages. He was finally convinced to do one himself, ours.

As we journeyed around the world together, it became more evident why he had won the Nobel Peace Prize. While I experienced many new cultures and ways of existing in the world, the archbishop helped to refine my understanding of myself and my interconnectedness to others.

My first encounter with the archbishop happened right before the other students got on board. My mom and I had a small audience with him and other staff as he helped set the stage for an inspiring voyage.

At the small gathering in our grand performance hall, which would fill with hundreds of students in the coming days, the archbishop spoke about the meaning of our interdependencies as human beings. He emphasized how we would be meeting people from all walks of life whom we would depend upon and that our shipboard community itself was full of individuals from every background, including those among the staff and faculty, the students, the captains of our ship and our crew who needed each other to make it through. To successfully circumnavigate the globe, we would need everyone.

Exploring our interconnectedness, he spoke about how we aren't human without other human beings. Each of us has something unique to offer the world. So much so that no one is ever truly alone because we all rely on each other, whether we realize it or not, including those who paved the way for us and those who are there when we least expect someone to be there for us.

He contrasted that with our ability to inflict such hate and destruction upon one another, emphasizing that the same people capable of such love are also capable of such violence. He questioned why there were such things as a war in Iraq or genocide in Darfur, just like the similar contrast drawn in my philosophy class years earlier suggesting that we could all become Hitler or Mother Teresa. Yet somewhere in it all, we also have the choice to do the most good we can as individuals making up our local communities and moving throughout the world.

Using his Christian faith, he pointed out that one of the most radical things Jesus ever did was to tell Mary Magdalene to go and tell his brothers what had happened. He highlighted the word *brother* because the archbishop found it interesting that Jesus used these words for those who betrayed him and were ultimately not there in the end.

We may not like everyone in the world; we may even detest them, but whether we like it or not, they are our sisters, brothers, and others, and we are all the children of God—He, She, It.

I was thrust back into my campus life, realizing how much of what I had already done related to this. To live one's life in service to others, recognize the interconnected gifts we each bring into this finite life, and even still love those who saw me as *other*. His words beckoned me to continue bearing witness to the humanity all around us and to ground our voyage in the humility of being a part of the wider world we were about to encounter.

We arrived in the Bahamas to pick up the students and began our voyage. At first, most were star-struck with the archbishop. Who wouldn't be? We had a few opportunities during the first week to meet and greet him while grabbing a photo. But seeing the Arch as we sailed across the Caribbean and then on to Brazil soon became a casual everyday thing. Having met in our first few days, he and I struck up a natural friendship that would last us the rest of the voyage and beyond.

A few weeks later, I awoke to a phone call from my mother informing me that the archbishop had invited us to his cabin for a special service. "Good morning, Ryan." My mother said, "Please meet me on the ninth deck. I have a special surprise for us."

After just having had the most exhilarating time celebrating Carnival in Brazil, he decided to ask my mom and me, along with a fellow staff member, to join him in his cabin for a small commemoration of Ash Wednesday as we were disembarking from Brazil onto our next port of call, South Africa.

We met outside of the archbishop's cabin. As we entered, I immediately smelled frankincense, just like at my grandparents' house. He graciously welcomed the three of us and sat us around a group of chairs in a small circle. We each read scripture from an old, tattered Bible he had brought with him, seemingly everywhere, and spoke to the passages' meaning.

He passed me the Bible and had me read aloud to the group Isaiah 58: 1–8. The story reminded me of my sentiments from middle school about those who espouse that they have sacrificed for God on one day, but the very next, work against the spirit meant to bring us together.

We discussed how Ash Wednesday symbolized a rebirth, a rededication to living one's life in love and the spirit of action and manifesting the idea that all people, wherever they are, whoever they are, are intrinsically worthy of love and capable of giving such love to others.

Reflecting on it decades later, I see that moment in his cabin uniquely set the course for the rest of my life. A commitment to the service of others. Living every moment of your life in servitude to a higher calling. And as the archbishop would show me, not just every day, but in every moment of one's life. We each crossed ourselves and then parted ways shaking the archbishop's hand and giving him a small hug as we left his cabin.

As we continued our seven-day passage across the Atlantic Ocean, the shipboard community was made aware of our charted course. It was the same route that forcibly enslaved Africans had endured out of Africa into the Americas.

The archbishop gathered our shipboard community to pause and reflect on the countless lives lost at sea. We came to a calm part of the water where he presided over a small ceremony releasing white carnations into the ocean and honoring them. Many of us fought back tears as we contemplated the many lives lost to such an injustice and all those who would later suffer in forced servitude.

We returned to our learning while at sea. In our classes and community-wide lectures, we heard directly from the archbishop about his time growing up in South Africa's apartheid era. We were absolutely captivated by his first-hand account of facing oppression and fighting alongside Nelson Mandela and others to end discriminatory practices against Blacks and other people of color. His lectures were made even more illuminating as he further detailed the gruesome realities he had to explore through the Truth and Reconciliation Commission Mandela asked him to oversee and the national healing that took place as a result.

Sitting in observance and bearing witness to this man who had lived through such hatred and bigotry, seen such violence and bloodshed, and quelled violent mobs with his powerful voice was such a profound honor. In part, his leadership led to the liberation of millions throughout South Africa, as he led them in hymnals and worship, often reading from the same tattered Bible we read from in his cabin, calling for peace and justice.

It was a profound gift to hear directly from him. He often recounted his great admiration of young people. A huge reason he joined the shipboard community was the young people in South Africa were the ones who rose up to fight apartheid. It was also young people around the world, including in the United States, who pressured their governments to force the Afrikaans government to end their racist regime through embargoes and sanctions.

During one of his many ship-wide lectures, he taught us about the African philosophy of ubuntu, which guided his life and teachings, including when he led the Truth and Reconciliation processes. Translated to English, it means "I am because you are."

Understood by the Bantu people that populated much of Southern Africa for centuries, I came to appreciate the origin of the word emanating from parents instructing their children not to think only of themselves but to see themselves within the broader communities they were a part of. I didn't see it as a conformist word either, as in people should be the exact same as each other or sacrifice only for the good of the whole. But instead, all of us have bountiful gifts that can be extrapolated and combined to serve a much bigger purpose—all of this as we completed our seven-day voyage across the Atlantic.

The morning we arrived in South Africa was overwhelming. After everything we had just learned from the archbishop, we awoke in the early dawn hours to see Table Mountain appearing over the horizon of the Atlantic in the distance. The purple hue mixed with the rising sun as the mountain's silhouette gave me a glimpse into a continent that would become a place of such beauty to me in my life.

I started thinking about all the continent had endured in one way or another—from its colonial pasts to famine, war, and poverty. It caused a deep pain within me as I reflected on the unbearable torture many unjustly faced—especially from outsiders exploiting the good nature of many African people. Yet at the same time, the incredible beauty before me was breathtaking and awe-inspiring. It told me so much about what the continent held within it and all it offered to the broader world. Cultures, philosophies, ancient civilizations, modern poets, artists, ideas, and untapped innovations. Indeed, it was the cradle of humanity and all that was possible within our species as guardians of the earth. It felt so overwhelmingly beautiful I began to cry.

At one moment, the archbishop passed by. I briefly placed my arm around his shoulder and just stared into the horizon and the rising sun as we crept closer to Cape Town.

As we arrived at the port, the archbishop received a greeting worthy of the national treasure he was. Hundreds came to see him waving from the shore as he briefly returned to his home country. A lecture was held that evening on the ship with guests who had stood by him and helped to rewrite the national constitution during the reformation of the South African government, sharing their vision for the peace and prosperity of their nation.

They touted the importance of ubuntu in redefining their nation's constitution. This meant respecting the rights and freedoms of all people, no matter their walk of life. They stressed this is why South Africa was the first nation in the world to enshrine the right to marriage equality between same-sex couples.

South Africa was an incredible place to visit with the archbishop by our side. As we continued our travels throughout the world, he would be greeted like royalty wherever we went. At one point, the famed photographer Annie Leibovitz came onto the ship to do a photo shoot with him for a special issue of *Vanity Fair* magazine focused on the continent of Africa (Leibovitz 2007). He had been featured on the cover with President George Bush, Bono, Brad Pitt, the Gates, and other luminaries in an article highlighting the efforts to end the HIV/AIDS epidemic through programs like the President's Emergency Plan for AIDS Relief, otherwise known as PEPFAR.

With his every breath and every action, he offered an example of how to act one's way into being. It was not only his speeches and profound words of wisdom but also his lived example in the mundane, day-to-day ways of being. How he treated each moment of his life and each person with whom he interacted, his lived example itself, moved me the most. He was who he said he was.

When we docked in the country of Vietnam, just outside the ship, a set of dignitaries greeted him. They arranged to take their photo with the archbishop, and as they set up for the shot, the archbishop halted everything. He said, "Wait, we aren't all together yet."

Puzzled, those gathered looked at each other, wondering what he was talking about. Then the archbishop walked over to the driver of their vehicle and said, "He isn't in the picture yet." He guided the driver back to where the dignitaries were standing to include him in the photo.

Back on our ship, he first greeted each of the crew members serving the meal before he greeted anyone in the dining halls. He remembered their names, their kids' names, and their stories and always asked follow-up questions about how they were.

"How are you, Martin? How are your children, Xan and Marie? How did they do on their math tests?"

He also loved children. He spent hours and hours with the children on board, who traveled with their parents for the voyage. He treated them with such love and tenderness.

On the program was a little adorable baby boy named Ryder, the son of one of the professors. He was the archbishop's favorite child. The whole shipboard community loved both of them. Many would collectively *"awe"* whenever they saw the two together as they walked into one of our ship-wide lectures.

Whenever the Arch passed me in the hallway or after he had gotten done saying hello to the crew, he briefly poked me and asked, "How are you today, Ryan?" Chuckling his distinct laugh that everyone around the world seemed to know. His laughter was so infectious.

His lived example was so profound to our entire voyage, especially mine.

As we continued our many adventures, his teachings would inform every interaction we had along the way. We made many human-to-human connections. Emotions and feelings bonded us closely with all those we encountered. Through the archbishop's guidance, I saw the world in richer, more meaningful ways that struck to the core of who I was and the spaces of my heart I had so ached for.

It wasn't only in South Africa that I found the concept of ubuntu. I began to see it everywhere we went and how everything was somehow, someway, related to one another. As the Universal Declaration of Human Rights declares, our interconnected, interdependent, and intersectional lives are woven together as one (United Nations General Assembly 1948). Our humanity is not separate and apart but shared.

When we visited the Favelas in Brazil, the Townships in South Africa, or the slums in India, we carried the archbishop's messages with us. In each of these places, we were greeted by caring, loving, and kind individuals whose humanity we saw in their whole light. People who had nothing yet opened their homes and lives to us. All with laughter and love.

We also bore witness to so much pain throughout the world. I couldn't fully comprehend how our fellow human beings could so suffer. This was particularly true during our experiences with street children around the world. We met many kids who begged and sought our attention. Stern adults on our ship told us to be mindful of these children, for many were pickpocketers not to be trusted. Sometimes, our local guides would swat away at them like flies. "Go away!" they would coldly shout.

I couldn't help but think of all the children I had met back at Disney World, feeling such depths of empathy for the circumstances that might have led to these children begging on the streets. Despite the warnings, I'd use some of the same nonverbal, cross-cultural tricks I learned while at the Jungle Cruise to joke and laugh with the kids. They would laugh and often bare mouths with broken, jagged teeth.

While I couldn't do much to take away their suffering at that moment, having a brief laugh seemed to open us both up to see one another through tiny moments of connection that mattered.

Children were a huge part of our trip. We visited AIDS orphans in South Africa, met with disabled children in Malaysia, and worked with marginalized Children's groups in India who were outcasts from their societies because of what social caste they had been born into.

We also visited sites of historical atrocities. In Japan, we visited the atomic bomb site in Hiroshima. I was caught off guard when we arrived because it was eerily quiet for such a large area. You could hear keys jingling a block away. As we walked around, everyone remained silent.

I learned Japanese culture, particularly the Taoist tradition, believes in the *Ma* or *the space between*. Not only is there a you and a me, but there is what is between us. In the Taoist tradition, it is important to honor those spaces that bring us together and hold us as one by remaining quiet, especially in sacred areas such as the location where the atomic bomb killed over eighty thousand people (2020).

Nearby, the Japanese had built a memorial dedicated to all whose lives had been lost or maimed by the scars of war. The museum offered a brief history of the violent day that stole many lives. Volunteers who had survived the atomic blast as mere children were on hand to share their experiences and advocate for deterrence against the use of nuclear weapons.

As an American, what struck me most was how welcoming and forgiving those who worked at the memorial were to us. I felt like they had every right to hate us and to stand in opposition to us, yet they held out their hands and embraced us, sharing their own calls to find ways of connecting as human beings and never harming others in the ways that previous generations had been harmed.

Despite our language barriers, I continued to see more fundamentally the spirit that existed in them and the humanity in us all. We weren't that different; their calls for peace were as human beings to other human beings.

This became intensely personal to me on one of our Semester at Sea-sponsored trips in India.

We took an early morning train in India from New Delhi to Agra to see the Taj Mahal, sitting in the front car reserved for upper-class passengers, trailed by dozens of other train cars crowded with hundreds of people packed to the brim.

We had assigned seats and plenty of space in the first-class cabin. It felt almost like a hospital room. The windows were spotless and offered a wide purview of the waking world outside.

Most of us took a moment to rest on the two-hour train ride by sinking into our huge Semester at Sea hooded sweatshirts and listening to music in our headphones, drowning out the world around us, eager to get to our next destination and ignoring everything else.

Soon the train started to come to a slow roll.

As I picked up my head to see what was happening, I noticed we were coming through an encampment full of thousands of people.

It was a community of Dalit villagers, known as untouchables or lower caste people, who lived in extreme poverty. The Indian caste system is a hierarchical social structure in which individuals are born into a particular caste and deal with restrictions to certain occupations and social interactions based on their caste status.

Small fires were smoldering from the night before, and several mats made of cardboard were strewn about where people had been sleeping alongside one another. With the rising sun, and as our train slowly passed, it appeared we were waking them from their slumber. Several had evidently slept on the train tracks that we were passing through. People started picking up their entire belongings off the rails, forced awake by the arrival of our train and the rising sun.

Little children yawned and stretched while their parents hurriedly picked up their belongings so we could pass. They all were covered in dirt and filth from days and days without bathing. There were flies on their faces as some looked up at the passengers going by in the passing train, some instinctively holding out their hands and gesturing to us for food.

Everyone around me was still sleeping.

Suddenly, there was a break in the clouds. The rising sun cast a glare of light across my body, causing a reflection on the window in front of me.

As I continued to look out among the Dalit villagers, I suddenly was jolted into seeing myself among those just on the other side of the thin glass between us. There I was among them in their worn-out clothes, clutching all their belongings and facing the elements of each moment of life, day by day.

What if I had been born there, living in such conditions? Who would I have become? What would I have made of my life? Under what circumstances might my life have been shaped differently? What would stay the same?

I also questioned the same of those human beings on the other side who were just like me. Human beings who could have easily sat in the seat next to me or even in my place. What might have become of their lives? Their hopes? Their dreams if they had been born in my shoes?

But by the accident of birth, we found ourselves fated to our current realities. Yet we were all human. I am because they are.

It was no longer for me *"those people over there"* in the observable world from the safety of my train car. But I had the realization that, no, these very people were also just like me. What heroics went into their daily lives? What was the joy expressed by the laughing children? What was the pain they may have been hiding? They just happened to be born into their lives, and I was born into mine.

It was a powerful realization for me—connecting to and understanding the fundamental humanity in them and all of us.

Something I know that the archbishop sought to illuminate through all of his life's work, and one I became committed to carrying forward in everything I did.

That moment would inform so many other moments throughout the rest of my journey and my life. All people, everywhere, held a humanity deserving of fundamental respect and dignity—the same I sought to be seen for as I faced those who would harbor such prejudices and biases about my own worth as a gay man, something that fundamentally makes up my personhood and has shaded the colors of my purviews into the world.

As we neared the end of the voyage, the most powerful lesson I realized was the beauty of my own fundamental humanity and how tied I was to everyone, everywhere, including those in the camp that fateful morning. I began to see that the gay rights I had been fighting for back home intersectionally linked to the rights of all people everywhere, from those struggling for racial justice to women's rights, disability rights, and so forth. And intersecting through it all was tied to something even larger: our shared human rights as people with distinct backgrounds and perspectives from all walks of life and every geography and point in our human history.

To think, in my youth, I had been so afraid of my feelings of connection and love, even shamed into believing they were somehow wrong, blinding me to the rest of the world. To then, that moment on the train in India, realizing how fundamentally my existence, in itself, no matter the identity or shape it might take, was full of meaning and gifts and how connected I was to each and every person there in that camp and on the rest of the planet.

I was no longer just a gay rights activist but a human rights advocate. I had found my humanity and was wholly inspired by how deeply connected we all were. You, me, us them.

ACT THREE

ABYSS

What you spend years building may be destroyed overnight. Build it anyway.
—MOTHER TERESA

In our own ways, we are all broken. Out of that brokenness, we hurt others. Forgiveness is the journey we take toward healing the broken parts. It is how we become whole again.
—ARCHBISHOP DESMOND TUTU

Men who do not turn to face their own pain are too often prone to inflict it upon others.
—LAWRENCE REAL

LIFE UPENDED

Returning home as a newfound global citizen and committed human rights champion, I was ready to take on anything. Little did I know I would find myself in a series of events that would test my greatest resolve and challenge my core underlying beliefs in love itself, including all I had just learned, upon returning to the United States.

As we sailed into the final port of the US, we docked in San Diego and said our farewells to those we had just circumnavigated the globe with. On land, hundreds of parents were eager to see their children for the first time in months. They held large signs welcoming them home. My dad wasn't there.

At the same time, several students held signs for their parents to see as we docked, many of which said, "Mom and Dad, Thanks for Giving Me the World." And it was true.

I was incredibly grateful to my parents, who had made many personal sacrifices so I could have such an experience. I thought about the many hours they worked to help me travel around the world. It was only because of their encouragement, support, and financial backing that made my trip possible.

As we disembarked, I looked back at the ship in awe at all it had offered us.

I was in one of the happiest places ever and felt at peace. It was like a rebirth. I discovered so much about the world and, in turn, myself. I had an entirely new outlook on humanity itself.

My mom headed straight home to Spokane while I stayed for a few more days to spend time in California with some of my new Semester at Sea friends and visit Disneyland.

A few days later, I returned home to Spokane, where my dad and sister picked me up in what appeared to be a new car he had purchased while we were away. We got home and sat down to dinner at our family dining table as we had done for years.

Our family finally reunited after my sister spent the year studying in Italy while my mom and I were away on Semester at Sea. Sarah cracked jokes as she recounted her many adventures from her time in Florence. I shared a little more about my time with Semester at Sea.

My parents were relatively quiet, but in our excitement to be together, Sarah and I didn't recognize much as being out of place.

After dinner, we cleaned up and moved to the living room, where we spent time with our dad looking through our travel photos. Soon after, Sarah packed up her things and returned to the dormitories at Gonzaga, where she would work as a Resident Advisor that summer. We said our goodbyes, and then it was just my dad, mom, and me.

My mom, who energetically led entire shipboard discussions on Semester at Sea just a few weeks earlier, sat quietly on the couch, staring off into the distance.

"Mom, what's wrong?"

"Ask your father."

Concerned about my mom's demeanor, I turned to my dad and asked, "Dad, what's wrong?"

He led me down to my room, where he proceeded to tell me he was divorcing my mother.

My immediate reaction was first shock and then concern for him. "Dad, are you okay?"

"I'm just unhappy and want to be alone. I was always that kid who sat in the corner playing with my toys by myself. That's all I want. To be by myself."

"Okay, Dad, well, I hope you are okay. I'm sorry to hear this." Trying to take it all in while also growing concerned for him.

My dad was the most respectable person. In our family's eyes, he was perfect in every way. I was in such a state of shock I couldn't fully process what was happening. His actions seemed so out of character.

My mom was entirely devastated. She went from having a life-changing experience to suddenly having the floor pulled out from under her.

They were soulmates, according to her. On the ship, we had many conversations about what an inspiration my father had been to her. He was the only person she had ever loved. They spent what felt like a lifetime together after over thirty years, moving around, having kids, the whole nine yards. She couldn't imagine life without him. What would she do now?

Friends and family often designated our family as a *Leave It to Beaver* family, one many strived to attain. It was a point of pride for all of us. My parents' relationship was something I aspired to have for myself, the penultimate of which my belief in love and advocacy rested upon.

I recounted the many times my parents would come home from work every day and give each other long embraces, so much so our Samoyed Winston would always howl and want a hug too. From their times leading team building exercises for my youth soccer team to how they both supported me throughout my journey, coming out, to the love they showed at their twenty-fifth wedding anniversary, their love gave me inspiration and hope.

The news that my dad wanted a divorce seemed so out of the blue. We were all in shock and struggled to process it all.

To compromise and as a gesture of goodwill, my mom agreed to move into on-campus housing. I went with her—just days after arriving home from Semester at Sea. My parents decided my dad would have the house for a while, and we could visit when we wanted to. My mom would go back to work, and I just kind of hung out around town and on campus.

At some level, she held out hope that maybe my father might come to his senses with some time.

However, one afternoon my mom returned to her car from work to find the official divorce papers on the front seat of her car—another unsuspecting blow to my mother's fragile state. Not only did it make it that much more real, but the coldness of such actions was so unbecoming of the man I once knew.

As the weeks went on, things didn't feel right. I tried to learn more from my dad and get answers from him regarding his reasonings and rationales, but he wouldn't budge. I even asked, "Is there someone else? Promise me there isn't someone else."

To which he responded, "Of course not, Ryan." I can't even imagine dating someone for another year."

At one point, he started getting visibly angry at me when I continued my line of questioning and sternly said, "It's none of your business. This doesn't concern you."

None of my business? Divorcing my mom and providing no explanation whatsoever other than he wanted to be alone? No demonstration he had done any examination of the impact of his decision, nothing to explain why he may have been unhappy. He refused to talk about it. This made me even more worried for him.

Traumatized and still in shock, I felt I needed to get away.

I drove across the state and stayed at my old roommate Madison's house just outside Seattle. We had dinner with his lovely parents, who comforted me about the divorce. I detailed to them what happened, and they offered their sympathies while, at the same time, they were a bit suspicious.

"Ryan, this doesn't seem to add up. Are you sure there isn't more to the story? Something he isn't sharing with you all. Is it possible he is having an affair?" Madison's mom finally asked.

"No, of course not! My dad is the most upstanding individual I have ever met. He would never do something like that."

Still, her words stuck. I couldn't get them out of my head.

When I returned the next day to the apartment where we were staying, it felt nothing like home. It was cold and empty, with piles of dishes in the sink—in complete contrast to our trip sailing around the world less than a month prior, where literally the whole world was before us.

My mom and I wanted to grab a few things from our old house, so the next day my dad gave us the okay to go back and hang out while he was away. I met my mom there, and with the words of Madison's mom ringing in my head, I decided to snoop.

On our dining room table, my dad had left his briefcase. I opened it up and dug around for something that might offer a clue as to *why* he wanted a divorce. A month and a half after he broke the news to us, he still hadn't fully explained what led to his sudden shift in disposition.

Then there it was, a letter to another woman detailing his seemingly pubescent feelings for her, "as if he was back in high school," full of butterflies and nervousness. She "made him feel alive in ways he hadn't felt in years" while they were out to dinner a few weeks before.

As I read the letter, I dived deeper into shock.

I was appalled. All the benefit-of-the-doubt and serious concern I had for my father's welfare left my body. I had trusted him my whole life, even in those fragile moments when he said there was no one else. I always sought to live up to his words of wisdom. He was my moral compass. His words had always aligned with his actions, yet for what felt like the first time in my life, it became abundantly clear that his initial reasonings for the divorce were a complete fabrication.

As I was finishing the letter, my mom came out of her old bedroom with a look of shock on her face. She held up a hanger with a woman's clothes, which clearly weren't hers. We both realized at the same time what was truly happening.

Even until that moment, my mom had held out faith my father was still the same honest man she had known since they were in college together. She, too, had been pushed by her close confidants against her intuition to consider there might be something more insidious beneath the surface. She, too, couldn't believe them.

I confronted him directly about the affair when I met up with my dad and sister at the house later that week.

"Dad, how could you? How could you do this to Mom? To us?"

Caught off guard, he angrily responded, "How dare you go through my things. It's none of your business."

I pressed further: "Who is she? How long has this been going on? Why didn't you think about our family? How would you feel if someone did this to my sister or me?"

Without answering a single question, he continued to press on about how violating it was for us to go through his things. "How dare you look through my briefcase!"

I felt a cold distance between my father and me at that moment. It was as if I was speaking to a complete stranger. I had no idea who this man was standing before me. He was nothing like my beloved father. His demeanor turned so very cold toward me, angered I had somehow revealed the secret he was hiding. I had to question everything that had taken place the previous month.

I felt as if the bottom of a floor had collapsed beneath me as it hit me that he appeared to have considered nothing. Not my mom's feelings or my sister's and mine. What would this do to his relationship with us? Did he assume we would be okay with him treating our mother that way and go along with it? Or worse, did he know what would happen and didn't care?

With all I had suffered and fought against, even to be able to have the right to love in the first place. All the years of toiling and wondering if I would even find someone to love, let alone marry. The years I aspired to have what I thought my parents had. Marriage equality wasn't even legal yet in the United States. It was a sacred right I was fighting for in my life, yet it felt as if his vows to my mother and his commitments to our family no longer even mattered to him.

There were so many questions and painful truths I would be forced to face. If the love between my parents and the light I derived from the profound love they gave to me was somehow imperfect, what did that even mean about who I was and all I had come to build my life around in my activism? Was everything I just experienced on Semester at Sea, and the purviews I built my newfound understanding of the world around, some farce or lie?

In one final parting shot as my sister and I left the house to return to campus, he said, "You're so ungrateful. How dare you speak to me in that way."

This so hurt.

He was the man whose example I did everything to live up to. I made daily choices to ensure both of my parents were proud of me and that they knew every day of their lives how much I loved them. There were so many of the tiniest moments throughout my life when I chose to honor their teachings, even behind closed doors and in my private life.

That he would dare question the love and loyalty I had for him. As if the torture and anguish I displayed weren't out of the profound grief for the man I had loved my whole life?

I was devastated.

A few weeks later, it was time for me to start an internship in Colorado. Given that I had done Semester at Sea, I only needed the classes in the spring to graduate. I had the whole fall to do something else.

Still in shock, I was glad to get away from it all and put my efforts into a new advocacy organization. My sister agreed to drive down with me so I wouldn't have to be alone during the drive.

I packed up several of my belongings from the campus apartment where my mom and I were living, put them in my Honda Accord, and we were ready to go.

My sister and I said goodbye to my mom, and for the first time in my entire life, she completely lost it. All those summer months we had gone through, she still tried to put on a brave face for my sister and me.

As we were leaving, she began to sob uncontrollably. Tears rushed down her face with heavy gasps and sighs between her breaths. It became hard for her to stand as she fell into me, hugging me goodbye. There was nothing we could do but say our goodbyes and watch her as we drove away.

I became numb.

NUMB

After our long, eighteen-hour drive, my sister and I arrived in Colorado, grateful to be embraced by our chosen family, the Stills, Samars, and my old soccer coach, Greg. In my numb state, it was difficult to process everything as it happened.

Greg, and his wife Amanda became such godsends. They offered to host me and put me up in their spare bedroom while I would commute to my offices in downtown Denver. It felt like I was living with my older brother, who offered a quiet place to land as I returned from a devastating blow. That space alone served as a saving grace for me during such a trying time.

Over the fall, I worked at a national nonprofit working to support LGBTI equality across the country.

My main goal was to assist in building up a web-based resource database to act as a one-stop shop for LGBTI youth across the country to access services. Looking back on my own childhood, having such a place would have meant so much. As a result, I spent hours reaching out to LGBTI community centers nationwide and other organizations serving LGBTI-identified youth to request information about their respective services to list on the website.

I also bartended three to four days a week in the evenings at a local gay bar called Hamburger Mary's.

Throughout my time back in Colorado, I was more or less going through the motions. I'd go to one job, then the next, go to bed, and start again. I enjoyed many meals and deep conversations with Greg and Amanda, with whom I'd often spend weekends relaxing from our busy weeks. Still passionate about LGBTI rights around the world, I continued questioning my purpose in life and what I was supposed to do next.

I tried to remain relatively optimistic about the future. I wanted to carry out and apply the lessons I experienced traveling on Semester at Sea.

However, I found myself interacting with a group of fellow advocates who carried out their work differently. I had a carefree attitude and a sense of possibility of where the work might go, especially coming from my college activism.

For some of the advocates I worked with, it seemed to be just a job. The work was work itself, not necessarily their passion project like it had been mine up until that point. To their credit, there likely had once been a passion, but it became a livelihood.

When we would have ideation opportunities to share our thoughts on specific initiatives or add our flavor or perspective to what we were doing, my ideas were often met with skepticism or some form of jockeying. I suggested we create a podcast. I wanted to go to pride festivals and proactively reach LGBTI people. I wanted to have interactive graphics for the website. But they chided me and shut down my ideas for not knowing my place as an intern.

I felt like I was putting my life on the line, protesting and openly speaking out against injustices, whereas the work they were doing was more methodical and intentional—an approach I didn't fully appreciate at that time. My youth also didn't help me.

Like my time in our gay-straight alliance at Gonzaga, my effervescent and hopeful personality seemed to rub others the wrong way. We, too, were at different places as queer people navigating the oppressive world. Of course, it didn't help that I was still trying to numb the reality of my parents' divorce.

At my other job, I enjoyed the Denver nightlife and learned more about its gay culture—something I hadn't experienced as a closeted youth an hour north in Greeley. It was a space I could drown my troubles from back home. I started embracing the ways of the world I had once avoided. I didn't care as much to live up to the same values my father had instilled in me. That was all bygone. I started drinking heavily. Love wasn't as important to me when I met guys. And I started smoking. As much of a health nut as I had been as a former athlete and asthmatic, who cared anymore? So what if my dad wouldn't approve?

I tried to keep in touch with my parents, but I also used the time to avoid what was happening. I certainly didn't have any luck in love myself. I hadn't heard from James, and the guys I dated in Colorado felt temporary, knowing I would be gone in a few months. So, my experiences with them were mostly just avenues to my vices, temporary cessations from the well of pain I felt underneath.

Every once in a while, I tried to connect with my dad to ask him about this new person in his life in an attempt to reach him in one way or another. I wanted to still find an appreciation for my father with respect for the fact that, despite how painful the divorce was, in reality, sometimes people change and must move on.

I accepted as unfortunate as the circumstances were, he, too, was hurting and was still the loving father I cared so deeply for. I often wondered about the frightened little boy inside of him who had gotten lost along the way. Why he never felt safe in one respect or another to honestly share with us how he truly felt—his family who so unconditionally loved him.

Unfortunately, he didn't have much to say as a man of few words. We attempted to connect. "Hi, Dad, how's it going? So, tell me about her. Who is she? What's her name? What does she do? How did you meet?" Nothing.

When my internship ended in late October, I moved North to Fort Collins to live with the Stills, who hosted me for a few weeks before celebrating Thanksgiving. Like Greg and Amanda, they comforted me in my darkened state.

When my sister and mom joined us for the holiday, we took our usual trek up the mountains to Estes Park. Our families had spent nearly every Thanksgiving together for the prior two decades, renting a huge family cabin at the YMCA of the Rockies. We'd play games, hike, share meals, and revel in one another's company.

It was so lovely to get away. It was an important holiday for us to all be together. Our first without my dad. But the Stills and Samars were all there, loving on us and helping us press forward, despite not knowing what was supposed to come next for our family.

Leaving Colorado the following week, I realized how much Greg, Amanda, the Stills, and Samars were there to catch me when I needed people the most. The small conversations. Letting me express my doubts and fears. The moments when they allowed me to exist alongside them without having to say a thing. I hadn't appreciated it at the moment, but I didn't even know I needed them that much because I was so numb from everything happening in my life. Where would I have ended up if I hadn't had the love and support of my chosen family?

I started my final semester in school the following spring. I lived in an on-campus apartment with a guy I never really got to know. He was barely there. I went to my classes in a constant gloom, never really engaging. I moped around.

Over my spring break, I finally got to see James after not seeing him for nearly a year and a half. He invited me to stay with him and his girlfriend in Seattle for a few days. I also visited other people in the area.

When I pulled up to his parking garage, he met me outside to help me park. He smiled, saying with a coo, "Hey, guy," like he always did.

He hopped in my car and, while looking in my glove compartment, saw my cigarettes and immediately tossed them aside. "What is this, and how could you? These aren't good for you!" I never smoked again.

We went up to his immaculate apartment. He was so excited to see me, and I was beyond happy to see him. We started with small talk and then began reliving our favorite memories together. My favorite part was how he kept turning to his girlfriend to tell her how amazing I was.

We decided to stay in the first night and played a board game. We toured around the city the next day and had a great time. James made us breakfast, and at their long rectangular dining room table, his girlfriend sat on one side, and I sat on the other with two chairs between us. James sat in the chair next to me.

That night we planned to go to a gay bar with their new friends from work. They were gay too. It was the first time James had agreed to go with me to such a place, but it meant the world to me. Before, he had always been so nervous about how others might perceive him and what others might think if he went anywhere with me, especially at a gay bar.

He was still quite nervous but took a few shots before we left.

We first stopped at a cocktail bar they loved, just the three of us, for a drink before meeting up with their friends. We spent the whole time talking to his girlfriend, reminiscing about our adventures together in college. James and I sat close to each other, our knees touching under the table as his girlfriend sat across from us while we enjoyed the ambiance of our surroundings.

Then we met their friends at the gay bar. I was so excited for him to be there. We all got a few drinks and began chatting as we vibed with the music and enjoyed our surroundings. I was finally in a safe place with my best friend and did my best to ensure he felt comfortable.

I tried making him laugh. I got up and danced a little provocatively but comically. I returned to the table, turned to James, and told him, "Gay bars are amazing!"

With a few more drinks, I kept dancing, having a free moment to be beside such an important friend in my life. I started to get in my head and then approached James and his girlfriend, grabbing their shoulders as they sat on two of the bar chairs surrounding our table.

I hugged her and then looked her in the eyes and, with tears forming in my own, told her how much "I had loved getting to know her and how happy I was for James to meet such a wonderful person. All I had ever wanted for him was his greatest happiness, and I wished them all the very best from the bottom of my heart." I meant every word of it.

I don't know what triggered me at that moment. Maybe it was thinking about the immense love I still had and would always have for James. Perhaps it was the realization that I most likely wouldn't be with him in the eventuality of my life in that way, which I had come to accept.

But as I've reflected on it more, I believe I was genuinely happy in their presence. After a year of feeling so numb, I finally felt safe. It was as if he was the only person in the world with whom I felt I could be one hundred percent myself. And I began to cry. No, I began to ugly cry. I could no longer keep all the pain from the last year within me. Sobbing uncontrollably, I quickly ran down a short, dimly lit hallway and found a place to let it all out. And it all came out.

Everything I had suppressed that entire year regarding my parents' divorce. All the uncertainty of what the future held. All my grief for the loss of my father, or the version of him I had thought I knew, came pouring out of me. I cried for my mother, who suffered greatly and was the person whose character remained steady, even during her darkest hours, and had never deserved such pain.

It was a release I needed all that time, and all because I was with James in a safe place.

To my surprise, James quickly followed me down the hallway to see how I was. He wrapped his arms around me, facing me, and we held each other around our waists for what felt like an eternity. Interspersed with both crying and playful teasing, I told him I loved him so much, he meant the world to me, and I was so grateful to see him again. It didn't need to be said, but it was what I needed. He told me he loved me, too, and would always be there for me. I razzed him for not seeing me sooner, but with a smile on my face and gratitude to have seen him at all.

While in that embrace, his girlfriend walked to the back where we were to check on us and saw us. She looked like she had seen a ghost and then quickly turned around. James and I followed shortly, and we decided to return to their friends' apartment for more drinks.

We then called it a night and went back to their apartment.

The following morning as I said my goodbyes. We hugged in a long embrace, not knowing when we would see each other again. We said I love you. Then I drove back to Spokane to finish the year.

I found the relief I needed, if even temporarily.

At the end of the semester, my vast extended family came together for the first time since the divorce to celebrate me and my sister's graduation from Gonzaga.

There was an awards ceremony in which my sister and I received recognition for our contributions to our campus community. I received praise for my contributions to campus culture and how I brought people together despite our differences.

The awards ceremony was the first time my mom and dad were back in the same room together. My mom and I sat at a round table at the front of the room with other award recipients. Meanwhile, my dad and sister sat across the room at another table.

My mom dressed in this flowing red dress and jacket, and as a testament to her spirit, she stood graciously, crossed the room, greeted my dad, and wished him well. While pomp and circumstance were happening on stage, I couldn't help but tear up and enter this deep haze as I watched it all unfold. My dad could hardly even look at her.

Graduation day was difficult because it was the first of many instances in which my sister and I would have to navigate the experience of divorced parents, both of whom we loved very much.

Our whole family had come in, including my maternal grandfather, paternal grandmother, aunts, uncles, cousins, and chosen family. My little cousin, Tommy Ray, was a hit with all our friends. As joyous as the experience was supposed to be, it all felt like a blur.

The year as a whole, I could barely think straight. I was thrust into a tug and pull between the person I had always been and confronted with the present circumstances of my life. I wanted to follow my passion for LGBTI human rights and ached to be back out in the world, continuing to pursue a career in advocacy. But I had no idea what that would look like, where to turn, or what to do next. I felt entirely lost.

CLOSE

James and I were asked to be groomsmen at my former roommate Madison's summer wedding. After seeing James over spring break, I was excited to see him again for the bachelor party just a few weeks after graduation.

Madison's family owned a small cabin in the Snoqualmie mountains, no more than forty-five minutes from where Madison grew up. We decided to all rendezvous at Madison's house and spent a day at the cabin celebrating Madison's nuptials.

I felt a sudden sense of ease and comfort when James walked in.

We spent the first evening with Madison's lovely parents. His mom made us a lovely dinner, and then we went to a few bars with his dad. By the end of the evening, the seven of us found ourselves lying in a field, looking up at the stars and laughing.

All the guys at this point knew of my profound love for James. Even Madison's dad knew. However, not many really knew of James's feelings for me.

As we lay there, Madison's dad drunkenly started to make light of the situation between James and me. "Ryan and James, kissing in a tree. K-I-S-S-I-N-G," he slurred.

Everyone laughed. Not me.

I was a bit embarrassed. I didn't say anything. More importantly, I found myself worrying about James. I wanted to protect him while avoiding my feelings about the situation.

Who wants to constantly have to be the PC police when you are just trying to have a little fun with your friends? I knew Madison's dad meant no harm. I took it as a bit of hazing, like I learned to do in middle school, and quickly let it go. However, it wouldn't stop there.

The next morning, we carpooled to the cabin. We'd end up taking three cars. Before anyone could decide who was going with whom, James immediately said, "I'm driving with Ryan." It was nice to have him want to spend time with me.

In my car, we talked and talked as we always did. Our ebb and flow came so naturally to us. We were together—just us.

When we got to the cabin, we set up our stuff and took a short hike before continuing our debauchery from the night before.

On the hike, the guys picked up on the razzing from Madison's dad.

"Hey Ryan, staring at James again? Hahaha."

"Ryan probably shouldn't walk behind James, or else he will get too excited," and so on. I was the joke.

I let it slip off my chest as I had done my whole life. At that moment, it seemed James had done so too.

We continued drinking and played typical bachelor games when we returned to the cabin. As the best man, James had gotten some X-rated games standard of the Catholic school kid he was. A poster of a scantily clad woman with which to play pin the kiss on the woman.

As we drank some more beers, we began to move to a nearby picnic table to play a game of cards. I sat down first. Then Madison's brother-in-law, Bobby, sat next to me.

"Hey, I want to sit next to Ryan," James said to Bobby as he approached the table. So, Bobby moved as James took his place beside me. Everyone else joined. We started playing, laughing, and enjoying one another's company. There didn't seem to be a care in the world.

Six inches or so of the bench was between each guy around the table. On the other hand, through our natural gravitational pull toward each other, James and I sat with the entire sides of our bodies touching. It felt so natural. It didn't seem at all out of the ordinary. It's just how we were.

As the jokester he sometimes was, James turned to me and whispered, "Look here," gesturing just under the table. He was cheating and held a few high cards in his hands he had stashed from a previous round.

He chuckled, and so did I, and as I did, I playfully tapped the top of his thigh to give him grief for cheating, thinking absolutely nothing of it—a millisecond. A quick pat and went back to the game.

In a flash, James went from laughing with me to suddenly becoming ferociously angry, like I'd never seen him before.

"How dare you try to grab my dick! Don't you ever do that again, or I will be forced to teach you a lesson!" he threatened me.

I was so unnerved. I couldn't understand the sudden shift. Most of all, I was so angered James would accuse me in front of every one of something I felt he should know I would never do. For gosh sake, as a gay man in society those days, I knew better than to overstep boundaries. Knowing Matthew Shepard's story and countless others like him, I had feared reprisals like this for much of my life. It was an everyday stressor for me, worrying about violence from others.

Let alone the deep love and respect I held for him, which included his bodily autonomy. I would never harm him in such a way, and for him to accuse me of such a violation, especially in front of our friends, made me furious.

How could he believe I would ever violate the trust in our friendship or the love between us? Why was that where his mind went?

Sitting there, while angered, I simultaneously found myself protecting him. I didn't want to embarrass him further. He had made me feel all those years like a secret. A burden if others ever knew. I knew a part of him was still working through what it meant to be my friend and love each other as we did. I couldn't defend myself and say not twenty minutes before, he was the one who nuzzled up next to me. I couldn't say anything because I didn't want to hurt him, even at that moment when he was hurting me.

Instead, out of pure frustration and hurt, I pushed back on him in my own way. I did it again—a quick, gentle pat to the top of his thigh, no longer than a millisecond.

He bolted out of his seat, got up, grabbed me by the head, and dragged me into the dirt next to the table. Before I knew it, I was looking up at him with his foot inches above my crotch as if to stomp on me, shouting at me, "Never do that again!"

I was dazed. Confused. Embarrassed. Shocked. What had just happened?

How could someone I love so much, someone who meant the world to me and loved me too, do such a thing? I said nothing. I got up and dusted myself off. Ironically, we returned to the table, sitting again, side by side.

As dudes sometimes, no often do; minutes later, there was some silence, and then we went on playing cards as if nothing had happened. I was still in shock, but we kept going. Eventually, the awkwardness subsided, and we continued with our fun—though my mind kept reeling from the trauma of the event I had just endured.

I could only rationalize away James's behavior as him simply working through his own stuff, things I had started to tire of. While it wasn't okay, I knew societal impositions were working themselves out at that moment, far beyond what actually occurred. His action resulted from the deep-seated work he still needed to do or, at least hopefully, might one day overcome. But that wasn't the day.

As evening came around, we sat around a campfire. The guys began harassing James and me again, specifically me, for being in love with James. I finally had had enough and eventually snapped at the group, "Stop it!" I exclaimed. "Yes, I love James, but I deeply respect him. He is my best friend. You guys are being ridiculous and have been ridiculous this whole time. Leave us alone." The group went silent.

James said nothing.

Just before bed James and I entered the cabin alone. We were chatting, and he began to change into his pajamas and snapped. "Are you looking at me?"

He seemed far more consumed with our relationship than I was. The other guys had clearly gotten to him. All I wanted to do was go to bed.

After a weekend bombarded by unexpected comments and outright homophobia directed my way, zeroing in on my relationship with James, we headed home to Madison's house for one last breakfast. James drove in someone else's car.

Madison's mother already had breakfast waiting for us when we arrived at their home. She eagerly began asking us about our weekend. "How did it go? What all did you boys get into?"

Well into the conversation, there was a point where she asked the group, "So, who is going to be next to get married?"

No one replied. After a long pause, she responded, "Well, when you meet the one, you just know."

Immediately I had an internal dialogue with myself. "Don't look at James. Don't look at James. Okay, well, maybe just a quick look." James and I turned our heads and looked at each other without skipping a beat at the same exact time, as if in slow motion. We locked eyes and paused, seeming to know what the other was thinking. We then each withdrew our gaze.

Even though it was brief, it was a tiny reprieve from the blistering day just before. I knew, beyond a shadow of a doubt, he truly loved me.

Yes, he and I had our ups and downs that weekend, but a part of me believed he was my soulmate at some level, whether as friends or more. Whatever we were to be, I knew we were meant to be. Some form of divine intervention had a hand in bringing us together. We knew it deep down.

It was also gut-wrenching to have such confirmation, even in the subtlest of ways. It only deepened the confusion I had about what he truly wanted.

I will always have to think about that moment for the rest of my life and what it might have meant.

I knew he loved me for a fact. However, for him, what we had was dangerous. It was scary. It was something others wouldn't hold on high as they do in all the fairy tales, even at the same nuptials we were there to celebrate. Instead, it would be the butt of jokes and face our peers' ridicule. What kind of choice is that? As if my tender gazes, my vulnerabilities I only experienced with him, were ever a threat.

After wrapping up breakfast, we drove back to our respective homes dozens of miles away in every direction. For weeks upon weeks, I pondered what it all meant. James's struggling duality only confirmed for me the ongoing ordeal he experienced whenever he was around me.

How does one reconcile this? How does one protect the one they love without losing themselves? Why should I lessen myself when what brought me joy also brought him such shame?

I knew I needed to find a way to get away. It was all just too much.

VILLAGE LIFE

Maybe if I was six thousand miles away, I could escape the unraveling of my family and the pain I had just experienced with James.

To find some semblance of my former self and relive what I had experienced through Semester at Sea, I decided to travel to The Gambia, West Africa, on a service trip to escape it all. The confusion and outright homophobia during the bachelor party a few weeks prior certainly inspired a desire to get away to rest my heart.

I took out a personal loan as a graduation gift to myself. I needed to return to the international space to reclaim what had inspired me the year prior on Semester at Sea.

My friend Megan, whom I met and stayed in touch with since high school, invited me to join her newly created nonprofit, A Hand in Health, to provide health services and education to villagers around oral healthcare.

We were the kind of friends who always had deep, existential conversations about our purpose in the world. When we were seniors in high school, we often drank hot cocoa on my family's back porch late into the winter evenings staring up at the stars, mesmerized by it all and wondering how we each might change the world someday.

She went on to graduate school to pursue becoming a dental therapist. Her nonprofit sought to enhance oral healthcare efforts worldwide, which many don't readily have access to. It worked within a more expansive program called Operation Crossroads Africa, which Megan had done the previous year and inspired the creation of her nonprofit.

Considered the "progenitor of the Peace Corps" by John F. Kennedy, the program started in 1958 to establish greater connections between Americans and young Africans (Operation Crossroads Africa 2023). It is believed one can truly enter another culture only by living and working in it. Operation Crossroads Africa sent hundreds of students annually throughout the continent of Africa on assignments ranging from agriculture to education programs or addressing the health needs of a community.

I and two women from Megan's dental program, Dua and Erin, would be her assistants. She could use all the help she could get in rolling out her specific mission.

As I started to learn more about The Gambia, I was apprehensive about going on the trip. Not because of the treacherous elements we would encounter living in a remote village or the risks we faced from unknown contagions from the dense underbrush of the forests and rivers nearby, but because of the growing homophobia in the country.

I learned days before I left about the deeply homophobic, highly controversial dictator who ruled there, President Yahya Jemus Junkung Jammeh. Following a bloodless military coup de Tate in 1994, he declared himself ruler of the country. He governed with an iron fist for the next twenty-three years. He was known to terrorize individuals throughout the country (Human Rights Watch 2008).

Just before my arrival, Jammeh announced that his government would introduce legislation against homosexuals that would be "stricter than those in Iran" and that he would "cut off the head" of any gay or lesbian person discovered in the country."

I certainly was a little paranoid about going to such a place, fearing someone would realize who I was. I was escaping one form of homophobia and entering another.

When I arrived in the capital, Banjul, Megan, and the head of the hospital where we would work, Dr. Badgie, were waiting for us. We piled into a white medical van packed to the brim with medical supplies and headed to the hospital.

After our fifteen-hour plane ride from the United States, we sat on top of one another as we began the three-hour drive into the heart of the country to Bwiam, the village where we would be living. The red dirt road was full of potholes the size of our van, which we had to maneuver, especially where the heavy summer rains had made the roads nearly impassable. A lush forest covered parts of the road with tall Baobab trees towering on either side.

Our arrival felt disorienting. We arrived at the village around dusk. Rows of small shacks made up the village along with a few small farms scattered about. People were walking around as children, goats, cows, dogs, and chickens played in the streets.

Just on the outskirts of Bwiam was the run-down open-air hospital with six wings made up of concrete walls covered in chalky white paint. Sulyman Junkung General Hospital was built a few years earlier, in 2003, and saw around sixteen thousand patients a year. It was the central hospital for hundreds of thousands of people living in different villages throughout the region.

Members of the hospital staff greeted us, and then we joined the other fifteen medical students in the program. We were shown to the residential wing where we would all live for the short time we were there. Megan did her best to make us feel welcome as she showed us to our rooms. Those on the program shared a small space, with two small mattresses on the floor surrounded by mosquito netting, with lockable doors.

The Operation Crossroads Africa program brought medical students each summer to the hospital tasked to work closely with local health providers. They treated HIV/AIDS and Malaria patients, helped mothers deliver their babies, provided vaccinations, managed wounds, and cared for the villagers' general health needs.

Megan often shared stories of her summer before watching babies delivered by candlelight. On their daily twelve-hour shifts, they gained invaluable experience as future health professionals.

We settled in for the evening and rested until the following day. After unpacking and getting into bed, I was overwhelmed by the sweltering heat, some one hundred degrees, with no reprieve even at night, and surrounded by a chorus of bug noises as I tried to fall asleep.

What am I doing here? I thought, tossing and turning from my jet lag.

The next day, Megan took us to the village chief's house to get his blessing for our work. She had quite the rapport with him as he warmly greeted her.

"Welcome, my friends, to Bwiam. Here we believe in looking out for one another. We are dependent on each other. We appreciate you stopping by. Please, tell me more about why you have come to our village."

"Chief, we are here to help villagers think about their tooth pain and how we might help them. We plan to work with the village dentists, Fatu and Katy, to offer them support as they see many patients in one day," Megan said.

"Ahh, yes, this is very important. Please go forth and treat my people well," he said.

We shook his hand and headed to the administrative offices of the hospital. We were to meet with members of Dr. Badgie's executive team. As elders within their community, it was important we also received their blessings.

We crowded into their office, located near the front of the hospital. They looked us up and down and decided to give each of us a unique Gambian name for villagers to better pronounce and get to know us. One of them gave me the name "Landing." We thanked them and headed to the hospital ward, where we would begin our work.

We came to a large room with high ceilings and a bank of windows along the far wall with a door to the central hospital wing. Outside the entrance to the dental clinic was a waiting bench. In the room were piles of expired supplies, a combination of different dental tools, and a rusted-over chair. Near the bank of windows was a second recently donated dental chair still wrapped in plastic.

As we entered, Fatu and Katy greeted us. Between them, they probably had a year or two worth of formal training as dentists.

They were the primary caregivers for villagers throughout the region who sought them out when they experienced severe tooth pain. Our task was to assist them in examining patients as they came from miles away. I was to greet the patients at the door. At the same time, Megan, Dua, and Erin, three dental therapy students, prepared the materials, helped to clean, and offered Fatu and Katy support as they worked.

Given their poor infrastructure, lack of supplies, and limited training, Fatu and Katy could rarely provide anything other than an excruciating extractive process or a micro-dose of the very limited supply of pain medication they had on hand if it was available.

Fatu and Katy used instruments that had to be regularly sterilized in Dr. Badgie's house in the residential wing, in boiling water from the nearby river atop the one stove in the village. The instruments in many US-based dentists' offices may have been used once before being discarded. With the limited supply in Bwiam, they had to get as much use out of the tools as possible.

During an extraction, I saw a stark contrast compared with my own experiences of going to the dentist in the United States. Many patients came in presenting what they considered to be "tooth pain," pointing to the area of their mouths hurting.

In Gambian culture, one's medical needs are first presented to a local medicine man. Tooth pain is considered a wicked spirit. To cleanse oneself of the pain, the medicine man would place a grub atop the sore tooth and wait for it to heal. A bitter-tasting concoction would be made, and the individual would drink to rid themselves of the *evil spirit* causing them agony. When patients finally arrived at Fatu's dentist's chair, they often presented with an advanced degradation of their tooth, necessitating extraction (Rerimoi 2017).

This differed from the typical extractive process in a Western dentist's office. There was no suction tool. No sink in which to spit. No sterilized room or bright light to support the procedure. No gas or even pain ointment to numb the area where the procedure was taking place.

As the procedure proceeded, it was never a clean tooth pull. While the decay often eroded parts of the exposed tooth, numerous roots were still embedded deep within the patient's gum. Even the tiniest roots needed removal to ensure proper extraction.

As Fatu dug into the gums with metal clasps, she'd pinch the bleeding gums, moving them left, right, backward, and forward while digging, scraping, and uncovering the remaining bone with her other hand all while constantly washing away the oozing blood.

The excruciating procedure took place for over thirty minutes to an hour. Each patient was asked to hold the accumulating blood and other remnants from the process in the back of their throat. They would then spit into a bucket next to the bed every few minutes.

As word got out that Westerners were offering services for tooth pain, patient after patient arrived, often traveling for days just to have us examine their teeth.

In those moments, sitting off to the side as I greeted upcoming patients, I was aghast at the poor conditions these villagers had to endure in contrast to what I considered to be a basic health service. Most people in the US would never think twice about it. How could this take place in the modern world? Why didn't they have better facilities, supplies, or better relief from their pain?

While I struggled with what I saw these local villagers endure, simultaneously, I was in awe of them. During these procedures, one after the next, each patient showed a tremendous level of self-control. Barely anyone screamed out in agony.

Of course, every once in a while, a small child would cry. But, even then, collectively, it felt as though, en mass, these individuals were withstanding the pain to the best of their abilities or at least hiding it. Something I would never be able to do.

I later learned in Gambian culture, showing any pain is of poor taste (Rerimoi 2017). This is to the point where mothers giving birth are slapped by their doctors if they scream out in pain. Pain is something you endure, which you inevitably experience and go through.

I felt a profound respect for the capacity of human beings to endure such pain. Their bravery. Their resilience. It was something I was shaken by. I couldn't even hold a light to my experiences of suffering compared to what they had endured.

As we continued our work in the village, we also sought to provide community education on oral healthcare. In our off time, we would go to local schools, village meetings, or other large gatherings to help share why it was necessary, dispel common myths, and share brushing techniques.

One of my favorite aspects of our preventative efforts was getting to know the village kids. We became fast friends with the kiddos, who ranged in age from five to fifteen. Their playful energy and curiosity about the world electrified me. Despite my exhaustion from our long shifts and the beating sun, I, of course, wanted to connect with them.

Every day, like clockwork, they came by after our shifts and shouted up at our hospital wing to join them. They were primarily boys, as it was the expectation of the girls to stay and help their mothers in the home. Megan, Dua, Erin, and I would join them to swap stories and go on various adventures throughout the village with them. Like my playful time with guests at Disney World and other children I met through Semester at Sea, I found ways to laugh and be silly with all of them.

I played soccer with the older boys. We swam in the nearby Gambian River. We helped plow the field for the forthcoming rainy season. We visited the local medicine man who made us a small ankle bracelet of charms. We sat in the shade and discussed our lives.

Many young men we befriended often asked about our experiences in America. They wondered about the mirage of material things that existed there. Our gadgets enthralled them, and they saw them as out of this world. I remember the innocence on some of their faces as they examined my solar-powered battery charger or my digital camera.

It was truly magical. Many expressed a desire to come to America one day. They shared dreams of seeing what they heard was like an emerald city. A beacon of opportunity beyond their wildest imaginations.

Having deepened my appreciation for their culture, I quickly felt a certain kind of hesitation and even dread. From my unique purview, I understood how they might be drawn toward our culture and way of life. However, I also felt that while I had come to address a particular type of poverty—a poverty of resources, there was an entirely different type of poverty back home in the United States—a poverty of spirit.

I observed over my time in the village a shared purpose. I watched when a heavy rainstorm came and caved in the thatch roof of a villager's home. The entire village came out to assist them in repairing it. Villagers were one another's keepers and looked out for each other in ways I hadn't experienced in the United States. I barely knew my neighbors.

This was a whole other way of life, wildly contrasting with my life back home. Our rugged individualism created a poverty of spirit, made up of loneliness and depression. Neighbors barely knew each other, families went months without talking, and lives seemed disconnected from the broader realities of our world. Most escaped to virtual worlds where they could ignore the broader, more uncomfortable truths surrounding them. Moreover, our culture heralded one's accumulation of wealth when a single purchase might have been one of those villagers' entire incomes for the year.

While getting to know the villagers, I met a young man who stood out from his peers, Landing. He was a leader in the group, but rather than being overly energetic with us, he stood back as if already a wise elder. We bonded after learning that we shared the same name, and he became my guide throughout the village. He took my hand, introduced me to his family members, and answered my questions about his life.

As I got to know these kids in an even more personal way, as the human beings they were, I soon let down my own defenses. The youthful spirit most of us recognize in ourselves gave way to bountiful curiosities about the world. They wanted to be a part of something.

What especially moved me, as a gay man, was how they openly expressed affection with each other, the same thing in childhood I felt so frightened to even express. Even as a recent graduate, I was all too conscious of it in my everyday life. I felt forced to tightly control my every move, every touch, every stare, and even thoughts. Even as James and I were so naturally inclined toward one another, as if second nature, only for it to become some foreboding thing the moment consciousness was brought to it.

In village life, holding your friend's hand or sitting closely wasn't perceived as gay or feminine as in the West. I noticed how common it was for men to sit very close as they would talk about their days. It was totally normal and came naturally to them like anything else. There was a fluid mess to their presentation of themselves and who they were. I started to feel safe in my own skin, not only as a gay man but also to recognize how fundamentally human these feelings, emotions, desires, and expressions were. It was natural to be close and connected, even physically. It also confirmed what I had experienced a few weeks prior, sitting next to James on that bench, was fundamentally an aspect of our human connection. Something each of us aches for at some level. How beautiful it was to see them express their connections to each other so openly as who they were.

Connection, affinity, and love were all embedded in and realized by these young adolescents who were simply, wholly, and fully living their lives without second-guessing their every action. This translated to their individual relationships and the broader community they were a part of. I felt so connected to them in my short time there. We were all just human.

While I risk romanticizing their realities, what I took away was ultimately the comfort in knowing that what I was was no different.

That I, too, loved, cared for, and felt a connection to those whom I most admired, respected, and valued in my life, and my longing to exist, to express that love outwardly, even to sit close, hold hands, or be in communion with someone was as authentically and wholly connected to my human capacities as any other aspect of who I was. Every day with them was beautiful.

Near the end of our time in the village, we took a quick reprieve from village life alongside those on the program to the coast of Banjul to spend time relaxing for the Fourth of July holiday. We all piled into the same white hospital van that had picked us up, drove to the Capital, and found a nice shack on the beach with a few hammocks just outside.

Being a Muslim country, drinking was not common. Still, we found a way to let loose a bit after finding a few bottles of wine at a local shop. That evening we celebrated the holiday by coming together on the beach, singing, dancing, and taking a few dips into the sea lit only by the light of the moon.

I was having a great time, free from the cares of the world, when there opened up a moment I had to myself in my inebriated state, where the tumult of my family's breakdown back home seemed to bubble up out of nowhere.

In the dark of night, I had been gazing west from the beach, thinking about returning home in just a few days and all that was there. I thought of the adolescent boys I had met in my village, my wishes for them, and all the villagers who persevered through so much pain. Their heroics and what their fundamental humanity had shown me. I thought about all I had experienced over the past year with my family and the pain I had endured. I wondered about the limitations found back home in America, which contrasted with the freeing ways in which I felt the world around me while there. And I thought about my dad.

For the second time since the divorce, and not since the moment in the gay bar with James a few months prior, I started to sob uncontrollably, kneeling in the ocean waves. It was another release of all that had built up within me, offering a brief reprieve from the well of pain still within me.

Once we were all done frolicking, we headed back to the shack. I fell asleep under the stars in the hammocks outside, listening to the rolling ocean waves as they crashed upon the beach.

The next morning, we returned to our friends in the village and spent a few more days there before it was time for us to head home. I left in tears, knowing that I would likely never return, leaving everything I had carried with me that I could. I handed out my T-shirts, books, and other items to the village kiddos I had come to befriend. I took Landing aside and offered him a book on Buddhism. I thought it might help him center the calm energy he carried within him as the future leader I knew he might become. The book was full of all my leftover cash—whatever I could find to ensure he and the others had whatever I could give.

The villagers had given me so much simply by living their lives and so lovingly welcoming me and others into their homes. Without knowing us, they showed such love and hospitality. I was forever touched and felt a deeper connection to the sacredness of our shared humanity.

ABANDONED AND ESTRANGED

A month after returning from the Gambia, we returned to Madison's hometown for his wedding.

This time I had my eyes open. Rather than wilting away at James's behaviors, like a tree bending with the winds, I decided to sit back and observe him from a knowing space. After spending the summer with the young men in the village, I knew even more profoundly the love I had for James and expressed was of the most human form. It was a beautiful gift those young Gambian men reminded me of. I indeed was and always had been a true friend.

I tired of being caught off guard after moments of intimacy and accused of being the only person gravitating toward our mutual connection. So rather than just going with it, as I typically had done before, I would make sure, this time, to pay attention.

What a telling weekend it was.

All the groomsmen and bridesmaids arrived a day early to attend a rehearsal dinner. We were put up in a hotel next to the wedding venue. Ironically, my room was at the end of a long corridor right next to James and his girlfriend.

During the many wedding events, several subtleties showed more of James's hand, convincing me, once and for all, I wasn't crazy for loving him and wanting more from him in how he owned his love for me.

James inspired me endlessly. At the rehearsal dinner, I gave a brief toast in tribute to the love I discovered through him.

Gesturing toward Madison and his soon-to-be wife, I began, "This is such a powerful moment being surrounded by all your loved ones supporting you on your special day. You must remember this moment whenever you may face rough seas along your journey together."

I paused and gestured to the whole room, inviting them to join me in singing the song "Itsy, Bitsy Spider." We did.

Turning back to the bride and groom, I said, "Sing this song whenever you are facing troubled waters and remember the profound support you have at this moment from all of us and our collective belief in your love. Remember it when you sing this song to your future children as you scare away the monsters under their beds. And hum to yourselves as you close your eyes each night, after a long day, that this love exists, here and now, in hope and support of your wedded bliss. Not everyone gets to have what you have. Congratulations!"

Those gathered brushed back a few tears. Then, after the toasts, we returned to mingling about with one another.

Out of nowhere, an older woman approached me and mentioned how James was staring at me during my speech.

"Your boyfriend looked at you with such love. You are so lucky."

"Oh, we're not together," I responded. "That's his girlfriend."

"He looked at her so differently than he looked at you," she said, looking puzzled before moving on.

Soon after, a few women from our friend group back at Gonzaga reiterated what the older woman had said. Maybe something was there? Their comments felt so out of the blue. Remembering my commitment to myself just to observe, I let it go.

The groomsmen met up before the wedding for a photo shoot at the church the following day. We changed into our tuxes in the back. As the close friends we were, James helped to straighten my tie, and I helped him straighten his collar. I helped lock a bracelet around his wrist while he did the same for me. Our intimacy felt so natural.

As we took photos in the empty church, dressed in our black tuxes, at one point, James and I found ourselves standing closely together, facing one another, alone at the altar—the very same sacred spot our friends would be committing their lives to one another an hour later.

I caught him tenderly gazing at me. With light shining through the stained-glass windows upon us, we locked eyes, just as we had done when Madison's mother suggested, "When you know, you know." This time, I had trouble looking away. It was as if there was no one else in the room.

The moment was so overpowering I tried but couldn't avert my eyes. "James… stop. I…" I stuttered under my breath in a hushed tone.

What if this was what our own wedding would have felt like one day? Might he have been thinking the same thing?

I felt his gaze so deeply hitting me at the core of my soul. His love struck every fiber of my being as if some divine presence was with us.

The bride and her bridesmaids entered the church to take their photos, disrupting us. James and I took our seats in a nearby pew. Away from the prying eyes of his girlfriend, we sat so close it seemed like he was sitting on top of me.

Shortly after, other wedding guests filed into the church. The couple lovingly exchanged their vows and were officially married.

At the reception, we found our tables, gave a few speeches at dinner, cut the cake, and had a grand time. James gave his best man speech, which was so touching. While sitting next to his girlfriend, I caught him gazing at me again from across the table. I intentionally turned away, only to look back to see him still warmly staring back at me and tenderly smiling.

It was a beautiful yet painful reminder of so many what-ifs. What if he really did love me, and in that way? What would the world be like if he wasn't ashamed of me? What might we have had if he had followed his heart? All the speeches about love, compassion, soulmates, and commitment—what did it mean for folks like me? Maybe us? Would I even have the right to marry, one day, at all?

As the reception turned to the dancing portion of the night, a couple appeared on the dance floor where one partner was in a wheelchair, with her doting husband by her side. They were the parents of one of my college friends, and her mom had been in a terrible accident years before, crippling her. I was in awe of their evident love and commitment to each other, like soulmates. Something I would have been for James had anything ever happened to him.

Their love reminded me of all I fought for. It's what my grandparents had after almost fifty years of marriage. It's what I thought my parents once had. That special space in one's life in which you find strength and love in all the manifestations love can offer through the different ways you show up for those who matter most to you.

With a few more libations, all I was trying to ignore that evening suddenly hit me. What might have happened to us with everything that happened that weekend and the things I struggled through with James over the years? All the dragons I had fought and the battles I endured to provide safe passage for folks like us?

I quickly left the wedding reception to find a quiet spot to release my overwhelming emotions, sobbing into my arms. Fortunately, no one had seen me leave. It was only the third time I could cry since my parents divorced.

I picked myself up, dried my eyes, went back in, and let it go. The rest of the evening was full of love and light.

As James, his girlfriend, and I returned to our rooms in the nearby hotel, they asked if I wanted to get into the hot tub with them under the stars. I said, of course.

James forgot his swim trunks, but I had an extra pair. So I went to my room, grabbed them, and knocked on their door. His girlfriend answered, ready to go in her bikini. From behind her, I heard James shout, "Just come in, Ryan."

I was confused. Didn't he need to change? I declined the invitation out of respect and wanting to give him privacy. I handed my swimsuit to his girlfriend and returned to my room to wait, thinking it would be just a few more minutes.

Not five minutes later, I started hearing odd sex noises coming from their room behind mine.

Caught off guard but not necessarily surprised, I decided not to let it get to me. Why had they invited me to their room just minutes before? Had it been an invitation to join them? And if not, why leave me alone waiting for them rather than giving me the heads up? Was it intentional, another attempt by James to counter his feelings for me?

I went to bed with a pillow over my head to drown out the noise.

The next morning, we had breakfast at a local diner. James asked me if I had heard what had happened. I told him I didn't take it personally. In fact, I even jabbed back at him. "Yeah, I heard. Funny. You were clearly thinking of me while you were doing it. Weren't you? You totally exposed yourself, dude." We awkwardly laughed.

"When will I see you again?" I asked, quickly changing the subject.

"I don't know where I will be. I might move to Europe or Latin America." His girlfriend gave him a quick glare. "Maybe I'll see you in ten years."

My eyes welled up. "You ass, that's far too long."

We wrapped up our breakfast and departed in our respective directions, not knowing when our paths would cross again.

That weekend confirmed what I had always known. James loved me too. He cared for me in ways that seemed unimaginable. What I often experienced alone was no longer something solely mine to carry, but I was no longer willing to accept his blatant disregard and irrational fear of me. The battle was within him, and I couldn't help him as much as I ached to be there for him, the love of my life.

I didn't know whether I would see him again. But I had many of the answers I needed after that weekend to know that my yearning and aching for him wasn't just something in my head. I also knew I had given all I could, and it was in his hands to fully appreciate me and all I could offer him if he so chose.

I returned home to Spokane.

I was living with my father after graduation while I looked for work—just us. I continued to think about what had transpired and what to do when someone takes you for granted or devalues who you are as a person, despite your love for them.

In 2008, the US stock market crashed, upending the global economy and placing millions of Americans into financial ruin (Kosakowski 2021). As a recent graduate, entering the labor market became next to impossible, no matter my accomplishments or good works, let alone the depression I was still fighting from my parents' divorce.

I saw the time as an opportunity to reconnect with my dad after the tumultuous prior year. He had yet to truly have a meaningful conversation to help me better understand his actions from the previous year. Sporadically, I tried to learn more about his relationship with the new woman, understand my father more, and give us all the chances to reconnect, especially before I struck out into the world.

My dad had a different idea. It felt like he saw my presence there as a burden.

Our paths would cross like ships in the night. He seemed to be always gone. Rather than spending time with me, he spent his evenings at his new girlfriend's house. I often wondered over that summer if my attempts to reconcile with him had been ill-conceived.

To my surprise, one night, he started making dinner. I was delighted, thinking we might have an actual meal together, like old times at our family dining table where so much had taken place.

Not five minutes before we were about to eat, he told me, "My girlfriend is coming over." My joy turned to anxiety. *What do I say? What do I do?* I thought.

The doorbell rang.

She walked in, briefly said hello, and we all sat down at our family dining room table. My dad sat on one end next to her. I was on the other side. Like him, she wasn't much of a conversationalist, the exact opposite of my mother.

Despite the clear power difference in our relationship and my profound discomfort, I found myself trying to be welcoming to her. I told myself, "I'm an adult. I can handle this."

I asked her about who she was, where she grew up, what her hobbies were, and more. As my parents had taught me, I offered her the general politeness I would afford any guest in our home. I made it through supper.

We cleaned up and moved to the living room, where we began watching the Beijing Olympics, which would last late into the night. They sat beside each other with my dad's hand on her leg. While discomforted, I told myself, "I'm an adult. I can handle this."

After an hour or so, they headed to the hot tub downstairs while I stayed upstairs, watching the Olympics. Again, I thought, *I'm an adult. I can handle this.* Whatever they were doing, they had their time downstairs. Then they returned to the primary bedroom just opposite the main living room, where I was still watching TV, barely acknowledging me.

Not fifteen minutes later, I heard them having sex.

As a sexual and reproductive health advocate, a sexual liberationist, and a feminist, I was not mad they had sex. I believe sexuality is but another expression of the human experience, and we should feel free to experience this aspect as fundamental to who we are.

What I did not expect, especially coming from my father, one of the most beloved figures in my life, was to hear them making so much excessive noise, knowing full well that I was just on the opposite side of the thinly constructed wall. It was unbelievable. I was in shock.

I just met this woman. Had they even considered the immediate impact upon me? Or the more prolonged implications it would have on whatever future relationship we might have?

I couldn't believe my dad would do that to me. I was so hurt.

The next morning, after she left, I confronted my dad. "Dad, how could you do that to me? You knew I was watching the Olympics right outside your door?"

"What do you expect me to do? Change my whole life just because you are here?" he coldly replied.

I couldn't believe it. It would have been one thing had my dad mistakenly acted in such a way and apologized. However, his blatant disregard for our relationship and its already tenuous state shut a door I naively thought was still open.

Over the next several weeks, we'd get into small arguments. There was no longer room for acquiescence. As with James, I tired of having to endure such blatant forms of disrespect in an effort to salvage something, but only at my expense. My dad became increasingly annoyed at everything I did. Nothing was ever good enough for him.

One evening, we were back to having dinner, just the two of us, and I turned to him amid a heated discussion and said, "You know what, Dad, I don't know that I will ever be able to see her as anything other than your mistress."

"Well, if that's the case, you can get the fuck out." When he looked at me, it was as if I meant nothing to him. He got up and went to his room.

Stunned, I went outside. I felt so empty and alone. It had been my biggest fear since childhood—abandonment. While not because I was gay, it was happening.

The only person I knew to call at that moment was James.

"Hey, guy. What's going on? You just called three times? You all right?"

"No, I'm not all right. My dad just kicked me out of the house." I started crying.

He calmed me down. "You're going to be okay. Just figure out what's next."

It would be one of his last moments of love toward me, despite doing the same thing to me just a few weeks before.

Next, I called my best friend Megan. She invited me to live with her in Minneapolis. This way, I could be near where my mom now lived in Wisconsin.

I packed up my belongings and moved out of my dad's house by the end of the week. I didn't say goodbye. I drove halfway across the country, only to realize when I arrived, as kind and loving as Megan's gesture was, her small studio apartment would not suffice for us to live together in the long term.

Without question, my mother lovingly opened her home and heart to me to live with her an hour and a half away while I figured things out. When I showed up on her doorstep a few days later, I began to weep uncontrollably, holding her close.

What was to come of my life? I felt entirely lost.

OVERCOMING DARKNESS

My greatest fears came true. The person who revealed to me my capacity to love was afraid of me. My own father treated me as if I was just a stranger in his life.

I felt at the bottom of a pit, one I couldn't imagine ever escaping.

As I settled into my mom's home, I continued striving to make meaning and purpose out of the crumbling world around me. I fumbled through TV channels while lying on my mother's basement couch, surrounded by piles of dirty dishes, feeling empty. I entered a dark depression, not knowing who I was, what my life was about, or what I was supposed to do next.

In many ways, who I was, had been so inspired by these two men. Their love provided me with a form of strength I couldn't live without. I still loved them and profoundly cared for them as I always had, but I would have to create a distance far and away from where they seemed capable of going and the prolonged pain they had caused me.

My father was the rock by which I could lean on and whose example I strived to live up to each and every day. It was always through his actions that I knew deep down he loved me. How, of all people, could he not know the mortal wounds he would inflict by kicking me out of my house and treating me the way he did? Does one accept such treatment, even from those they love? Unfortunately, I could no longer trust that his words would align with his actions. I was so worried for the beautiful man I knew him to be, deep down, hoping he was somehow okay.

James was a love of my life. I believed we were soulmates. For so long, I became less and less of myself to accommodate his insecurities about our relationship. I saw him struggling with the things I once struggled with and wanted to offer him something I never had, someone to lean on. Despite his treatment of me, I forgave him repeatedly. I just wanted him to be happy. I thought that's what you were supposed to do for someone you loved.

I learned the hard way no matter how much you give, you can't carry someone's pain for them. There are certain gates they have to pass through solely on their own, no matter how much you may want to be there on the other side, waiting with open arms. However, it's also not my place to force them through any gate if they are unwilling or unable to do so.

Sometimes, you must choose yourself, even if you have to make such a seemingly impossible choice. You may even have to let them go.

In my depressed state, I continued to ponder my life's purpose but without them. I was still set on pursuing a career that would somehow allow me to continue my advocacy for LGBTI human rights and gender justice, particularly tackling harmful norms around masculinity—the same masculinity James and my father seemed to struggle with.

I had no idea where to begin. What types of careers applied to my deep passions? Where would I even look? With the economy in shambles, pursuing such a niche career was even harder. I applied for job after job, but nothing seemed to bite even though I checked all the boxes in college to get a decent job—good grades, extracurriculars, numerous internships, global experiences, national notoriety, etc.

While now estranged from my father, he occasionally called to see if I'd gotten a job yet. He'd complain I was lazy when I told him I hadn't figured it out. My mom was more understanding but also pushed me to continue looking.

They wanted me to take a practical job and couldn't understand why I was so hell-bent on pursuing such roles as working for a human rights nonprofit. It was far and away from the profession in education that they had sought. To them, my ideas weren't something they could wholly conceptualize. So, I had to strike out on my own to discover a new professional pathway.

Beyond the practical realities of finding a job, I had to question the existential purpose behind my drive. I was stuck not only in my professional development and growth. I was also stuck emotionally and spiritually.

How could I pursue a career that would allow me to share all I'd come to know through my life experiences? What on earth was love if it could lead to divorce, abandoning one's children, or entrap a person in a place where thirty years later, they just wanted to throw it all away? Was this worth fighting for anymore?

Were all those awards and accomplishments, the profound moments of insight, or the inspiration I gleaned from my grandparents, James, the Shepards, or Archbishop Desmond Tutu, just happenstance? All the love I felt so deeply—was this just a matter of naivety?

Why strive to be the good son my parents raised me to be? Why sacrifice for individuals I cared so deeply for when I could become an aberration to them?

I struggled for months with such questions. Some days, I couldn't get out of bed.

Everything was in a heavy fog where nothing seemed to make sense.

While in my darkened state, moments of enlightenment here and there reminded me of what mattered most. I continued to be inspired by poets, authors, and creators from around the globe as I pored over books, watched movies, and listened to my favorite music from times when I was happier, including the CD James had given me.

My saving grace was my mother. While broken in many ways by the circumstances of the divorce, her sense of self, her knowingness of the world, her central repository where she stored her greatest truths, remained constant.

She remained faithful to the person I always knew her to be. She was the same sage guide who answered all my questions, held space for me, and was patient and kind during my darkest hours. She didn't shy away from the hard conversations about our new reality, one neither of us fathomed would be our truth.

"Ryan, I finally understand the darkness you went through as a child. I never knew such depression until the divorce. I see you."

Her patience with me was, in itself, such a gift and kept me going.

I visited Megan in Minneapolis frequently, where we'd have deep conversations about life and continue navigating our seemingly parallel paths toward our mutual social justice missions. As unemployed, free-spirited dreamers in the cold arctic air of the upper Midwest, we spent many nights reminiscing about the wonder of the world. She became like chosen family, similar to those back in Colorado.

During those long months, I struggled to understand why what happened to me had happened. Yet at the same time, I knew all too well.

So many of the barriers of masculinity I encountered with James, my dad, and other men I felt forced to fight against throughout my life. The fear of closeness itself, the suppression of one's feelings, let alone the expression of such emotions, and the fear of love emanated from harmful gender norms around manhood and the masculine ideals pervasive in our Western culture.

Indeed, it was one of the fundamental areas my advocacy efforts underscored. So much of my work wasn't solely about LGBTI individuals like me. The homophobia I experienced emanated from these terrible ideas about what it meant to be a man and the undergirding social norms that perpetuated sexism, racism, ableism, and so on. The same unspoken rules held against me as a child were also held against James and my father in their own light. Things they too clearly grappled with.

What kind of pressure builds inside someone considered the perfect father and husband like my dad?

What kind of suffering manifests when you feel such deep love for another person like James and I did but it also provokes such conflict within the societal expectations surrounding it? Even if it was purely plutonic.

Both homophobia and sexism buttress up masculinity in our American culture. Acting outside of one's prescribed gender role, let alone caring for and loving other men, was seen as counter to the societal ideal of manhood. I long struggled with this myself because none of what I knew about being gay in my youth applied completely to who I was. I was not all the horrible stereotypes projected onto me. The beautiful feelings I came to feel were not the evil I was told they were supposed to be, but in fact, were liberating forces within me that connected me to the world around me.

I recalled, even as an out gay man, being constantly compared to something far and away from what anyone really knew. For some people, I wasn't gay enough while to others, I was too gay, and even more, others thought I was only gay.

Fellow activists would critique me for not having known enough queer theory in my arguments or that I should be more into shows like Ru Paul's drag race. I wasn't gay enough.

Some were embarrassed by my level of comfort in who I was and often dismissed me as being too much. I was too gay.

Still, others condensed my personhood down to a stereotypic idea they had picked up somewhere along the way, not the unique person I was with a vivid lived experiences and attributes worth getting to know, even learning from. I was only gay.

My lived experiences were neither solely masculine nor solely feminine but fell along a continuum of my lived reality.

American society feminized the mere act of loving itself. As a male, society viewed being kind, caring, and tender as a weakness, associating weakness with femininity and homosexuality—the opposite of my experiences in many other cultures. At the same time, being bold, taking action, and stepping outside the norm was seen as heroic or masculine in many ways, but one couldn't stray too far. Yet I experienced the continuum of it all—masculine, feminine, and everything in between.

From this space, I saw whole new worlds and ways of being from my unique vantage point. The authentic self, possible within me, gave possibility to humanity as a whole. What if these boundaries around gender and sexuality were more blurred than the worlds we presently occupy?

I could only imagine the countless individuals around the world who experienced a profound sense of love for each other and came alive in whole new ways but were too afraid of what it might mean. How could that ever be wrong? To love someone so deeply in the way I came to love James? Yet the world still perpetuated such deep fear around this beautiful thing.

Despite no longer having James by my side, I needed to continue fighting for this. After bearing witness to such a profundity, how could I not? It became my calling long ago before I even could fully name it.

I also grew out of the deep suffering I experienced with my father. I sought to better understand the contexts in which he, too, faced the world. While I struggled for the freedom to express my most authentic self outwardly, so did my father.

In hindsight, my father, for my whole life, seemed to struggle to really put words behind his emotions. To fully grasp his life's spiritual, emotional, and relational aspects, or at least express them. Maybe he did. Perhaps it was because he grew up in a small town, and the expectation was to be stoic and brave, not express his feelings—like the villagers of The Gambia. Maybe it was because he considered himself shy and introverted. And maybe, just maybe, he also grew up in an era in which, as a boy, he was told not to value his emotions, to not dive deep into understanding oneself in those ways, to as a husband and a father, live stoically in servitude to one's partner and children and to sacrifice his own feelings and emotions.

Over time, I think family life just got the better of him. I know as his son, I certainly took him for granted. I don't know that he knew where to place those bubbling thoughts of discontent. When your life is measured by what you do, your family life as a husband and a father, I imagine this has to be a lot of pressure—especially when, for the majority of my life, my dad was nothing but the most upstanding father. I know my mom would claim him as an upstanding husband as well. He was "Saint Barry," as my aunts lovingly called him. What happened?

The tell for me was in his final actions. How could you treat so egregiously those who are closest to you, idolize you, look up to you, want the best for you, and love you unconditionally? How could he treat me, his own son, as if I was a complete stranger?

My dad is not alone in his actions. In the United States, over half of marriages end in divorce (Bieber 2023). It's commonly understood that men experience *midlife crises*, but little is done to examine what's underneath. So many people throughout the world, particularly men, struggle to examine and embrace those parts of themselves hidden within. We raise boys lacking the skills and capabilities to express their feelings. When they do, society puts them down and even punishes them for doing so.

It was, in a sense, easier for me because being gay felt like there was something on my face I couldn't hide. Therefore, it was easier to fling my hands in the air and say, yes, fine, I am. But on the other hand, as a straight man, my dad had to live up to an archetype his whole life, with no grace to fall or maneuver outside the predefined parameters of what so-called manhood prescribed. In many ways, he was a man ahead of his time. He was a girls' basketball coach, supportive of my mom's career and of me.

In my travels abroad, I saw how these errors of our ways and misconceptions around gender and sexuality were built around centuries of ideology that had consequential impacts not just on individuals or families but on entire societies.

If it's important to be stoic and unshakeable, what happens when war is on our doorstep? When power and domination are what we strive for, what do we do when we need to rely on one another when an existential threat such as climate change faces us all? When we fail to see half of the world's population as equally deserving of the same dignity and respect, we demand for ourselves, simply because they are female, let alone due to their race, ethnicity, geography, ability, or more, what do we miss as a result?

Let alone in minimizing the complex realities of gendered identities and expressions into just two categories—men and women.

At the end of the day, after all those months of toiling in my misery, I realized my struggle was not solely my own. It was one countless people faced in a myriad of ways. Including James. Including my dad.

Therefore, my liberation was not only my own but was also theirs and all of ours. Me. You. Us. Them.

The real-world impact of this underlying suffering is the devastation it causes to all of us. I couldn't close my eyes to all I bore witness to, experienced, and now knew. My capacity to love was not a deficit but a gift of the human experience, something we are all capable of and ought to strive for.

As a part of my existential questioning, I kept thinking about the lessons I learned from my global travels, through my journey as an accidental activist, and what the archbishop had taught me about the notion of ubuntu and the power of our interconnectedness as human beings. To me, this was what could push us all toward a penultimate kind of love, that which I felt so deeply within. Something these harmful gender norms around masculinity held us back from. Like looking at the sun, it was overwhelmingly powerful within me and hard to bear witness to.

Over that year, I would write the word ubuntu on napkins, leave them on bars, or hand them to strangers. I thought if someone saw the word, they might Google it and be moved to act. Then I had an epiphany.

Inspired by my transgender friends, who sought to align their inner and outer worlds, which often included changing one's name, I thought about changing my name to align with who I was.

Taking on ubuntu as a part of my name might have a similar effect. Its philosophy so aligned with what I wanted to dedicate my life to and had come to mean so much to me after all that had been imparted to us by Archbishop Desmond Tutu.

While my original name, Michael, was intended as a spiritual name taken from the Bible, it was given to me by my parents. However, its spiritual meaning held little weight for me, whereas ubuntu had such substance. A name that better aligned to my inner and outer worlds I now understood as myself.

After deciding, I emailed the archbishop and asked for his blessing. To which he responded, "*Haha, how wonderful. I'm touched that you should want to have ubuntu as your middle name. Now do you know how to pronounce your own name? Ha! Much love and blessings, Arch.*"

So, I took it as my name. But what was that, and where would I go next?

In the early spring, my mom's university hosted an alternative spring break for students and staff called the Civil Rights Pilgrimage. Students would spend a week visiting historical sites of the civil rights movement.

As a new administrator at her university, my mom eagerly signed up to learn more about the popular program. As she had done throughout my life, from Disney World to Semester at Sea, she suggested I join her on the trip.

At first, and in my darkened state, I was insistent that I didn't want to go. I had a lot of excuses as to why it wasn't for me. Hours upon hours on the bus? Going to the Deep South? I had no interest. I just wanted to stay home and sulk, as I had done for the previous six months. But through some nudging, she eventually convinced me to go.

And boy, did that trip change my life.

The ten-day trip took us across the Southern United States, stopping in various cities.

In Atlanta, we visited Ebenezer Baptist Church, where we sat in on a service and learned more about the life of Dr. Martin Luther King, who had been the primary pastor there at the time of his death. It was a powerful way to start our trip (Waxman 2021).

We visited Birmingham and Selma, Alabama, two cities where major civil rights actions took place in which civil rights protestors were beaten with batons, harassed, sprayed with fire hoses, attacked with dogs, and more. We saw the 16th St Church, bombed in 1954, killing four little girls. We walked across the Edmund Pettus Bridge in Selma, where John Lewis and others were beaten to a pulp as they sought to advance voting rights on what would become known as Bloody Sunday (Vang and Bowman 2021).

We spent a day cleaning up a section of the lower wards of hurricane-ravaged New Orleans, predominantly owned by members of the Black community (Williams 2020).

In Arkansas, we visited Central High School, where students known as the Little Rock Nine exercised their right to an education (Keyes 2017). They had to be escorted to class every day for a whole year due to the violence threatened against them for breaking the racial barrier.

At the Burkle Estate in Memphis, Tennessee, we learned about efforts of the Underground Railroad to hide and support formerly enslaved persons to escape slavery in addition to the Jim Crow South years later and beyond, the great migration out of the South by Black Americans (Bradley 2018).

Our final stop was the Loraine Motel, where Martin Luther King Jr. had been assassinated in the broad light of day (National Civil Rights Museum 2023). It was powerful to lay eyes on a place where such a sage leader had taken his last breath after breathing such light into the world.

Nothing could compare to having those direct experiences in such powerful places in American history. The entire trip reinvigorated my soul. It helped me draw linkages to the civil rights work I had conducted over the years while in college, the history of human rights advocacy I was a part of, and what my heart was pushing me to continue striving toward.

As a person searching for meaning in life, during this trip I discovered the Clinton School of Public Service in Little Rock, Arkansas.

While visiting the Clinton Presidential Library, I stumbled upon a brochure about the recently created program. The school touted it could help turn your "why" into your "how." Two-thirds of the master's program was experiential—just like my previous experiences. I was intrigued.

Through happenstance, fate, or mere serendipity, out of this dark place, I started to have clarity on what I needed to do next. So, I applied and waited for the gods to determine my fate.

A few months later, the program accepted me. Suddenly, I had an excitement again I hadn't had in years—a place to put my passions to work.

I could never even imagine all that might lie ahead or the exponential growth that was before me, where I could put my passion into practical use and turn my pain into purpose all around the world.

ACT FOUR

PERSEVERANCE

When will our consciences grow so tender that we will act to prevent human misery than to avenge it?
—ELENORE ROOSEVELT

The mystery of human existence lies not just in staying alive but in finding something to live for.
—FYODOR DOSTOYEVSKY

However long the night, the dawn will break.
—AFRICAN PROVERB

CLINTON SCHOOL

After learning about my acceptance to the Clinton School, a cloud lifted, and suddenly I felt like I could come up for air. I had hope again. After searching for so long to find breathing room to return to myself and what I loved most, I finally had a next step.

I felt called to the experience as if there was more ahead of me. My grandmother's presence was strong within me—something I always felt when I knew I was moving in the right direction.

I packed all my belongings into my tiny, deep purple 1994 Honda Accord and moved down to Little Rock, Arkansas, a place I could never have imagined I would call home.

Over the summer, I met my new classmates. They were all exceptional people. I entered this new community with far greater confidence and experience under my belt more fully as myself.

We had summer barbecues and brunches while getting to know each other in ways that would serve as a foundation for our program. I even found myself attending the sixty-eighth birthday of Minnijean Brown-Trickey, a member of the Little Rock Nine whom I had just learned about on the civil rights pilgrimage. Her daughter, Spirit, was one of my new classmates.

By September, the program officially began. There were thirty-six students passionate about thirty-six areas of focus. My passion was LGBTI rights and tackling harmful gender norms around masculinity. Others' passions were to fight climate change, reform voting rights, build a more just world for immigrant communities, and so on. Everyone was there to do something. Indeed, many of them already had. We all had our own drives and pathways that had brought us together on that same day in the same place.

Individuals worldwide joined our class, including those from Indonesia, South Africa, Uganda, Kazakhstan, Pakistan, Haiti, Mexico, and elsewhere. In addition, super volunteers such as return Peace Corps volunteers, AmeriCorps, and Teach for America alums joined our program. Graduates from state schools, historically black colleges, private religious schools, and trade schools were among our ranks.

We came from different socioeconomic backgrounds, genders, races, classes, and creeds. Many of us, in one way or another, had also experienced some form of hardship. Some came from war-torn communities, and others directly experienced the impacts of climate change or faced the brutality of unjust systems.

We all connected deeply based on our mutual desires to see our world improve and shape the future for a better tomorrow. We believed solutions to the world's most pressing problems were not impossible but merely improbable.

It was powerful. Not only because of the individuals in the room but the collective ways we all showed up in the space. There was a certain vibrancy we fed off one another—an excitement about doing meaningful work and an underlying belief that people were, at their cores, good. I was no longer the solitary activist but a part of a community sharing a common aim.

The program helped champions like us develop practical skills and know how to put into practice what we sought to change about the world.

During the first year, we attended several requisite courses on leadership, ethics, evaluation, civic engagement and advocacy, law, program management, and more. As we moved from course to course, we found that our professors were equally passionate with decades of experience, making the seemingly impractical possible.

I particularly remembered my professor, Dr. Arvind Singhal. Deeply inspired by the social change praxis of Mahatma Gandhi, on the first day of class, he had us all sit in a circle in our chairs. He turned out all the lights and then asked us to pretend we were aliens visiting from outer space, and we came to Earth and stumbled upon what many commonly call a chair. "Sit in that chair in a way you've never thought of sitting in the chair before." We had thirty seconds to figure it out.

When he turned on the light, we were all sitting on our chairs in thirty-six completely different ways. It was a powerful testament to how conceptualizing change could be, undergirding our entire program. If we wanted solutions, we had to be willing to suspend our belief in what we thought we knew and be open to what could be.

This framing was uniquely powerful because I felt the same about addressing prevailing gender norms, which limited the capacity of human beings to fully be themselves and live out their greatest truths. What if binary social constructs of gender actually limited us? After all, my experience breaking through such a false dichotomy helped me to see the world in a whole new light.

How we showed up to the work as leaders became a central aspect of our curriculum. In our leadership course, we closely examined different leadership styles and how to show up for the communities our efforts stood to benefit. They asked us to deepen our understanding of our why and expand on how to articulate it clearly. Love, after all, was my purpose on this Earth.

When we think about our individual agency, we also learned to think about the capacity within all of us to do something alongside one another. Through the concept of community philanthropy, we explored how we all have contributions we can make to our communities, which don't have to be some government grant or a bank loan or involve solely financial resources. We all have something we can give from our talents, time, and thoughtful engagement with our neighbors and loved ones.

From imagining the world in a new way to knowing how we showed up in it, we expanded our theory and understanding of how to bring people into the fold. In our civic engagement and advocacy course, we explored best practices for building consensus and finding common ground, shifting hearts and minds within society and government. I started to hone my abilities to reach different groups from different backgrounds around gender equality.

While our efforts for social impact might be ongoing, it's essential to demonstrate measurable results. How would you know you were making a difference? We sought to build in key indicators to help us know we were on the right path or adjust as necessary along the way.

While there were grassroots solutions to everyday problems, how would we ensure there was a systemic change? At the law school, we were philosophically challenged to expand our notions about the expanse, reach, and limitations of legal systems. How might policy better our societies or harm them? So many of the barriers everyday people face actually link to systemic failures. How could we tackle this core area of social change?

One of the best parts of the program was not only the classroom explorations of theory but the practical application of our required fieldwork. Our class was split into groups of three, and each group was assigned a community partner to address a prevalent issue within the surrounding area.

I was paired with two of my classmates to work with the Goodwill Industries of Arkansas, where we would strive to address the rising issue of recidivism. Recidivism is when an incarcerated person has served their time and then reenters society but then returns to the criminal justice system because they aren't able to adjust to the new world they reenter by reoffending (Simpson 2022). When a former offender is released from prison, they can often struggle to meet their basic needs like food, clothing, and shelter and make a living through gainful employment.

Using our newly formed skills, we met and worked with several stakeholders throughout Arkansas to identify barriers to reentry for former offenders and develop solutions to better assist them. We found that due to the reentry process, which is essentially starting one's life over, there were a lot of services individuals had to rely upon, but they needed coordination. Imagine you've been in prison for some time, and then suddenly, you must learn how to be in the world again. However, you have to go to one organization for one type of service, such as job training. And then you have to go to a different organization on the other side of town without access to a car for another kind of service for housing.

Our team sought to map all the services within a person's reentry experience and bring them together to make it easier for former offenders to identify and meet their needs. It gave me far more empathy for those incarcerated in our often-unjust criminal justice system within the United States, particularly toward Black and Brown individuals subjected to disproportional arrests and prison sentences compared to their white counterparts (Sawyer 2020). As our focus wasn't on individuals but rather systems, it was great to feel like we helped build a comradery among service providers so they could more aptly serve those in need.

While seemingly different than my life's passions, I particularly related to this work. As communities that were once criminalized in the US and remained criminalized in parts of the world, LGBTI people still interact with and are subject to the criminal justice system on a daily basis (Donohue, McCann, and Brown 2021).

It was a powerful way to see the academic work in the classroom translate to tangible outcomes in the real world.

The Clinton School also offered us a top-notch public speaker program to expand our thinking further. Each week, two to three luminaries came to Little Rock to speak about their lived experiences, public service, and commitment to social justice. Not only would the speakers come to the school to give public lectures, but they spoke directly to our classes, offering our small cohort the opportunity to ask poignant questions of them about current world affairs. For a select few whose personal missions aligned with the specific speakers, we'd then join the speaker for dinner.

Speakers who came during my time included former Secretary of State Madeline Albright, Senator Elizabeth Warren, Hans Blix, Rachel Maddow, Paul Farmer, CNN's John King, Michelle Rhee, DNC Strategist, Matthew Dowd, the Egyptian Ambassador to the US, Sameh Shoukry, Republican Strategist, Steve Schmidt, Former Governor of Michigan, Jennifer Granholm, Founder of Tom's Shoes, Blake Mycoskie, former Secretary of State, Hillary Rodham Clinton, and countless others. Imagine every single week interacting in your classrooms with luminaries from all sorts of backgrounds which you'd only previously seen on TV as a small-town kid.

I felt fortunate to attend and get to know three incredible speakers that aligned with and buttressed my passions for gender justice and LGBTI human rights. I met Mariana Iskander, the former head of the International Planned Parenthood Foundation; a leading gender justice advocate addressing the epidemic of manhood in the US, Jackson Katz; and I got to introduce and get to know Neil Giuliano, the then president of the Gay and Lesbian Alliance Against Defamation, or GLAAD. Learning directly from individuals whose paths had inspired me sometimes felt like a dream.

I was wholly inspired when President Clinton took time out of his busy schedule to give our class a three-hour lecture. We huddled into a classroom, dressed up as professionally as possible, awaiting the moment to hear from him. My friend and I got there early and snagged two front-row seats. The anticipation of finally meeting the namesake of our school was before us.

He came in and stood at the front of the room where we were seated. All our faculty and school administrators crowded at the back. He had us each briefly introduce ourselves. In my introduction, I mentioned I graduated from Gonzaga, to which he responded, "Oh, you all have an incredible basketball team!" And I replied, "Yes, but did you hear about our national champion debate team"—to which everyone chuckled, softening the tense mood.

As I had always heard but never knew firsthand, he had a mastery of making someone feel like they were the only person in the room. In such an intimate setting, my classmates and I had the chance over several hours to talk with him about his worldviews, perspectives, and how we might better the communities we came from. His book, *Giving: How Each of Us Can Change the World*, had recently come out, and he spoke to us at length about the power and privilege we held in being able to move the needle to better our shared world (2007). He noted his life experiences meeting all these inspiring world-renowned individuals along his journey of life and the way they were making a difference in their communities.

When it came time for questions, I eagerly raised my hand, and he called on me. Having been moved by my time on Semester at Sea and still struggling to make sense of it all, I asked, "You've traveled throughout the world and met with both world leaders and those touched most deeply by the scars of war, famine, and poverty. Yet you remain so optimistic about our collective agency. What have you learned about the human condition from your travels that keeps you so optimistic?"

He smiled and recounted several examples of his world travels. He highlighted his time working on AIDS relief in Africa when there were no drugs, and he met with patients dying in hospitals. He spoke about his work to address Middle East peace at Camp David with then-Palestinian President Yasser Arafat and Israeli President Yitzhak Rabin. And he highlighted his time as president working with those in the Mississippi Delta in the Deep South, the poorest part of the entire country, and the local community's resilience to persevere to better their lives.

Then he went into a short speech specifically about the word ubuntu and the notion of our intersecting responsibilities as human beings to look out for one another and build peace and prosperity within the world. He referenced he had learned of the philosophy from his friend, the former President of South Africa, Nelson Mandela. I knew it from Tutu.

I sat there, deeply moved. At that moment, it was clear that this program deeply aligned with my life's purpose. I was meant to be in that room.

As our first year came to a close, we made preparations for that summer. While the first year's practicum placed students into teams, the summer international public service project, or IPSP, would be led by individual students embedded in an organization somewhere out in the world.

After researching different LGBTI organizations, I stumbled upon the Gay and Lesbian Coalition of Kenya or GALCK. They were a loose coalition of advocacy groups that sought to advance the health, safety, and rights of LGBTI people in Kenya.

I had heard very little about Kenya at the time other than previous students who had done their IPSPs there. But, after talking with my point of contact there, David, and the work I would get to do, supporting the rollout of human rights training, this could be it!

By the end of that incredible first year, all thirty-six of us had selected where we would work, packed our bags, and shipped off to our respective work locations to work on thirty-six different impact projects.

What a summer it would be.

LGBTI HUMAN RIGHTS IN KENYA

I arrived in the middle of the night in Nairobi. I slowly exited the plane to find my host, David Kuria, waiting for me at the baggage claim. The only image I had of him at that point was from a Wanted poster.

I had been communicating with David about working at his organization GALCK, my scope of work in the country, and accommodations. Major academic institutions regularly asked him to detail the experiences of LGBTI people in Kenya to accompany one of their theoretical papers. I agreed to assist the organization in finalizing a human rights curriculum and rolling it out across the country to sensitize other LGBTI groups, government officials, religious leaders, and others on the fundamental human rights of all people, including those identified as LGBTI.

I also agreed to live with him. He had a small, two-bedroom apartment in a gated compound on the outskirts of town, about a thirty-minute drive from the heart of Nairobi. David and I had a quick drink and chatted briefly before heading to bed the first night.

The next morning, we woke up around 5 a.m. to make our way to the industrial area. On some days, depending on traffic, it could take a few hours to get in and out of town.

The offices sat above a mechanic shop and offered five large cubical areas. Given the safety concerns of those at GALCK, it was a safe location because of its obscurity, providing protection from those who might want to cause them harm. It was also the only place that agreed to offer them a place to rent.

Advocacy for LGBTI rights in Kenya was a new type of activism I hadn't experienced before. In a country with remnants of the colonial era penal codes criminalizing homosexuality with up to fourteen years in prison, being a queer person wasn't easy (Human Rights Watch 2019). While the LGBTI identity was still a relatively recent set of terms, there had always been a rich underlying life of queerness in Kenya, even if it wasn't labeled as such, just like many other cultures around the world. Many indigenous groups expressed homosexuality within their traditional practices (Buckle 2020). Variances in typical gender roles were more expansive than the Western binary construction of gender I was used to.

Like elsewhere, politicians and religious leaders often used LGBTI people as pawns in their crusade for power. This dangerous rhetoric created serious barriers for the average LGBTI person in Kenya and the wider East African region.

While the police only arrested some under the strict penal codes, the stigma and discrimination LGBTI people faced, simply because the law existed, was everywhere. As a result, people would lose their jobs and families, be kicked out of schools and homes, and in many instances, have to seek shelter elsewhere for the risk of being found out and being bludgeoned to death.

On the coast, in Mombasa, just before I had arrived, there had been a rumor of a gay wedding taking place at a local center that supported health services for those living with HIV—which happened to include patients who were also men who had sex with men. This rumor, out of the back of a barber shop, spread wildly among religious community members. Eventually, an angry mob stormed to the HIV center, demanding they produce the would-be grooms. Barricaded inside were the center staff, accused by the townspeople of supporting such abominable behavior, a gay wedding. They refused to leave until they could bring out the unholy homosexuals to punish them (AfroQueer Podcast 2018).

Soon, the police intervened and safely escorted the center staff out of the city. Not only did the service center have to shut its doors for a while, but the couple accused of getting married had to escape to a safe house somewhere in Kenya, fearing for their lives. The incident is just one of the most well-known in Kenya, but there are thousands of others whose stories never make it to the local paper or international press.

The work that David and a few of his friends had done to establish GALCK was meant to address the numerous incidents just like this and those even more obscure. Not solely to oppose the ongoing violence perpetrated against members of the Kenyan LGBTI community but also to serve as a place to provide information to the community and to address, at the systemic level, inequalities faced by LGBTI people.

GALCK had several sub-organizations that operated under its umbrella. Several international philanthropic organizations funded their operations, seeking to support efforts that would advance the rights of LGBTI citizens in Kenya.

Those who worked at GALCK were a lively bunch committed to their work while also having the typical in-group dynamics of any other professional environment where some personalities clashed amid office politics. My new friends and colleagues reminded me of my friends back home. I was in awe of their bravery, tenacity, and impact within their community—especially within the context of what seemed like such a hostile setting—and grew to love them all.

As I met my team, who operated under one of the five sub-organizations, it soon became apparent that there was a herculean effort to educate individuals about their fundamental rights as queer people. Just like when I came out, and my mom offered me information on LGBTI history, so too was the need to educate people about their fundamental rights. Members of the organization had taken the previous year to adapt the globally ratified "Yogyakarta Principles" to the Kenyan context, which applies an LGBTI lens to fundamental human rights principles (ARC International 2006). The principles outlined how gender or sexually diverse people should be afforded the same human rights.

Human rights were essential to advance throughout Kenya, from the right to live to have safe and affordable housing and the highest health standards to organizing and speaking out on important issues. It was an eye-opening experience that centered the policy discourse around human rights in Kenya as an avenue for advancing fundamental freedoms that should be afforded to any person simply because they are human, including LGBTI people.

I worked on the curriculum, building its various components and preparing the training to be delivered around the country. Then, after a few weeks of gathering feedback and identifying our key audiences, we produced a first-ever training on LGBTI human rights. It was full of interactive modules and illustrations that helped underscore the importance of LGBTI human rights to participants.

We delivered the curriculum throughout the country in hotel conference rooms and offices of local organizations. I traveled with my colleagues in matatus or small, packed buses for many hours throughout Kenya to get to the training venues in cities like Nakuru, Kisumu, Naivasha, and Nairobi.

Through the day-long training, we helped intake officers at the United Nations Refugee Agency, or UNHCR, better understand the rights of LGBTI asylum seekers from other countries and showing up in refugee camps. We delivered our training under a tent with a projector in the sweltering heat to HIV organizations, helping to dispel common myths. The Kenyan Human Rights Commission had us train some of their program staff to understand LGBTI citizens' rights better. And we worked with religious leaders and media voices to better understand how their harmful portrayals of LGBTI people would not only violate their rights but could cause irreparable harm to them. It was compelling work and gave me an unexpected education and foundational knowledge of the universal human rights I would go on to use later in my career.

As my colleagues and I got to know one another, I learned of their powerful stories of family rejection, lost loved ones, and standing up to stigma and discrimination within their communities. Some became refugees forced to flee their home countries. Others were living with HIV and sought to develop programs to educate others. Some had lost everything after being rejected by their families. GALCK was all they had.

One of my fiercest colleagues had battled intensely simply to be who she was. She was the first openly transgender leader in the country to successfully sue the Kenyan government for her right to change the gender on her birth certificate. In addition to her legal success, working alongside her, I felt her exuding energy from across the room.

Another one of the organizations focused on recording several stories for the None on Record podcast about their lives as lesbians living in East Africa. They sought to create a record of their experiences through oral histories so their lives wouldn't simply be erased. Each episode held guttural stories of facing hatred and humiliation, while others were profoundly hopeful about the future.

My time at GALCK helped me to fundamentally appreciate the shared experiences of LGBTI people within the East African context and worldwide. We shared many of the same characteristics, personality dispositions, group complexities, and dynamics as among my peers back home. I related in many ways to their experiences. I was so grateful to have gotten to know them. It reawakened that place in my heart I had begun undertaking as a sophomore at Gonzaga.

In many other ways, I also appreciated the unique context in which this work was being done. I hadn't initially fathomed the many sacrifices they were making. They had survived so much in their personal lives that it was striking to observe them giving back in the ways they were, risking possibly everything. I was so honored to work alongside them.

The most inspirational person I met was my host, David, who after our long drives back and forth to the office, I got to know in more profound, meaningful ways. We'd talk about what inspired his efforts to improve the lives of LGBTI people in Kenya. He drew quite a bit upon his faith tradition and how he felt he was living out a calling. He spoke about individuals in his life who suffered at the hands of bullies and found no refuge, even taking their own lives. He felt indebted to them and others still finding their way.

David was born into a middle-class family in Kenya, where he was one of six children. Knowing from an early age, like me, that he was different, he went into the seminary hoping to become a priest. Instead, as life pressed upon him his reality, and in keeping with his faith, he chose not to live a lie and came out of the closet while also beginning a life of activism and helping found GALCK.

I often cooked us dinner based on one of the six regular dishes my family once made, using ingredients from local markets. He always loved them. On Tuesdays, it became a tradition to stop by and have pizzas on our way home. We continued our conversations on his noble purpose within the world.

On the weekends, David introduced me to different places in Nairobi. We went to the botanical gardens and the movies, and at one point, we even took a bus through Nairobi National Park and saw tons of animals. We'd laugh and enjoy the world as much as we could.

While his grassroots efforts inspired me, it's also what he endured. Prior to my arrival, I learned David was the target of a brutal hate-filled campaign led by US-based Christian evangelicals and their Kenyan counterparts.

They made wanted posters with David's photo on them and a quote from the Bible claiming that those promoting homosexuality were against God and should be killed. These posters, designed in America, were sent to their Kenyan counterparts, printed, and plastered across the country.

Everywhere you would go, from matatus to buses and public squares, these posters hung. His face was everywhere. Not only did some declare him a public nuisance, but his life was endangered. Whenever we were in public, he would wear a hat and glasses to disguise himself just so we could get groceries.

I saw David as the Harvey Milk of Kenya, someone who risked his life for the greater good of his community. He was my hero.

After three long months, as my time in Nairobi came to a close, I began to see how the work of LGBTI human rights intertwined with an even broader spectrum of the human condition I had been fighting for all of those years. Getting to know local activists, particularly David, gave me a driving spirit to continue doing the work to advance human rights and to fight for the fundamental freedoms of gender and sexual minorities throughout the world.

I realized my life's work was far beyond the borders of just the United States and necessitated a way to return one day to Kenya to continue supporting the efforts of my newfound friends and loved ones.

RELIGIOUSLY BASED HOMOPHOBIA AT THE UNITED NATIONS

The religious hostilities that impacted upon my experience in college and which fuel modern forms of oppression in countries around the world like Kenya led me to tackle other forms of religiously based homophobia. Who knew those experiences would so inform the work I would go on to do, even at places like the United Nations?

In pursuit of a purpose-driven life based on the example of my family, friends, and experiences of profound love, I was more committed than ever to advancing LGBTI human rights. My friends and fellow advocates in Nairobi inspired me.

When I returned home, I moved to New York City, where I spent the second year of the Clinton School working on my final capstone project at a nonprofit exclusively conducting advocacy at the UN, the Unitarian Universalist—United Nations Office or UU-UNO. For my capstone, I assessed the needs of religiously based organizations conducting advocacy at the UN in favor of LGBTI human rights.

I went from working directly with local LGBTI activists to working with diplomats from all over the world.

The UU-UNO was one of the very few organizations with a dedicated LGBTI human rights program and exclusively conducted advocacy at the UN. It also was one of the very first organizations ever to hold ECOSOC status, meaning they were allowed to directly advocate to member states and institutional bodies. This was in contrast to other organizations, including the International Lesbian Gay Association (ILGA) or the International Gay Lesbian Human Rights Commission (IGLHRC), now known as Outright, who at the time, didn't have ECOSOC status.

Ironically, as I was taking on my fellowship in the first few weeks, the head of their LGBTI program moved on from the organization. So, in addition to my capstone project, I took over their responsibilities. I met with several different organizations and advocacy groups while convening numerous discussions around the significance of advancing LGBTI human rights.

This new work would shape how I understood the structural impact of homophobia and gay rights on such a body and the new paradigms with which to address such barriers through a human rights lens.

To think I was there, just over a decade ago, when discussion of LGBTI human rights was still considered taboo. In our own small way, we helped expand some conversations for the first time in such an institution and it was 2010.

Being a faith-based organization, we engaged in human rights advocacy navigating relationships with other religiously based organizations to build support for and advance LGBTI human rights.

I coordinated a consultation where we met with dozens of member state representatives and faith-based civil society organizations to identify possible entry points for LGBTI human rights advocacy. As part of our consultation, we worked with prominent religious leaders to counter extreme religious fundamentalism driving antigay legislation in Uganda, which threatened to criminalize homosexuality with life imprisonment like the same fundamentalist that printed Wanted posters with David's face plastered all over Kenya. It was sickening.

The consultation brought together representatives of member states, LGBTI-affirming religious leaders, and UN representatives from the Office of the High Commissioner for Human Rights. LGBTI leaders from Uganda joined us, including Frank Mugisha and none other than my new friend and inspiration, David Kuria, from Kenya. Through the consultation, we identified ways to offer a counter-narrative of pro-faith, pro-LGBTI leaders who supported Ugandan LGBTI people to confront the hatred coming from other religious leaders. At the end of our consultation, we emphasized the importance of mutual understanding, love, and seeing the humanity in all people, everywhere.

While David was in town, I thought it was fitting to host him since he hosted me in Kenya. We squeezed into my small dorm at the International House where I lived.

He visited during Human Rights Day, so we attended several events with human rights defenders from around the world. We went to several high-level meetings, including a meeting on LGBTI Human Rights, which was chaired by the UN Secretary-General, Ban Ki Moon, and featured US Ambassador to the UN, Susan Rice (Associated Press 2010).

We toured throughout New York City to speak to various audiences about his experiences as an LGBTI person living in Kenya. He spoke to classes at Columbia University and the New School on human rights. It was powerful to visit such prestigious institutions and watch him share his stories.

David and I also trekked down to Washington, DC, where we attended an advocacy meeting made up of LGBTI leaders from throughout the world. It was one of the highlights of my career. To be in the room with dozens of activists who deeply shared the same passion for the work I was so dedicated to in my life. We all became close friends in the years to come, fighting in our respective regions of the world for our fundamental freedoms to be free and equal.

While in DC, I attended a briefing session at the US State Department on the situation of homophobia throughout the continent of Africa, mainly fueled by American Evangelicals and their local counterparts. I looked around the room and so many advocates I had looked up to in my youth were there. We spoke to top diplomats overseeing African Affairs on behalf of the United States. There I was, beside them, in the room, asking poignant questions and hopefully offering some small amount of advice to help in their diplomatic efforts to ensure LGBTI Ugandans were not further harmed.

When I returned to New York, I moderated a panel on LGBTI human rights for UN Human Rights Day. The panel was made up of senior representatives of the Office of the High Commissioner of Human Rights (OHCHR), the United Nations Development Program (UNDP), and members of civil society. As the moderator, it was fascinating to curate meaningful conversations with leaders in a space that was still hostile to the advancement of LGBTI human rights.

Our work was but a part of a broader effort by dedicated advocates, diplomatic representatives, and organizations working at the UN. We fought to ensure LGBTI human rights were considered equal while ILGA, Outright, the Council for Global Equality, and others continued to press for recognition at the UN to raise the voices of LGBTI people worldwide.

All in all, the experience gave me a whole new lens through which to address LGBTI human rights. I could take on a thirty-thousand-foot view that I might not have ever had before. Through that lens, I continued to strive to understand the interrelated, intersectional, and interdependent rights we all share as human beings.

I left the UN with an unwavering conviction to continue dedicating my life to advancing calls for human dignity and worth. What a way to apply one's learnings through their capstone from their master's program to real-world impact?

Back on my campus in Little Rock, I presented to my classmates and professors on all I had undertaken in my capstone. I could see the exponential ways in which I had grown as a professional over the course of the past year.

I was more poised and confident having developed a richer knowledge of how LGBTI human rights are applied at a micro and macro level. As my former classmates, professors, and school administrators sat there, I saw the awe in their facial expressions after all I had accomplished and how the Clinton School had such a meaningful impact both on my life and out in the world.

What I valued most was realizing the transformative powers of chasing one's passions. The Clinton School fostered, and even encouraged, social entrepreneurship. If you had a dream, no matter how big, it supported you in making it possible.

I would never have thought during that long bus ride through the Deep South on the Civil Rights pilgrimage that I would end up two years later graduating with high honors. I could take tangible action toward my once seemingly unattainable goals.

At the end of the semester, the whole class came together again for my graduation. Many of our family members and friends from around the country were able to join us in celebration.

Both my mom and my dad came, along with my sister, my cousin, aunt, and grandfather. It meant a lot for them to be there. While still somewhat estranged from my father, he, through his actions, showed up for me as he had once before. It was wonderful to show my family my school and share with them all I had been up to while I was away. After all, my journey had been so inspired by them and the love they provided me throughout my life. It was a proud day.

President Clinton sent a video message reminding us that each of us has the power to change our communities wherever, whenever, and however we can. There are thousands of ways in which every moment of our life has purpose and possibility, and we have the choice to better our world. It was a powerful note to end upon as a class—both as individuals and as a collective group.

All thirty-six of us were shaped and molded by our experiences at the Clinton School. Some of us stayed in Little Rock and made lives for ourselves. Others went off to other cities to cultivate change. We were not the same people we were just two years prior when we walked into the school.

The program changed my life and opened doors I never realized were open to me.

The question, though, was—what was next?

GLOBAL ADVOCACY THROUGH THE INTERNATIONAL DAY AGAINST HOMOPHOBIA, TRANSPHOBIA, AND BIPHOBIA

After graduation, I'd like to say I landed the most incredible job, building off my amazing UN experience, my work in Kenya, my decorated advocacy work in undergrad, and graduating from two top schools. Maybe I would've led an international nonprofit. I thought I could do anything leaving the Clinton School.

In reality, it was hard to identify a full-time paying gig that leveraged my skill sets and capabilities to the fullest breadth of what I now knew was possible. So, I headed back to my mom's house in rural America to figure out what was next in my life.

Coming off the high of the Clinton School, feeling like I could do just about anything, not being able to find a job right away felt quite demoralizing. The world was still bouncing back from the global recession of 2008 just a few years earlier, and living in rural America didn't connect me immediately to the people who could make my next steps possible.

I felt very fortunate because my mom and I got to do another voyage for Semester at Sea, touring around the Mediterranean for the summer season. We started in the Bahamas, traveling across the Atlantic to Spain, Italy, Croatia, Greece, Bulgaria, Turkey, and Morocco. My mom was the dean of students again while I traveled as a companion voyager. Drawing on my time at Disney World, I supported the children's program, offering a summer camp-like environment for the staff and faculty's kids as we made our way around the Mediterranean.

As we embarked on the two-month voyage, so many memories from my previous journey four years before came flooding back. Returning to the ship reminded me so much of my transformation during that time. So much of it I wasn't able to even process because I'd been thrust into my parents' divorce.

I found a way to develop a deeper appreciation for the Semester at Sea program and the perseverance I would need as I entered the next phase of my life as a future leader. I was given opportunities to explore the countries we visited more independently this time while also leading a few Semester at Sea sponsored trips.

One trip I led, which forever shaped me, was with a group of about fifty students, staff, and faculty on a four-day hike over the High Atlas Mountains of Morocco. The mountains stretched across the country, seemingly dividing it in two, and were mainly populated by the Berber people, indigenous communities who'd been there for centuries.

Four Moroccan guides led us, each fasting for Ramadan, and twelve packing donkeys. As we ventured along in the scorching sun, our guides offered us water and made what felt like gourmet food whenever we stopped for meals. They'd pick a shady spot on our trail and lay out whole feasts for us. Their hospitality, especially during such a holy period where they wouldn't even take a sip of water during our long, hot hikes, was one of the greatest gifts of the local Moroccan people.

As the trip leader, I made several decisions to help the group work together throughout the hike across treacherous passes. On the first day, as we moved along, there came a particular moment as we climbed up a hillside. Several students rushed to the top while others struggled to make it from the mountain base. Once we got to the top, I gathered everyone around and told the group, "You all, it's not about being the first person to the top. It's about ensuring no person is left behind. We all have to work together to make it through this experience."

The group heard my call. Students started helping each other if they were struggling. We sang songs as we hiked. And most importantly, we laughed with one another the rest of the way. Each night after an average of ten miles worth of hiking, local Berber villagers graciously hosted us as we slept atop their flat roofs under the stars.

We'd drink mint tea and breakfast with them, celebrating Ramadan. Our group bonded, sharing who we were and how the journey impacted us.

I was deeply moved, again, by another Semester at Sea experience.

Following the summer voyage, my mom and I returned to Wisconsin, where I started my job search again. Months passed, but I was more encouraged than ever to put my life toward something meaningful. After all, I just passed through another gate within my life, discovering my capacity to put tangible results toward meaningful goals. I continued to look high and low for different opportunities. I met with individuals, sent in job applications, and attended several conferences.

After attending a national LGBTI conference in Minneapolis, I met the executive director of the International Day Against Homophobia, Transphobia, and Biphobia, or IDAHOTB. Founded a few years prior to commemorate the World Health Organizations May 17, 1990, decision to declassify homosexuality as a mental health disorder, the organization sought to advance the rights of people with diverse sexual orientations, gender identities or expressions, or sex characteristics (Cochran et al. 2014). The aim was to bring visibility to local activists worldwide facing stigma, discrimination, and violence and to offer global comradery to their cause while centering their local ambitions.

I told him I was looking for a job and wanted to help however I could. Soon after, he brought me onto his five-person team at the organization's secretariat.

We were based throughout the world. He was in Paris, France. My teammates were in Brazil, Argentina, and Belgium. I was based in the US and tasked to build up visibility of the day among US-based organizations while supporting the activities of activists worldwide.

I grew to profoundly appreciate my team's work and, most importantly, the thousands of activists around the world whom our work supported. Our executive director's philosophy was his insistence our organization and subsequent activities were only meant to serve those on the ground implementing actions in various contexts, particularly as the global secretariat.

It was not about us, nor should it ever have been. Instead, we helped select a global theme, offered ideas to activists based on prior activities in other countries, and then captured what we could from the information they shared directly with us or on their social media pages to share with the broader world on the official day.

Preparing for May 17, we worked closely as a team on our advocacy efforts. My skills were put to good use. I engaged activists worldwide to understand their needs better and leveraged my recent contacts in international LGBTI human rights organizations to get the word out in the US.

Through one of her incredible staff members, Jirair, I got Rep. Barbara Lee of California to put forward a proclamation in support of the day on behalf of the US Congress as well as the US State Department to issue diplomatic cables to all their missions worldwide to show their support to local activists (Lee 2013). Several hosted IDAHOT-themed events at local embassies. President Obama and Vice President Biden also issued proclamations in support of the day (Human Rights Watch 2012).

For a first-year rookie, this felt pretty empowering. But most importantly, the efforts helped amplify the work of local activists worldwide in their very real and immediate struggle.

As the day approached, I shifted from helping support activists develop their ideas for action to documenting and reporting on their activities. To bear witness to all that took place that year deeply inspired me, particularly to the degree to which activists from every country imaginable took on the task of bringing visibility of sexual and gender diversities within their societies, including those in which they faced violent repression.

In Eastern Europe, particularly the former Soviet states, activists planned to partake in peaceful marches in the streets to create visibility. Orthodox Christian priests and right-wing thugs violently attacked many marchers with bricks, batons, and teargas. In some instances, the police themselves beat and apprehended activists. From Albania to Georgia and Serbia, we saw many profound examples of activists putting their lives on the line for LGBTI human rights.

Solitary activists took action in defiance of the regimes under which they lived. For example, in Russia, activists displayed signs supporting LGBTI rights in front of the Kremlin and were promptly arrested. In Iran, photos were shared of activists' hands holding a rainbow flag in the foreground and the city of Tehran in the background—a risk that could be met with the death penalty.

Throughout Latin America, many activists developed campaigns around the theme "Cures that Kill" to address the prevalence of reparative therapies seeking to *cure* people of their diverse sexual or gender identities. Just like they tried to do on my old campus, right-wing Christians decided homosexuals needed to be *saved* and came up with harebrained approaches to cure them through the power of prayer. Many of the activists had been subjected to such harmful practices themselves, and as such, their trauma-informed their advocacy.

Several horrific stories from activists in those countries highlighted the harm done to those who identified as LGBTI. In Bolivia, they held prayer vigils for those who committed suicide. In Peru, they had a sit-in outside of a church. In addition, activists in Brazil, Chile, and Argentina produced and shared numerous videos and podcasts.

Activists throughout Asia sponsored unannounced and sporadic self-expressions of their LGBTI identities. They created flash mobs wearing rainbow-themed clothes and arrived in well-known public spaces like Beijing's Temple of Heaven and the Forbidden City. In Singapore, LGBTI people and their families came out by the thousands to form a giant pink dot supporting LGBTI rights. In Japan, an incredibly modest society, activists held kiss-ins in public spaces.

In Cuba, thousands of people took to the streets to celebrate LGBTI Pride. They also held drag performances and competitions to celebrate queer liberation.

Throughout the continent of Africa, advocacy organizations held vigils, community gatherings, and educational events. In Uganda, their celebration was a simple vigil for an activist, David Kato, who'd been murdered the year prior, simply for his outspokenness.

There were proclamations, discussion groups, film festivals, concerts, marches, works of art, policy dialogues, and more everywhere you went. The United Nations, World Bank, the Hague, the Organization of American States, and other global bodies all commemorated the day. It was fascinating to observe activists' bravery and resilience in some of the most repressive spaces in the world.

I'd go on to support IDAHOTB over four years, each year more inspiring than the one before. Now, it is a globally recognized day by hundreds of governments and international institutions. It's a powerful force that can't be matched.

While I loved the work, especially under the leadership of its incredible executive director, I only received a small monthly stipend for my efforts. Unfortunately, such small and uncommon causes don't always establish huge funds.

Continuing my passions came at a cost, especially while still living in my mom's basement. It was time for me to put more effort into solidifying opportunities allowing me to live out my dreams while also making a living.

I lived with my mom on and off for almost three years after graduating undergrad. I worked at a local Italian restaurant, but it wasn't even covering all the bills that were piling up, especially the student loans, which started following my graduation.

My mom continued to try to encourage me. While I appreciated her nudging, I was adamant about finding a job that aligned with all I'd been afforded. I had come so far to give up now.

I felt a powerful sense of responsibility, given all I was privileged to feel and experience. I couldn't look away from what I'd seen. I had to be out in the world evangelizing about the beauty I came to know within my life.

ACT FIVE

ACTION

Love and compassion are necessities, not luxuries. Without them, Humanity cannot survive.

—DALAI LAMA

All of our humanity is dependent upon recognizing the humanity in others.

—ARCHBISHOP DESMOND TUTU

We all do better when we work together. Our differences matter, but our common humanity matters more.

—PRESIDENT CLINTON

We did not come to fear the future. We came to shape it.
—PRESIDENT OBAMA

I don't know how much value I have in this universe, but I do know that I've made a few people happier than they would have been without me, and as long as I know that, I'm as rich as I ever need to be.
—ROBIN WILLIAMS (FORMER JUNGLE CRUISE SKIPPER)

DIVING INTO DEVELOPMENT

"You've got a great career ahead of you."

"I feel your passion for the work. Keep looking, and you'll find something."

I couldn't find a job.

I decided to go to where the jobs were. So, after nearly nine months of waiting since my graduation from the Clinton School, I planned a trip back to New York City and Washington, DC, to meet with mentors, confidants, and contacts I'd made the previous year.

I set up informational interviews with several contacts who were doing human rights work in the areas of sexual reproductive health and rights. I'd go to each meeting with such hope. I was passed from one person to the next, and then the next, and the next.

At one national LGBTI organization, I even received the *advice,* "Have you ever considered removing the ubuntu from your name? It sounds, you know… Black."

Sharing my story over and over again and not finding any inroads, I started losing hope. I resigned myself to the idea that maybe this was the end of the road for my work in human rights. During my last week, as I was about to give up, I met with a colleague of a friend who had some ideas on where I might go next.

First, I was late.

Second, my clothes were slightly disheveled after living out of a suitcase for a few weeks.

And finally, I didn't have my résumé printed out. I was a hot mess, and he noticed.

Though he appreciated my experience and, after printing me out a copy of my résumé, he made a recommendation I speak with a man named Kip, who might utilize my global advocacy skills at an organization I'd never heard of. Futures Group.

After reaching out, Kip agreed to meet with me. I arrived on time at the Futures Group offices on Thomas Circle in DC with a printed résumé, dressed to the nines.

Walking into the office, I noticed family planning products on the walls. Everything from old-fashioned lamb skin condoms and lubricants, birth control pills, female condoms, and other family planning products. There were also several documents on sexual health, HIV, and human rights framed and hanging on the walls.

I started to feel like something about this place spoke to what I had sought to commit my life to. Kip greeted me in the lobby and took me up to his offices on the second floor.

He was a fabulous gay man himself, and from Montana, with a slow cadence to his speech, just like my dad. He explained more about what he did and asked a few questions about what he saw on my résumé.

He, too, led national and international LGBTI movements and focused in his current role on refining various health policies across different country contexts to ensure people on the margins of their societies, particularly those living with HIV, were not disproportionally harmed.

He was working on a policy analysis and advocacy guide around global health and HIV specific to men who had sex with men, sex workers, and transgender women.

My ears perked up. I didn't know what he was talking about, but it sounded interesting. He went on to highlight how many laws around the world were used to repress the rights of LGBTI people and deny them access to high-quality health services. These laws weren't always overt and, in many ways, innocuous ones only enforced to discriminate against specific communities. I thought about laws in the United States requiring individuals to have trash bags in their cars—something unenforceable but could be cited as an additional infraction to further punish someone pulled over.

Most advocates I knew were only focusing on the criminalization of homosexuality, which remained in over seventy-eight countries (UNFE 2023). Often overlooked were the numerous other laws that prevented people from self-organizing, accessing legal aid, or were used to repress LGBTI people. Such policies violated people's human rights. A few laws existed but were not strong enough to be enforced, such as confidentiality policies within health clinics where gossiping healthcare workers often violated patients' rights by outing them as either HIV-positive or gay. The list went on and on.

He needed someone to assist him.

I was blown away and inspired by his vision. We shook hands and parted ways. I left feeling like I had just faced a firehose of information that was hard to piece together fully. It was fascinating. I didn't expect much walking away from the meeting and assumed it was just another one of the many conversations I had that week.

On my final day in town, I was at another meeting when I got a phone call from Kip. After our conversation and reviewing my résumé, he offered me an internship. He also wanted me there in a few weeks.

I was so full of emotions. There was so much to do in such a short period. I didn't fully grasp what he was doing, but I knew I was intrigued. This was my chance.

I returned home to Wisconsin, where I pulled together all my things, packed up my car, and a few weeks later journeyed to Washington, DC, to start my new role at Futures Group. It was all so quick, but it was something I knew I needed to do.

It wasn't until three months into my internship that I realized how incredible and impactful the work was. Even more, I started to learn about international development, which addressed some of the world's most pressing problems—from global health to education and economic development, providing humanitarian aid and assistance to millions worldwide.

My new company was one of the go-to implementing partners of USAID, the US government's agency for providing humanitarian aid and assistance to the world's poorest communities. The work was all I could have ever hoped for.

As I was only there for an internship, I continued to meet with individuals throughout DC to learn more about possible jobs. But the more and more I worked at Futures in the areas of sexual and reproductive health and rights, the more I realized I wanted to continue the work I was doing there.

As my six months started to come to an end, I was approached by the Deputy Director of HIV at the time, Ron, with an opportunity to stay on to continue supporting the work that Kip had started. I was in his office with the director of human resources, signing a contract to begin a full-time job with the company.

Coming from small-town America and a journey laden with such highs and lows, it was hard to believe it was finally happening.

I broke down sobbing at Ron's desk. I finally found something that aligned with all I dedicated my life to.

I soon found myself traveling for work, bringing me back to my love of international travel and working directly with frontline advocates.

One of my first trips was to attend the launch ceremony of a discrimination and redress reporting system we helped develop. It was being launched at the Ghanaian AIDS Commission's annual World AIDS Day event (Macinnis, Williamson, and Herstad 2013). As it was over Thanksgiving, many of my colleagues had already planned to celebrate the US holiday with their friends and family, so they offered me the opportunity to represent our team at the ceremony. Naturally, I jumped at the chance.

I hopped on a fourteen-hour flight from DC to Accra via Brussels and landed for the first time in Ghana. I took a taxi three blocks to my hotel that evening, only to wake up early the next day to load up on a bus with three dozen Ghana AIDS Commission staff as they headed to the far north of the country to the town of Wa. The bus ride was sixteen hours and very cramped. We spent much of the trip watching Nigerian soap operas, but getting to know my colleagues at the commission was a fantastic opportunity. We arrived late that evening at a small hotel in a rural city.

Along with the country's vice president and our US ambassador, we joined a series of festivities celebrating World AIDS Day. At the center was a large dirt area usually used as a soccer field. On one side was a large stage jutting out near the center of the field and had chairs fit for kings reserved for the national dignitaries and their guests. Several tents surrounded the soccer field with a large pathway outside of them. Around the ring of the fairgrounds were numerous booths various organizations used to share more about their work in HIV, including Futures Group.

People from all over the region came to the event. It turned out that each of the tents set up around the perimeter of the soccer field had been reserved for various chiefs of local tribes. As each arrived, they were followed by entourages of individuals dressed in tribal clothing.

People would move from booth to booth before the festivities to learn more. Free condoms, HIV rapid tests, informational booklets and brochures, and giveaways, such as that year's World AIDS Day T-shirts, were hot commodities.

As the festivities got underway, tribal performers put on these intricate dances and athletic displays that celebrated the Ghanaian culture while also telling the story of HIV. After several dances, we joined the Minister of Health, the US ambassador, and the Ghanaian vice president to read aloud an official decree from the president to officially launch the discrimination reporting system my team had worked on.

The next day I hopped on a bus, eighteen hours since we had a flat tire, and then jumped on the fourteen-hour plane ride back home.

After the trip and building on my work under Kip to better address stigma and discrimination, I had the chance to develop further and roll out the new stigma and discrimination reporting system in Ghana we'd just launched.

An identified barrier in accessing health services was people not coming forward to report instances in which their fundamental human rights were violated, particularly in the health care setting. People were hesitant to go to a hospital or the police because they feared their HIV status or identity as an LGBTI person would place them in further harm.

People experienced arbitrary arrests by the police, were kicked out of school, left out of housing or employment opportunities, or denied their HIV medications simply because of the stigma in their communities. In turn, people avoided getting treatment when needed or coming to the doctor to obtain prophylaxis like condoms or lubricants, which would have prevented unwanted pregnancies and lowered the likelihood of transmitting a sexually transmitted infection or HIV. There wasn't even education about safe sex in society, let alone as a same-sex loving person.

Our goal was to assist the Ghanaian AIDS Commission in sensitizing its staff and that of the Commission for Human Rights and Administrative Justice on the fundamental rights of citizens, regardless of their HIV status or their real or perceived identities, to access justice. We also prepared them to confidentially and respectfully take on local Ghanaians' cases so they could safely report instances of discrimination.

I helped conceptualize the needs that might arise from communities being marginalized or made vulnerable due to their personal characteristics or identities and ensured we accounted for this in our initial design.

As a follow-up to building the system, we recognized that just because you build it does not mean the people you made it for will come. Therefore, there needed to be incentives and tested methodologies that would allow people to come forward to share their vulnerable experiences about the discrimination they may have faced.

My work turned from supporting our team in building the system to identifying pathways to generate demand for it.

One of my most powerful experiences was flying back out to Ghana the following year. I spent two weeks traveling around the country alongside our local colleague, Vivian, interviewing individuals and local organizations representing marginalized groups about their experiences of discrimination. We flew from city to city and met with dozens of groups to learn more about how they supported people in their times of need.

We heard incredibly devastating stories from people about what they experienced. Local pharmacists withheld free life-saving HIV medications from people living with HIV unless they provided additional payment. A few women reported being kicked out of their village compounds by their husbands after learning they were HIV positive.

The reality was their husbands likely transmitted HIV to their wives but never disclosed their status to them. Only to blame their wives when they found out, leaving them excommunicated from their families and all they had ever known.

One man worked for a major company within the country. When he found out he was HIV positive and disclosed it to his employer, he was let go.

Many we interviewed reported they were denied medical care or experienced sub-par services due to their HIV status or their identity as a gender or sexual minority. Nurses often quoted the Bible to their patients about the evils of sodomy or shared what they learned about a patient with their fellow nurses or, worse, the next of kin who accompanied them to the hospital.

We met with a local police officer at a police station. They described their responsibility for responding to cases of community violence, particularly at the intersections of HIV and gender-based violence. As we sat there, behind them were two cells full of prisoners waiting to be sentenced.

At a local nonprofit supporting men who had sex with men, we learned of the recurring harassment young gay men would receive. They described one incident in which a young man, who was slightly effeminate, had been walking down the road one day. A group of other young men passed him by, and because he seemed a little *off*, they started beating him.

When a policeman passed by, he broke up the commotion. But when he asked why they were hitting the young man, and they explained it was because they thought he was gay, the police officer joined in. As a result, the young man was jailed for several weeks without an apparent reason for his arrest. There was little that local advocates could do to get him released. He later disappeared and was never heard from again.

In another gripping story, two men lived together in a neighborhood and were suspected of being gay. Neighbors eventually caught wind and ended up entrapping them in their home and lighting it on fire, murdered because of the bigotry of their neighbors and those in their community.

Matthew Shepard's story came to mind as I thought about these young men who face such violence. There are so many whose names we will never know and, as we uncovered on that trip, whose stories may never be reported. The struggle to affirm one's rights and to fight for justice was beyond simply speaking one's truth into the world but was indeed a matter of survival.

Once we completed the interviews, primarily led by my local colleague, we returned to our Accra offices. We summarized what we had learned to offer the Ghana AIDS Commission and the Commission on Human Rights and Administrative Justice ideas on how they might overcome people's trepidation in coming forward with their stories. We particularly stressed the importance of helping people understand their fundamental human rights and to be more confident that action would be taken if they reported what was happening to them.

We later returned to bring representatives of the government and local civil society organizations together. I continued taking on project assignments within the company and was fortunate to move on from my time in Ghana.

The work flew by so fast that I was already four years into the job. I felt incredibly blessed to be doing work where I could support local leaders in addressing the rights of LGBTI people throughout the world. Their circumstances were far direr than anything I had ever faced, but their resiliency deeply inspired me and showed me they could face just about anything the world threw their way.

FINDING OMAR

Over a decade had passed since Melissa and James opened those gates offering me a purview into my capacity to love. It still fueled my ongoing advocacy efforts to advance LGBTI human rights, yet I found that love seemed to evade me in my personal life. I began to believe it was inevitable I would never find someone who might live up to those adolescent dreams of satiating the well of loneliness that often consumed me, let alone the profound level of love I had come to know was possible within me behind closed doors with James.

While starting my development career, there was a lot of excitement about the work I got to do and the new city I lived in. Many refer to Washington, DC, as the *showcase* city because it has the best of everything in the United States. In many ways, it represented all I could have wanted as an adolescent dreaming of a better world.

I enjoyed the city's vibrancy as I began to feel my way around. DC has the highest number of LGBTI households in the United States, per capita, just ahead of San Francisco, California. In addition, I met many LGBTI people from around the world who called DC their home.

Despite an abundance of out gay men all around me, things never seemed to click for me when it came to dating. I had a few fleeting romances with some extraordinary human beings, but our schedules never aligned. I might have the most intriguing conversation in one moment only to realize they were gone for the next three months on an overseas assignment. It's still that way.

There was a cattiness to the city too. So many wanted to get ahead at any cost. They were so competitive. Vulnerability and spiritual alignment weren't top of mind for most folks looking to advance their careers or rise into power in the heteronormative rat race we all subjected ourselves to. A scaled-up version of the toxic masculinity that had already oppressed so many of us and was commonly used to discern inferiority. Who were you if you didn't know the right people carried the correct status, spoke with a certain cadence, and dressed a certain way?

My effervescent energy, positive outlook, and hopeful optimism weren't always taken seriously. I was often underestimated. After experiencing so much magic around the world, my soul deeply ached for a far deeper connection I was lacking in such a fast-paced, high-stakes city like DC. So many bore scars from their past lives, and opening up wasn't as easy.

I often thought, *Here I am surrounded by other gay men, all who have gone through some version of what I've gone through, who I likely could relate to in a multitude of ways, many who might equally be a best friend or confidant I'd always wanted.* Yet it felt like no one sought that deeper connection. Instead, like a game, everyone seemed to always be after the next best thing, even in dating.

Far away from the years when we were protesting on the capitol steps in Olympia, through the election of President Obama, marriage equality became a possible reality for millions of Americans (Obergefell vs. Hodges 2015). Something I always dreamed of finding when I was young but never believed would happen in my lifetime. But would it be possible for me?

After a few years, I got into a funk. Would I ever find love again? I started to feel unlovable. I'd been fighting in the name of love for nearly a decade, yet I hadn't had the opportunity to experience it myself other than the heartbreak that had driven it.

I was ready to give up on finding a soulmate.

Unexpectedly, one night I found Omar. What was supposed to be a quick hookup turned into an all-night love affair.

I met him in the middle of the night on a dating app and invited him to come over. We started making out before I even knew his name. As we lay next to each other and started conversing about our lives and who we were, I realized he was kinda cool.

He was there on business and was supposed to leave the following morning. He was from California and was in his first year at his new firm. He was a little shorter than me with olive skin and had the most beautiful brown eyes.

I was utterly blown away by what a charmer he was. His energy was infectious. I learned he was originally from Morocco. While born a citizen in the United States when his parents studied here, he grew up in Marrakesh and came back to the US for college.

As we lay there cuddling, he expressed wanting to see the city. While I usually would've passed on showing a stranger around town, especially at such a late hour, uncharacteristically I said yes. I felt this strange set of butterflies in the pit of my stomach telling me this was different. I hadn't felt that way in a long time.

We dressed, and I took him to different gay bars in my neighborhood. I especially wanted to take him to the Habibi night, where some of my friends from the Middle East and North Africa would go once a month to be with other gays from their home countries.

We had a fantastic time. Soon it was one in the morning. We started back to his hotel. As we approached, I suggested we tour the National Monuments. Walking around the Mall, we continued talking and talking, holding hands and briefly kissing under a cherry tree. Time flew by, and it was 4 a.m. I was completely enchanted.

We returned to his hotel, and I kissed him one last time as he left for the airport, thinking I'd never see him again.

But we kept in touch. He and I talked almost every day.

The more we got to know each other, the more enamored we became. We'd Facetime and share more about our lives and who we were. He'd ask me about the different artifacts and paintings I had around my apartment and what they meant to me. He had a way of appreciating the spiritual aspects of each object, not just their superficial meaning.

While his parents were back in Morocco, he lived his full life as an out gay man in the US. He was his parents' perfect son. He'd gone to a top school in California, had become an engineer, and now worked for a major company. He'd done all he could to impress his equally impressive parents. His father worked for a major development agency and, like me, was often traveling the world working on various projects. Omar's family was, culturally, also very religious. In Morocco, there is no separation of religion and state. So spiritual aspects were embedded across all aspects of life.

His sexuality seemed to torment him, and he lived this dual life, constantly battling between being the good Muslim son and living his life out loud.

When he was away from his family at college in California, he started to come out and got into the party scene. When we met, he was going to several circuit parties, full of thousands of beautiful gay men dancing together, which were notorious for lots of sex, drugs, and alcohol. But, as he recounted, it wasn't about finding himself in these places but escaping his inner turmoil.

He couldn't imagine how his two worlds would ever align.

I was one of the first people able to connect those two worlds. So much of my Catholic faith tradition overlapped with his Islamic faith. They were both Abrahamic faiths and held a lot of similarities, even sharing several of the same origin stories. As we spoke, he'd say things in ways that told me he was listening, and we took turns disclosing about our lives. He deeply valued my knowledge of what it meant to be LGBTI, especially my understanding of issues facing individuals in North Africa. I could empathize with a lot of the pain he experienced growing up. Heck, I had even been to his hometown, Marrakech.

Like James, Omar's dad worked hard to toughen him up. As he was gone for work, Omar's mother tried to get him interested in several activities. Like his older sister, he picked up ballet and started to love it. However, once his father found out, he was yanked from the program. Ballet was for girls, after all.

Omar spent much of his adolescence experiencing the barrage of teasing and taunting from his male peers, who punished him almost daily, for any hint of his femininity, often with physical violence. It toughened him up. He put his head down, worked hard in school, and sought to be the perfect son his father had always wanted him to be.

Wow, could I relate? Omar decided he wanted to come back to town for DC's Pride. So, a few weeks after we'd met, he flew out to join my friends and me, experiencing one of his first pride events in the Nation's capital. We walked around with thousands of other spectators and had the time of our lives.

We had such a connection—from the way we laughed together to the small ways in which we held each other's hands—as we walked through the streets. There was a strange confidence building in how we so naturally seemed to connect.

We'd catch each other saying something the other was thinking. Or in our mutual love of music, of all the songs he could choose, he would select some of my favorite tunes that held deep spiritual meaning to me. We seemed to think in the same exact ways at times. There were so many tiny coincidences. I started to feel as if some sort of divine intervention was at play, the same way I had felt around James.

The butterflies I developed on our first night together only grew and became overwhelming. Was it possible this thing I was aching for was finally happening?

On the last day of his visit, we had the time of our lives at a pride festival, drinking and listening to music. By midafternoon, we were heavily intoxicated, and it was time for him to return to California. So, we jumped in a cab and headed to the airport.

As I walked him to the security line, I asked, "If you could say any one thing to me, right here and now, knowing that we may never see each other again, what would you say?"

"I love you," he replied, hurrying off to his gate.

I was so struck. I started to feel that way myself, but given my past hurts, I was terrified of saying it out loud. But he said it first.

Since I graduated college several years before, I dated a few guys here and there but never really got to that same level of wonder and amazement I felt with James. But here, suddenly in the airport, was someone with just as much energy, enthusiasm, and appreciation for life as me, telling me he loved me. Wow.

We continued to talk by phone, and I convinced him to join me for the Fourth of July fireworks on the National Mall with my friends Chad and Gabe, who would be visiting DC that weekend from Florida.

We spent a day in Virginia wine country. Went to a ballet at the Kennedy Center. We had fancy dinners and drinks and watched the fireworks on the National Mall. It couldn't have been a more perfect weekend. Better yet, he got along fabulously with two of my closest friends. I was so happy.

I convinced him to stay for an extra day and took him to brunch with a close friend who was queer and Muslim. She had spent years advocating for human rights in predominately Muslim countries for LGBTI people. It was wonderful to introduce them. From our conversations afterward, he felt positive meeting someone doing such heroic work who was also like him.

A few weeks later, it was Ramadan. He taught me about its religious meaning and its significance in his life. Ultimately, I took away it was a time of sacrifice to appreciate what we have and give to others.

As he fasted, we talked daily about what he was doing. In honor of that faithful time of year, we chose to do random acts of service for strangers in our hometowns and talked about them together through video chats.

He planned to return to Morocco to be with his parents to celebrate Eid, the breaking of the fast, at the end of Ramadan. We kept in touch every day.

When he returned, we decided I would come and visit him for a long weekend. When I arrived, his energy seemed to have shifted. We started enjoying each other's company, but after prodding a bit about his sullenness, he finally said, "I'm not sure I can be with you anymore."

I started to cry. What was strange was he didn't seem fully committed to it. I asked him to give us at least the rest of the weekend to feel it out. After all, it was only the first evening, and I was there for the next few days.

So we did, and we had another fantastic time together. I met his friends at a house party. We went zip-lining on the beach. And we'd lay in bed watching movies together as we fell asleep. Then on my last day there, we went to a bar on the beach overlooking the ocean and started talking about our relationship.

We discussed the bubbling love that had emerged within us. I began to tear up, believing it might be our last moments together. And I said, "Given that it probably won't happen, I will just say it. I thought you were the person I would marry."

At that moment, he lost it, saying, "Me too."

We both sat there crying with a bucket of fried calamari and coronas before us as the ocean breeze cooled us on the otherwise perfect day.

We got up and took a walk on the beach one last time. As we were walking, he pulled up a random song on his phone and played it. Of all the songs he could have played, it was "Kissing" by Bliss, a song I had often played in my college dorm room, dreaming of finding someone to quell my loneliness. Another sign we had been destined for each other. He pulled me close, and then we started kissing with tears in our eyes.

I asked him again the next morning if he still wanted to call it off. He replied, "Yes," in a colder tone, and then I left, brokenhearted.

Our situation reminded me of my relationship with James. Omar's internal conflict seemed to prevent him from fully embracing the connection we so clearly had. Everything I had felt with Omar, I had felt with James. Only this time, Omar was out as gay and could openly express his love for me without the shame James always carried when we were in public together.

I was devastated. I felt closer to a God or Divine being than I had ever felt when I was with Omar. I felt my grandmother's presence constantly. There was some energetic wavelength between us. Everything that had ever mattered to me somehow came out through him. I finally experienced all that love could be. Losing him brought back all the loneliness I had escaped by being with him, making what I had lost much more palpable.

A few months later, I had another work trip to Kenya. While I was there, there was a terrorist attack on the Westgate Mall, a popular place for many ex-pats. Some eighty-five people were killed, and hundreds more were injured (McConnell 2015). It was one of the worst terrorist attacks in Kenya's history.

I had been on my way to the same mall with my friend David that day to have lunch when we decided to go somewhere else at the last minute. When we got to the restaurant, we watched in horror the live news feed on the screen of hundreds of people bloodied and fleeing for their lives, reminding me of when I watched the Columbine massacre as an adolescent

Our finite time on earth became more real to me that day. I, of course, thought of Omar, wondering where he was or what he was up to after having been made a believer again in the possibility of a soulmate out in the world.

When I came home a few weeks later, I visited my friend Megan in Wisconsin. With tears in my eyes, I told her about my love affair with Omar, how much he had meant to me, and how deeply I still ached for him. I reminisced about our last moment on the beach, how he had played the song "Kissing," and how I saw it as some divine sign of our ordained connection.

Seconds after telling her that story, I received a long text message from Omar. On a jog that evening, he ran by a group of young men playing rock music. As he passed, the song "Kissing" suddenly came on—a stark contrast to the music they had played moments before. After hearing it, he started to weep uncontrollably, thinking of all we had had and what he had seemingly lost.

I couldn't believe what I was reading and felt even more divinely connected to him. Was this another sign?

Omar was back in DC for work the following month, and we decided to meet for coffee. When we did, all our feelings came flooding back. We knew our bond's strength and decided to try it again.

I invited him to my aunt's house in Orlando, Florida, to celebrate Christmas with my family and ring in the New Year with our friends Chad and Gabe. He agreed to come.

My family was so excited to meet the person who had made me so happy. They all welcomed Omar with open arms. His first action was to apologize to my mom for having broken my heart just a few months prior. He then started calling her "Mama Beth."

My family tried to show us their love and support in numerous small ways. My aunt changed our traditional ham dinner, one we had every year since I was a child, to a beef dish to ensure Omar felt welcome and his Islamic faith was respected. We went to Disney World, my happy place, with my sister, and the two seemed as if they had known each other their whole lives. My cousins loved him. At one point, after he shared his fears about his family's rejection, my cousin turned to him and said, "You will always have our family." While on the other side of the country, my dad even sent us a gift card to treat us to a nice dinner together.

When we opened presents on Christmas morning, my family ensured that Omar also had gifts. We each opened presents, one by one, all chuckling and laughing as we always did. I made him a small photo book of our first six months together with a letter in the back. He started tearing up, perusing through its pages as we continued opening presents. And then I surprised him with one last gift—tickets to Machu Pichu, Peru. He cried.

I couldn't have been any happier. As we were leaving, my grandfather pulled me aside, placed his hands on my shoulders, and said, "Ryan, he's a good man." His small gesture meant everything to me, just like when he helped me put up the AIDS Quilts years before at my university.

Omar and I spent many more long weekends visiting each other in our respective cities. He had moved to Delaware for a year, and I would visit him in his new home. I even helped him decorate.

He came to DC for Valentine's Day. It was one of the most romantic weekends of my life and felt straight out of a movie. Everything we did felt more meaningful because we were so deeply in love. We went to a play, went ice skating, and then did a cooking class. Everyone around us knew it, too, as we laughed and interacted with fellow patrons everywhere we went.

We started talking about moving in together. He kept bringing up the idea of when we would get married repeatedly. Almost subconsciously. It was beautiful. I, too, wanted that. We walked around and looked at neighborhoods to move into. We were also excited about planning our trip to Machu Picchu in just a few months' time.

But as we were talking about such big life things, and especially after spending time with my loving family, Omar started to feel like it was important to finally tell his own family about who he was. After all, the double life he continued to live was beginning to weigh on him. So he decided he wanted to come out to his mom, who would visit in a few weeks.

I offered all my love and support. I reviewed the letter he planned to write her. He also got advice from my mom, and on the day he planned to come out to her, my sister called him that morning to wish him luck. And so, he moved forward with his plans.

Wanting to know how it went, my mom, sister, and I waited anxiously to hear from him. But as the hours and then days passed, we heard nothing. Then after three or four days, he texted, saying things didn't go as well.

Evidently, after reading the letter, his mom started sobbing uncontrollably. She told him, "I love you, but I will never accept that part of you."

I couldn't be upset with him for his reaction. A mother's love is so powerful. But suddenly, the things he so loved about me became deficits. He began to pull away from me.

He started trying to numb himself and retreated to the old, dual world he had previously built for himself before meeting me. He started working out obsessively and becoming overly concerned with his looks while judging me on mine. He wanted to party and seemed more concerned about meeting more guys at circuit parties. I wanted to give him the space he needed because I knew the pain he must be in, but I also felt him pushing me away.

We had a brief reprieve from it all when we traveled to Machu Pichu. Finally, I had my Omar back.

Peru filled us with wonderment. We visited all the ancient archeological sites. We climbed to the top of Machu Picchu. There even came a point where he wanted to take a picture of us kissing on top of the mountain. I was the one a little nervous about being in a foreign country and not being sure of their attitudes toward LGBTI people. It was entirely blissful.

We returned to the States, and the following weekend I visited him in Delaware to celebrate our first anniversary since we had met that fateful night, touring DC. Again, he expressed his profound love for me, and it appeared as if all had returned to where we had been. While he still needed to work through his feelings with his parents, we seemed to be on a positive path forward. He even introduced me to his new boss from work at dinner that weekend, where he had just come out.

A few weeks later, we attended a retreat meant to provide a safe and affirming place for queer Muslims. It had been established by the same friend Omar had met in DC when he came to town the summer before. I had recommended the retreat to him to reconcile that which he seemed to continue struggling with. I offered to be by his side if he wanted me to. And so he asked me to come, and I obliged.

When we arrived at the retreat, I surprised Omar with many beautiful letters on the first night from several mutual friends we had made along our journey together, including my mom and sister. There were also letters from some of his close friends in California he had mentioned in passing. I had gotten the idea from the spiritual retreats I had led at Gonzaga. After reading them, he felt deeply touched and wept. We fell asleep holding each other tightly.

At the next day's retreat, I did my best to give him space while attending different sessions. Over the weekend, I saw him grow and thrive. He even led a call to prayer for the community at one point. I was so proud of him for the journey he had been on. I was so in love and committed to him that I even briefly contemplated converting religions.

At the end of the retreat, we made such an incredible community of friends. It was tough for everyone to leave. Most participants hung around until the very last minutes when we had to leave. Omar went back to Delaware, and I went back to DC. It was yet another divine gate I believed we passed through to connect on such spiritual planes.

Omar returned to DC the following week to visit for his second Pride. I asked him to come a little earlier and surprised him with tickets to one of his favorite artists from his youth and one of mine, Jack Johnson. He once described how he sang in a band in Morocco, and they played Jack Johnson's covers. I was so excited to see the look in his eyes when we finally got to the concert.

My love for him had grown by leaps and bounds, and while many things still needed to be addressed in the reality of our lives,

I was sure he was the one. I found myself wanting nothing more than to make him happy. It's how I knew.

When we finally met to go into the concert, he seemed a little off. While off-putting, his sour mood didn't seem to hit me as much. I figured he had a long drive and was a little grumpy.

We entered the amphitheater and placed a large blanket on the grassy knoll overlooking the stage. Thousands of other concertgoers soon surrounded us. We got a few drinks and sat in anticipation of the show. But he was still moody. So I began to poke and prod him to see why he was so gloomy.

He finally gave in and blurted out, "I don't want to be with you anymore. I think I have only ever really cared for you as a friend. I never loved you."

Caught completely off guard, I didn't know what to say. Not only was he breaking up with me, but in a sea of people nonetheless. He said he never truly loved me. I couldn't believe what I had just heard.

In utter pain, I sought out the nearest bathroom stall and cried my eyes out for thirty minutes. Alone.

As I returned to our blanket, the sun had set, and the concert had started. He angrily asked, "Where have you been?" I said nothing and just stared off over the crowd in a daze. We sat, not talking the entire concert. And then drove back to my place.

Like before, we committed to seeing how things went over the weekend.

He oscillated back and forth as we continued being gentle and cuddly. As we started unpacking what he was experiencing, there was a point where he broke down in tears, sobbing to himself. "I don't want to lose my parents," he said before correcting himself and emotionally shutting back down.

On the last day, I asked, "So, what's your final decision?"

"I can't be with you."

I sobbed uncontrollably, as deeply as I'd ever sobbed before. I got down on my knees and just held him before it was time for him to leave.

This time my tears were for me. Even uglier than when I cried in James's arms in Seattle. This was the last gate to test me, my last gasp of air, as my hope for love was slipping away—the thing I wanted most of all.

Omar picked up his belongings. We hugged. And he left.

A month later, I was in Wisconsin with my mom, sister, Aunt Karen, and grandfather celebrating my mom's sixtieth birthday. I learned Omar had emailed her, "Mama Beth," apologizing for having to break my heart again. I sobbed as they all came around me, offering their sage love and support.

I'll never fully understand why he ultimately left. Was he suffering and conflicted between what his mother had said and his love for me? Was he in danger of hurting himself? Was what he said honestly how he felt?

I felt misled if I believed his last words to me, that he never really loved me. Because of what he said, I had to question every moment we ever shared. Was he just using me? Did he mean any of it?

If this wasn't love, what else is? He had previously told me I was the love of his life, his soulmate, and how I made him the happiest he had ever been. Now he was saying he didn't mean any of it. But which was the truth? Then? Or now?

Just like with James and now with Omar, nothing was as it seemed.

The world outside eroded and tore away at what might have been. On the one hand, I've had to accept that this was, in part, our interpersonal struggle. There were many ways in which both of us had much more room to grow within our relationship.

On the other hand, what would the world have been like if it had been more accepting of our love? What if his mom had turned to her son and said, "I love you for all of who you are." What if we lived in a world that didn't view the love we experienced as evil, perverted, or grotesque? Where would we have been today?

I will never know.

What I do know is for the briefest moment, the love we experienced allowed me to know the full breadth and capacity of my humanity where I felt utterly seen and alive in every fiber of my being with another person.

I had to carry on.

PARADIGMS FOR UNDERSTANDING GENDER AND SEXUAL DIVERSITY

Turning my heartache into hope, I brought my pain back into work, recognizing the transformative power of shifting hearts and minds around the beauty of gender and sexual diversity across the human experience throughout the world. Maybe folks like Omar's mom might one day understand. Perhaps others who experienced what I had felt might get to actually find their Omar or James one day, even if I never got to.

On Human Rights Day in December of 2011, right around the time I started at the International Day Against Homophobia, Transphobia, and Biphobia, Secretary of State Hillary Rodham Clinton made her infamous speech in Geneva at the UN Security Council "Gay rights are human rights, and human rights are gay rights," building on her 1995 speech in Beijing where she declared

"Women's rights are human rights and human rights are women's rights. (Clinton 1995)

It was a profound tipping point in the global movement for LGBTI human rights because it solidly positioned the United States as a leader in the area. While many countries previously supported such efforts, given the large footprint the US has on the world's stage, its stated position created a wave of support for LGBTI people worldwide.

Her declaration was not only philosophical in nature but also established several initiatives under the Obama Administration, spurring greater support. A public-private partnership was established to fund LGBTI leaders around the world. Policy changes were made at the US State Department and how the US would show up to support those facing human rights abuses in their respective countries. And an end to discrimination against LGBTI people within our US Foreign Service and National Security apparatuses was declared.

To supplement such efforts, the Obama Administration set aside funds to ensure such change. Adequate training was put in place for the thousands upon thousands of US foreign service staff and foreign nationals working at our embassies and US missions throughout the world. The aim was to ensure those staff clearly understood what LGBTI human rights were and how they pertained to the US government's ultimate aims.

As this happened, I started to understand and see the trend lines as they moved further throughout the State Department, including at USAID, my company's primary client. And so, as an intern, I pitched to our senior leaders to do something similar within the realm of our work with USAID and PEPFAR—the President's Emergency Plan for AIDS Relief.

Our team began discussions with our counterparts at the agencies around the possibility of starting such training with a focus on HIV. As a result, our company was allocated funds to develop and implement a PEPFAR-specific Gender and Sexual Diversity training for its staff worldwide and their implementing partners.

Building on my advocacy experience and my budding knowledge of global health and HIV, a few teammates and I began developing a day-long sensitization course for PEPFAR. It would help PEPFAR staff worldwide learn how LGBTI rights impact their everyday work, how to be good colleagues to their peers within the workplace and how LGBTI human rights extended out to and were essential in understanding the HIV epidemic.

According to the World Health Organization, in 2019, 49 percent of all new HIV infections came from those deemed key populations (UNAIDS 2022). While HIV infection rates globally were in decline, it was only among key populations where rates had increased. Further, there continued to be ongoing issues of stigma, discrimination, and violence targeted toward gender and sexual minorities, the same things I uncovered during my time in Ghana.

As our team got underway, we built upon the successful training designed by our peers in the US State Department. We wanted to ensure greater representation from local community members, so we invited several organizations to provide their insights to sustain the learning well after we were gone. And to make the training practical, we designed real-life case studies to conceptualize better what training participants had learned.

To draw linkages for individuals around the world encountering these issues outside of a Western framework and to better ease them into discussing the rights of marginalized persons in their local communities, we called it the Gender and Sexual Diversity training. After all, everyone has a gender and a sexuality, which made the training much more relatable. Additionally, it was important to explore difficult topics on harmful gender norms, which led to stigma and discrimination against gender and sexual minorities.

Once the training was almost ready to go, we started to identify co-trainers throughout the world. The first training of trainers we conducted was in South Africa. We rented out a large bed and breakfast and held a week of training with around thirty facilitators drawn from throughout the continent of Africa. We sought not only to teach them the training as we had intended but for them to add considerable value and weight to the training itself within their contexts and experiences.

As we deployed the training around the world, we started to receive incredibly positive feedback from those we trained. Many reported having powerful examinations of what it meant to be a gendered being roaming the world. Specifically, they reported having a more profound empathy for those who may face stigma, discrimination, or violence within their communities due to their real or perceived sexual orientation, gender identity, or expression.

On my first trip, I was fortunate to go to India, which would be one of my life's most meaningful experiences. I went with a colleague, Anita, a close friend from India, Tushar, and our USAID colleague, Amelia. It was an incredibly inspiring experience to work so cohesively as a team to deliver the powerful training.

There were several illuminating conversations with those in attendance about how individuals show up across an entire spectrum of gender and sexuality away from societal expectations. Participants started connecting the dots to their work in sexual reproductive health and rights and HIV. We heard the powerful stories of local advocates doing incredible work in their communities to advance human rights. It deeply moved us.

Our training team developed a deep bond with one another in such a short time there. Building on the day's topic, that evening in the hotel lounge, we shared a few of our own stories about love and connection and our professional and personal struggles at our evening nightcap over a meal. It was truly what the training opened us up to. I, of course, briefly shared about James and Omar.

On our last day in India, we saw a little of the city before returning home. I was grateful to visit the Mahatma Gandhi Museum, which told the story of his life and his impact on South Africa and India. There was even a picture of Archbishop Desmond Tutu, holding his tattered Bible, receiving the Gandhi Peace Prize from the Indian government in 2006 (Kalbag). Just like the other historic cities I'd visited, it was a powerful reminder of the possible impact we all can have in bettering our communities.

As we continued to roll out the training throughout the world, I delivered the training in another dozen countries, primarily throughout the continent of Africa. As many facilitators will tell you, you often learn just as much from the training participants themselves. From Kenya to South Africa, Zimbabwe to Ghana, and Nigeria to Tanzania, delivering the training was an incredibly powerful experience and a rare honor.

In many trainings, we'd start the day in a small, windowless conference room where many individuals would sit defensively, arms crossed, prepared to distance themselves from the training content. We had several participants give short speeches as to why they were unhappy to attend the mandatory training on gender and sexual diversity. Some professed their religious viewpoints, which the training never dismissed or affirmed. We simply stated facts.

By the end of the day, several of those same individuals would give more moving pronouncements about how they had been changed. One woman proudly affirmed her strong persona and somewhat masculine expression were, in fact, incredible gifts and who she was, nothing to be ashamed of or change.

In one training, one of our local panelists experienced estrangement from their family members due to having come out as lesbian. Unbeknownst to us, one of their relatives was a training participant that day. As a result, the relative had to sit and listen to the story of their niece as they shared the pain and prolonged suffering of being pushed out of their family. Following the training, they reunited and could work through, if only for a moment, what they previously couldn't discuss.

One participant expressed how she had a friend whose daughter came out as a lesbian and faced family rejection. The daughter committed suicide just days before. The woman was the primary support system for the grieving family and felt taking the training that day, of all days, was of divine providence.

Months later, I attended a conference on gender equality and social inclusion. One of the conference speakers began talking about her experiences in Nigeria, addressing the rights of gender and sexual minorities and all her work to train people in rural villages on the topic.

Drawn to what she presented, I introduced myself after the session and my work developing and delivering a similar training. Before I knew it, she pulled out of her purse a crumpled, tattered handout from one of our GSD trainings, covered in dirt, and explained how she used it where ever she went to help educate about the fluid nature of sex, gender, and sexuality. She'd take it to remote village after remote village and use it as a prop to share with those communities. I was blown away by how far the training had reached. I had designed the handout! I immediately raced back to my office and retrieved five dozen more to bring to her the next day.

The global training was ultimately delivered in forty-plus countries to over five thousand PEPFAR staff and their implementing partners. It remains a required course for incoming PEPFAR staff to this day.

An evaluation of the training impact demonstrated a statistically significant difference in how participants shifted positively in supporting gender and sexual minorities and being willing to take some level of action to improve the lives of those facing marginalization or discrimination within their workplaces and within PEPFAR programs (Poteat et al. 2017).

The training was so well-received that it was adapted to multiple country contexts and an online course. I had the honor of working closely with local advocates in Kenya, including David, and in Jamaica to take the shell of the training and integrate a more nuanced and country-specific adaptation. It was a powerful few years working to adapt the curriculum and help train local facilitators from diverse organizations to deliver the training themselves.

Working in Jamaica was particularly harrowing, given the country was deemed in 2006 by *Time* magazine to be the most homophobic country in the world (Padget 2006). Many gender and sexual minorities were harassed and violently attacked. Several had to seek asylum in neighboring countries. It wasn't uncommon for individuals suspected of being gay to be *burned out* of their homes as attackers set their houses ablaze, often with them inside.

Many street children were homeless because their parents thought they were gay, simply because they were effeminate, particularly young boys. They lived in poverty, under bridges, and often got into trouble while trying to survive.

While harrowing, the local organizations we worked with were several of the bravest activists I'd ever met who often dealt with the aftermath of such tragic circumstances. Their resilience to these hostilities and ability to thrive advocating for the rights of their community taught me so much as we adapted the training to their specific context. Over the course of two years, after refining the curriculum and training, it was made available to local advocates.

While helping to adapt and deliver the gender and sexual diversity training, uncovering and learning about some of the most appalling and discriminatory realities facing LGBTI people around the world, and trying to address them, the ongoing importance of such work hit home very personally.

While in Kingston, I got a call from my mother informing me one of my cousins, Tommy Ray, had committed suicide. He came home from school upset after something had happened. He grabbed his father's gun, went to his room, put the gun in his mouth, and pulled the trigger.

His mom, my aunt, found him moments later on the floor with his eyes open. At first, she thought he was playing a cruel joke on her, only to realize what had happened after seeing the blood covering her hand when she tried to lift up the back of his head. Her beloved and only son had committed suicide. He was just thirteen years old.

We will never fully understand why Tommy Ray took his own life, but I couldn't help recalling the previous Christmas when he disclosed to me, my sister, and my mom that he was struggling with his sexuality and thought he was gay.

When he told me, I pulled out a handout from my training to educate him on what it meant to be gay and who he was. However, I didn't want to pry too much without the consent of his parents.

My aunts often playfully teased they had a "little Ryan" in the family. Tommy Ray frequently expressed his thoughts on his favorite artists and movies that were always a little queer, like Ru Paul's Drag Race and Lady Gaga. He felt closer to my sister and shared even more with her about who he was. He even tried to come out to his mom at one point. He was twelve at the time, "How could he possibly know?" she thought. "He needed more time to be sure."

For many years, he faced relentless bullying from his peers because he was different. Like I was, he was this effervescent kid with a larger-than-life personality and couldn't help but stand out, no matter what he did.

Middle school had been hard, despite having several friends and joining the tennis team, where he found an evolving passion. But unlike me, he couldn't escape the bullying when he left school.

In the modern world and the technology connecting us all, he received hundreds of harassing messages from his peers, even calls to his home to pick on him. Had I gone through what he had gone through, I don't know if I would have had the strength to survive it, either.

He was the brightest kid I'd ever met. At an early age, he was obsessed with ancient Egyptian civilization and could name all the Pharaohs, the pyramids, ancient philosophies, and other realities. He even knew the steps to mummify a body.

Despite the bullying, he was well-liked by his peers. When they heard of his passing, his whole school was shocked and in mourning. He was so intelligent and had a whole life ahead of him. If only the world were safe enough for kids like him.

As I continued on with my work, adapting the gender and sexual diversity training to the Jamaican and Kenyan contexts, and later several more countries, I couldn't help but reflect upon the irony that despite all I had gone on to do in global LGBTI human rights—from my advocacy work at the UN and the trainings around the world to the country-specific work I was doing—there were many more for whom I still couldn't reach, including those within my own family.

His death only made the work to advance LGBTI human rights more significant to me and perpetuated my drive to continue doing what I could.

And I pressed on.

WHAT MIGHT THE FUTURE HOLD?

As I press on in my work, I remain committed to LGBTI human rights and tackling the world's most pressing problems by considering how harmful gender norms, the hushed ways in which we discuss sexualities, and the invisibilization of what makes us human might be addressed in micro and macro ways. I particularly seek to support those susceptible to stigma, discrimination, and violence simply because of who they are or whom they love, as I once was when I was just a lonely teen in middle school.

I continue, alongside others, seeking to expand how we might conceptualize our interconnectedness as human beings. How do we ensure that the human experience, including those of our inner worlds, make up the total vantage point in how we view our shared humanity?

How do we center the perspectives and lived experiences of those who've been forgotten within the pages of our history books—those who've faced erasure and discrimination through no fault of their own? How can we unearth these shared spaces to expand notions of what is possible within this life and what we might ultimately attain? As Archbishop Desmond Tutu passed on to the students on our ship, "Umuntu ngumuntu ngabantu—a person is a person through other persons."

For me, there is no single issue or single solution. The work very much needed in the world is not only our technological advancements, systems thinking, economic development, global health, peace, and security, or climate change. We must step further back to better empathize with our fellow human beings. The things we've often devalued within ourselves, like love and vulnerability, need to be reassessed and centered, including our abilities to feel deep empathy and compassion, to relate to one another, or to dare love each other. Indeed, like the African proverb, it is only together that we will go far.

We must shed the hypocrisies, lies, and misunderstandings of the past for a more hopeful, prosperous, and collective future that includes everyone everywhere. It is possible to be both our individual, magnanimous selves while also appreciating the greater whole we are a part of as human beings.

We each bear secrets to the universe only we know. This includes how we have crafted an understanding of the socially constructed gendered ways of being, which include but are not dependent on our sexual identities. We need to stop denying ourselves the forms of love that bring out the best in us. What undergirds so many of the world's most pressing problems, like war, famine, overpopulation, climate crises, and more, has to do with the stories we've told ourselves about gender and sexuality and, in turn, power and dominance, right and wrong, this or that. The feminine is rising and is the immovable force that will save us all, a worldview that moves beyond false binaries that limit our way of existing.

Building on my work around gender and sexual diversity globally, I've sought to work toward more human-centered solutions as I've delved deeper into development work. Working alongside countless others from all walks of life who share this vision, I've sought to advance more nuanced considerations of how we might reach everyone everywhere through inclusive development practices. Drawing on the same passion as the archbishop, I've become deeply inspired by the next generation of youth leaders. Their drive, resilience, and nuanced appreciation for how gender and sexuality play out in our lives give me hope for what solutions we might identify to address the world's pressing problems. What if people around the world had adequate education about their sexuality? Wouldn't this help us all when we think about our growing populations or the harmful gender norms that too often pit us against each other?

From the local to the global level, I've also had numerous opportunities to contribute meaningfully to conversations at the highest levels about how to expand and explore our global conceptualizations of gender and human rights across the field of development. From authoring numerous thought pieces to speaking on several high-level panels and joining several consultations and boards, I've advised and advocated for more inclusive approaches within our complex and pluralistic world. How can you solve the world's problems without including those most impacted by such problems?

As I've looked outward, I've also helped the organizations I am affiliated with to look inward. I've worked to help my fellow change-makers and development practitioners think about their positionality within the complex world in which we live to consider how our practices could do more harm than good. I've sought to work alongside others to build a more comprehensive understanding and expertise around inclusive development approaches. This includes examining how we think about concepts like diversity, equity, inclusion, and accessibility and the importance of addressing historical wrongs that undergird so many of the issues we face today. What would happen in a world where we achieve gender equality? How could healing and atonement be achieved through the act of reparations for the descendants of the millions who were forcibly enslaved in the transatlantic slave trade? Who would we ultimately be if we let love in? We must leverage our differences to bring out our greatest gifts and strengthen our global solutions to better our world.

A former president and a former secretary of state recognized me for my efforts. In 2021, I was named an Out Leader in National Security and Foreign Policy, compelling me to keep going and helping to shape our shared world alongside other human rights advocates.

While I've circumnavigated the globe, met with world leaders, and had numerous life-changing experiences, I'm constantly reminded much more must be done to advance human dignity and rights. The life I've uncovered remains perilously close to being erased, forced back into the shadows, and demonized by rising tides of hatred and bigotry. The love I preach and the seismic shifts in consciousness I have witnessed through my experiences remain threatened. I still have to question what the future might hold for someone like me in every aspect of my life. Frankly, I'm so tired of playing the villain in someone else's story, especially when they don't know me or what I've witnessed and revealed about my lived experiences throughout this memoir.

In my day-to-day life, I still face numerous impositions on my being, from being labeled as too nice to being overlooked or underestimated. I've lost friendships and continue navigating the realities of being a queer person roaming this world. I've continued to have to consider the freedoms of where I choose to live, to navigate the complex realities of gender and sexuality within my relationships, and to question what my life holds as I age and evolve. I even continue to face different forms of intolerance simply for being me, often in the subtlest and not-so-subtle ways.

I was at a bar recently and told a nearby friend I thought a guy across the bar was cute. Someone standing beside her drunkenly decided to pull me aside and tell me I made people uncomfortable by saying such things. Mind you, he and our buddies were doing just as much, if not more, to several women in the room. When I tried to explain to him his discomfort might not lie within me but was likely something within him he might want to work on, he interrupted me and told me he wanted to hit me in the face.

That he even felt in the position to tell me how to be and exist in the world, in and of itself, is how some people still treat me. As if I am below them and there is something about life, I just don't know that they've magically figured out, doubting my own lived experiences and ways of bringing myself into the world. To even say I'm gay at one point was controversial, and to still choose every day to lean into myself is not an act of naivety. It comes from a deep knowing that my life is full of wonder and beauty that is equally deserving of respect and dignity, just as any other person's life.

The work is ongoing.

The story in 2013 of eight-year-old Gabriel Fernandez in Los Angeles, California, being locked away in a cupboard, severely beaten, and tortured to death by his parents because they believed he was gay, simply because he was a bit feminine is too common of a story (Villarreal and Brennan 2020). The countless individuals throughout Latin America who are forced to undergo conversion therapies, including ice baths, forced rape, mutilation, and psychological torture, are still practiced (Guzman 2022). Families in other parts of the world conduct *honor* killings of their LGBTI relatives (Yurcaba 2021). Discriminatory laws are being passed in places like Russia, Uganda, China, or here in the United States, where even talking about LGBTI issues is criminalized (Angelo and Bocci 2021). In China, they've recently passed laws banning *sissy* men from national media in an effort to salvage the masculine identity in Chinese culture (Wang 2022). In Florida, they are banning books having anything to do with queer life and racial justice issues. In Uganda, legislation passed criminalizing even knowing someone who is LGBTI and not turning them into the proper authorities with life imprisonment. Sixty-nine countries still criminalize homosexuality, sentencing individuals to decades of imprisonment, even death.

Still, many struggle with the daily stressors of simply living life, facing microaggressions, stigma, and discrimination within their heteronormative communities.

At the same time, I wonder what the world would have been like had I never experienced all the stigmas and stereotypes I had. What if I had just been able to feel the profound love I have experienced throughout my life without fear or worry? Would my friends have stuck around, even been proud of all I've accomplished, unburdened by the shame of associating themselves with someone like me? Would I have ended up in the same place, or might I be sitting along some creek in the mountains beside my chosen family, leaning my head on the shoulder of the love of my life, watching our daughters explore the forest floor, hoping they might one day turn out half as amazing as my sister, mom, or grandmother, and just existing as a family? A simpler, less complicated life. I sometimes dream about this. What if?

I remain hopeful about the countless young people championing change in their communities and seeking to advance the rights of all people everywhere by confronting the systemic challenges that perpetuate the notions that love is somehow taboo, that to express oneself fully and wholly is somehow degrading. The work of organizations like the Family Acceptance Project are so important identifying all the different ways families of all types of backgrounds can support their LGBTI children like my family supported me.

What I've learned most about my journey as an LGBTI human rights advocate is that to love itself is resistance. To embrace my gender fluidity and to wholly value and care for those who mean the world to me and to tell them so is what life ought to be about. To experience authentic joy and to express thoughts and feelings fully—matters. As Desmond Tutu taught me, it's always about the simplest of acts, the kind gestures, and the smile to strangers that make the ultimate difference in our every action. It is possible. We simply need to make that daily choice.

What I wish most for all those who have come through my life on this already long and grueling journey is to know just how much they have meant to me and how they have made up the totality of my world. Wherever I have gone, whatever I have done, I have felt accompanied by their warmth and presence. The love and guidance, the wisdom and strength, the vulnerability and authenticity I have experienced throughout my life alongside them have helped me to know and find myself, to understand and empathize with others, and to have a fundamental belief in something bigger and more expansive than any one person could ever imagine.

Our humanity. In me. In you. In us. In Them.

From my soccer coach, Greg, to our family friends, the Stills and Samars, the Shepards, the archbishop, the Clintons, to my friends from Disney World, Semester at Sea, and the Clinton School, along with those I've met around the world, to my professors and sage guides along the way—I remain strengthened by how they provided safe passage for me throughout my life.

I was grateful to recently join the Stills alongside my sister and mom in Costa Rica to celebrate Melissa's wedding to the love of her life, Omar.

After several years of estrangement, I'm grateful to have reconciled with my father. I've sought to more deeply understand and value his own personal journey outside of and away from the pedestal I always placed him upon. I've come to appreciate and care for his wife and their life together. Our relationship as father and son, two human beings roaming this planet, continues to evolve as new gates of life approach us.

I am eternally grateful to my sister Sarah for growing into an inspirational figure who has carried forward many similar lessons into her own life to give her heart to those in her orbit and to be a rock for those she loves, including me. She is making waves within the world, too, helping build partnerships across university settings around the world and being the loving, caring friend she has been for so many others throughout her life.

My mom remains a light in my life, whose example I strive to live up to and whose love and guidance remain that safe space as it has always been for me to be vulnerable in the sacredness of her full presence within my life. The warmth and love she espouses in her every waking moment are awe-inspiring. How many people get to say, "I want to be like my mom when I grow up"?

I'm not sure that James and Omar will ever know their profound impact on my life, nor all the ripple effects the love we found together set in motion. Our love opened the gates for me to know myself and feel profoundly connected to the mystical world within me and all around us. The love I deeply felt for them perpetuates itself through me to this day in search of passing it on to a future generation who might be more readily able to receive such gifts from a universe we are only just beginning to understand in our relatively short human history.

And, of course, I continue to deeply feel my grandparents' presence in my life and the incredible example they set the stage for me to build upon. My grandmother was the person who could get off a plane in the middle of Russia and know someone. I can do that, too—maybe in Kenya, Malawi, or South Africa. I hope they are proud of me in whatever form of energy or spirit they might be watching over me from in this moment.

My hope for humanity is that we might all push ourselves to think more openly, not take for granted the love we are capable of giving, and to give it as freely and widely as we can each and every day. After all, when we think about the air we breathe, our time on this beautiful earth, and most notably, the bountiful gifts in me, in you, in them, and in us—even if we are simply sitting on a plane—we are all interconnected. Each and every one of us. Our past, our present, and our futures depend on one another. It all starts with a smile, a hello, a "How are you?" and allowing one another to be our full and authentic selves and to love wholeheartedly those that come into our everyday lives.

Such everyday acts should also lead us to be more open to solutions to the world's most pressing problems impacting upon us all. What would happen if we actually took the time to imagine those suffering from war, poverty, or injustice as ourselves? What would our solutions be if we broke free from the social constructions that have limited our collective growth? What might be possible if we not only dream of but work toward that ideal world we all know, deep down, is possible? What could we achieve together, standing side by side?

To those who may call themselves queer or are working through their gendered and sexual realities, our authentic, unbridled joy matters. May you come to see the profound beauty and gifts in all you are, including and most notably, your own capacity to love others and find communion with those in your chosen family.

To those who may be struggling to feel fully understood—take a chance, reach out, pay attention to that which your heart aches for, and keep going.

To those struggling to express all that is inside, but because of whatever societal expectation around vulnerability may be holding you back, choose to let go and embrace that vast horizon of love you know within you is possible. You just have to speak it into the universe. Tell your friends you love them and mean it—all the time.

To men, specifically, we often suppress whole worlds within ourselves, and likely experience shame or fear surrounding our capacity to love. It is essential we push beyond such societal influences that would dictate such limitations. You possess far greater potential than what you may believe is possible. Discovering it requires nurturing our relationships with one another. Let the world in. Give from the authentic spaces within your heart and soul. Honor the many people in your life, particularly those who identify as women, who have held you up, stood by you, and sacrificed on your behalf. Stop taking such people for granted.

Never forget, as my friend Amanda once shared with me, especially in today's world, to love in and of itself is one of the most radical things we can do to shift the tides of hatred, bigotry, and violence that feel all-consuming these days. After all, I am because you are.

As I close this chapter of my life, I think back to the kid who was so afraid of the world and my place within it, wanting to fall asleep and never awake from my slumber. To think of all that has been lived during my short time on this earth thus far. What might have happened had I chosen not to wake up?

As I stand and blow out the candles of my fortieth birthday cake, surrounded by the friends and family I love more than anything, my mom, my sister, my aunt Mary, Megan, Amy, Greg and Amanda, my cousin Allen, and others, I breathe back in the beauty and energy all around me, hopeful for what the future might hold, choosing to believe in all that is possible.

I know I've lived every day, giving my best effort with what I have been given and dealing with everything that has come my way, whether I wanted it or not.

May tomorrow or sometime within the next forty years bring renewed hope and continued faith in the humanity I feel so deeply connected to, simply because I dare love so profoundly within my life.

EPILOGUE:

WITH GREAT PRIVILEGE, COMES GREAT RESPONSIBILITY

But by the accident of birth, I am here.

I easily could have been born among those living in the Dalit slum we passed through that fateful morning in India. I could have been born among the villagers in The Gambia. My life would have been very different if I lived in Kenya, Ghana, or Jamaica as an out gay man. What if I had been someone else's son or brother? What if my first love wasn't with James but someone else? What if I had been born just a decade earlier or a decade later? What if I had grown up somewhere else, gone to another university, or never gotten on that bus to undertake a Civil Rights Pilgrimage?

What if Matthew Shepard never met Arron McKiney or Russel Henderson?

As I close out this memoir, I want to call into the world all those whose sacrifices, love-lost, doubt, fear, and even death paved the way for me to experience the world as I have.

To the kid who started the gay-straight alliance at my high school. The kids that came out in rural towns. The friends who didn't turn away from the love they felt for each other. The long hard walks home fearing harassment or violence. The conversations held in the dark and late into the night. The protests, the kiss-ins, the debates, the forums, panels, speeches, and more. Those who simply got by, barely so, woke up, put on their clothes, and existed for another day.

Let alone all those who have fought, battled, organized, stayed active, built chosen families, created safe spaces, taken in and sheltered those abandoned, treated the wounds of the beaten, pressed for social change, leveraged their seats of power for good, and continued to remember all those who would have otherwise been forgotten.

Those who came out when coming out meant risking everything.

Without such everyday sacrifice, hardship, pain, authenticity, vulnerability, and loving out loud, I wouldn't even know my name.

I have been so fortunate and blessed to have experienced such authentic joy. I've also faced profound loss, suffering, stigma, alienation, abandonment, and darkness—not something the world always chooses to see or accept. After all, I'm such a positive person. My high school classmates even chose me for class superlatives as the most optimistic. But many don't realize I am so because I'm grateful for what I have, knowing all I might have lost.

Nonetheless, my story is vast and can only be partially captured here.

I want to acknowledge the danger of a single story. My story here is but one of infinite moments throughout my life. Similarly, of the infinite moments in my life, so too are there infinite moments making up the lives of countless others worldwide whose stories are equally compelling, full of triumph and defeat, joy and sorrow, hope and loss. Stories that may never be heard or seen but are as deeply important to the interconnected and interdependent nature of all our lives that make up our shared humanity. My story is but one story.

I recognize that while I have faced seemingly insurmountable odds, I also reaped huge rewards from the social constructs of our modern world, shaped to benefit people like me. Much of my life experience and worldview I hold comes from a certain privileged purview I acknowledge and never take for granted. Even my own capacity to love so deeply and richly within my life has come about through a unique form of privilege. I had parents, family, and friends who loved me. Not everyone has that.

I strive daily to perpetuate and give back what others bestowed upon me. A part of that is bearing witness to and evangelizing what I know now, which I feared so deeply once before.

In honor of the love I hold in my heart and its ever-expanding capacity to simultaneously feel interconnected to all things, everywhere, all at once, I want to honor all of those who have helped to move and shake my consciousness, those who have lifted me, shaped me, inspired me and who themselves have stories to tell, gifts they have to offer the world, inspiration to provide, and worlds within worlds they have created.

All of them illuminate and keep aflame my perpetual hope that light will find its path wherever there may be darkness. Like a root growing its way through the tiniest crack in a boulder and then breaking it apart, so too shall our ceaseless efforts to challenge the oppressive states that prevent us all from being our fullest, brightest selves in communion with one another. All of us, everywhere. You. Me. Us. Them.

Wherever there is hatred, love will surely find its way.

ACKNOWLEDGMENTS

What would one have done without the incredible support and inspiration of those who believed in this memoir before it even took flight? Thank you to all the individuals who joined my presale campaign and helped this book take off the ground.

Those individuals include Andrew Aboujaoude, Aday Adetosoye, James Agan, Indira Ahluwalia, Myeashea Alexander, Wayne An, Michael Armesto, Joe Ballard, Alex Barba, Mary Barber, Michael Barnett, Brendan Beardsley, Joel Bervell, Cory Biggs, Trevor Blake, Brett Bovio, Andrew Brandt, Ti Bui and Curt Flickinger, Katie Burns, Ben Bynum, Kim Caldwell, Jessica Campbell, Rhonda and Doug Campbell, Dara Carr, Chris Carver, Danielle Cendejas, Rudolph Chandler, Kevin Chiang, Casey Clark, Dr. Farley Cleghorn, Jennifer Collins-Foley, Ben Conard, Brian Cookstra, William Corley, Brian Crimmins, Kathy Culig, Christopher Davis, Adriano de Bernardi Schneider, Dean Victoria DeFrancesco, Paul DeVido and Rick, Vlad Donets, Karlene and Joe Doupe, Elizabeth Drachman, Dr. Rosanna Duncan, Kristin Duquette, Sandra Duvall, María José Espinosa Carrillo, Kellie Evans, Kent Ford, Garrett Frey, Bob Gee, Bruce Gillispie, Neil Giuliano, Francis Graham and Melissa Schnure, Gary Gray, Reggie Greer, Jaynee and Rolf Groseth, Cristian Gulli, Jeffrey Haddad, Dr. Shannon Hader, Dwight Hahn, Shari Haines, Bob and Karen Hankinson, Karen Hardee, Rebecca Hazlewood, Michael Heflin, Katie Heinzen, Dr. Beth Hellwig, Scott Hellwig, Ann Hendrix-Jenkins, Chloe Faaiuaso Holmes, Daniel Horgan, Jin-Soo Huh, Micheal Ighodaro and Jirair Ratevosian, Husam Ismail, Merna Jacobsen, Mandeep Jangi, Vinny Johl, George and Jen Johnson, Dr. Stefanie K. Johnson, Saira Johnson-Qureshi, Ryan Kaminski, Lisa Kasha, Rebecca and Ben Kaufman, Laura Kim, Eric Koester, Rachel Kosberg, James Kostek, Ivy Lam, Cathy Lavoie, Jack Lofton, Abe Lopez, Panagiotis Loukopoulos, Glen Lubbert, Spencer Lucker, Fiona Macaulay, Ron Macinnis, Nick Martin, Jay Mathias, Saraounia Mboka-Boyer, David Mbote, Gel Medina, Gabe Medina and Chad Riddle, Christopher Melhauser, Sarah Menzies, Crystal C. Mercer, Lea Metz, Tim and Phyllis Meyer, Greg Miraglia, Marise Montrose, Tamarah Moss, Tina Nations, Liz Nerad, Scott Nuckols, Bethany O'connor, Anthony Oddo and Dave Freeburg, Raul Olivo, Allen Olson, Barry and Cheryl Olson, Sarah Olson, Howard Ou, Nathanial Owen, Ishani Patel, Troy Patterson, Amelia Peltz, Jenny Peterson, Rebekah Pfaff, Billy Pick, Susan Pitcher, Charles Radcliffe, Kiyan Rajabi, Margaret Reeves, Nicole Reichenbach, Eric Reinsvold, Danilo Rodriguez, Lianne Romahi, Michael Ross, Skip Rutherford, Roupen Sadyan, Sophia Said, Serkan Saka, Adan Salinas, Amy Samar, Diane Samar, Kimberly Sarotte, Rob Segan, Sandeep Shamasunder, Travis Shumake, Anne Simmons-Benton, Dr. Arvind Singhal, Perry Stamp, Caitlin Still, Michael and Robyn Still, Melissa Still Miller, Tuesday Stott, Marshall Stowell, Hunter Strodel, Anna and Aaron Strong, Kaelan Sullivan, Sharon Testor, Jane Wothaya (TJay) Thirikwa, Alex Thomas, Carol Thompson, Rebecca Venezia, Megan and Louis Wahl, Christine and John Ward, Greg and Amanda Watts, Krista Weih, Dr. Sue

Weitz, Jennifer Williams, Adam Wolf, Jason Wright, Carol Yee, Sj. Simon Zachary

APPENDIX

PREFACE:

Vaid-Menon, Alok. 2023. "'Center Dinner 2023: Visionary Award Recipient Alok Vaid-Menon." LGBT Center NYC. April 13, 2023. 11:00. https://www.youtube.com/watch?v=0924UWOBmaY.

INTRODUCTION:

Acosta, Nelson. 2010. "Fidel Castro Takes Blame for 1960s Gay Persecution." *Reuters*, August 31, 2010. https://www.reuters.com/article/us-cuba-castro/fidel-castro-takes-blame-for-1960s-gay-persecution-idUSTRE67U4JE20100831.

Gupta, Alok. 2008. "Alien Legacy—Origins of Sodomy Laws in British Colonialism." Human Rights Watch. December 17, 2008. https://www.hrw.org/report/2008/12/17/alien-legacy/origins-sodomy-laws-british-colonialism.

Isaack, Wendy. 2018. "'No Choice but to Deny Who I Am': Violence and Discrimination against LGBT People in Ghana."

Human Rights Watch. January 8, 2018. https://www.hrw.org/report/2018/01/08/no-choice-deny-who-i-am/violence-and-discrimination-against-lgbt-people-ghana.

Pink News. 2016. "This is how Fidel Castro persecuted gay people." November 28, 2016. https://www.thepinknews.com/2016/11/28/this-is-how-fidel-castro-persecuted-gay-people/.

SAFETY AT HOME:
Elliot, Jane. 2016. *A Collar in My Pocket: Blue Eyes/Brown Eyes Exercise.* USA: CreateSpace Independent Publishing Platform.

Francaviglia, Richard V. 1996. *Main Street Revisited: Time, Space, and Image Building in Small-Town America (American Land & Life).* Iowa City: University of Iowa Press.

SERVICE TO OTHERS:
Allen, Greg. 2011. "Children of Cuba Remember Their Flight to America." *NPR,* November 19, 2011. https://www.npr.org/2011/11/19/142534943/pedro-pan-childrens-life-altering-flight-from-cuba.

Bardon, Jonathan. 2012. A History of Ulster. Ireland: Blackstaff Press.

Brockell, Gillian. 2021. "The Long, Ugly History of Anti-Asian Racism and Violence in the US." *The Washington Post,* March 18, 2021. https://www.washingtonpost.com/history/2021/03/18/history-anti-asian-violence-racism/.

Conde, Yvonne. 1999. *Operation Pedro Pan: The Untold Exodus of 14,048 Cuban Children.* New York: Routledge.

Davis, Jimmie and Charles Mitchell. 1940. "You Are My Sunshine." New York: Southern Music Publishing Co., Inc.

History.com Editors. 2018. "1968 Democratic Convention." History. March 16, 2018. https://www.history.com/topics/1960s/1968-democratic-convention.

López, Segrera and Francisco Lopez. 2011. "The Cuban Revolution: Historical Roots, Current Situation, Scenarios, and Alternatives." *Latin American Perspectives* 38, no. 2 (March): 3–30. http://www.jstor.org/stable/29779317.

Shulman, Alix Kates, and Honor Moore ed. 2021. *Women's Liberation!: Feminist Writings That Inspired a Revolution & Still Can.* New York: Literary Classics of the United States, Inc.

BULLIED AND BROKEN:

Fitzsimons, Tim. 2018. "LGBTQ History Month: The Early Days of America's AIDS Crisis." *NBC News,* October 15, 2018. https://www.nbcnews.com/feature/nbc-out/lgbtq-history-month-early-days-america-s-aids-crisis-n919701.

Halkitis, Perry. 2012. "Discrimination and Homophobia Fuel the HIV Epidemic in Gay and Bisexual Men." American Psychological Association. April 2012. https://www.apa.org/pi/aids/resources/exchange/2012/04/discrimination-homophobia.

Ryan, Hugh. 2015. "Why So Many Disney Villains Sound 'Gay.'" *Vice*, July 14, 2015. https://www.vice.com/en/article/5g9e4d/the-number-of-gay-animated-villains-will-surprise-you-456.

A CLIMATE OF FEAR:

Goldstein, Dana. 2019. "20 Years after Columbine, Schools Have Gotten Safer. But Fears Have Only Grown." *New York Times*, April 20, 2019. https://www.nytimes.com/2019/04/20/us/columbine-anniversary-school-violence-statistics.html.

Sheerin, Jude. 2018. "Matthew Shepard: The Murder That Changed America." *BBC*, October 26, 2018. https://www.bbc.com/news/world-us-canada-45968606.

Shepard, Judy. 2010. *The Meaning of Matthew: My Son's Murder in Laramie, and a World Transformed*. New York: Hudson Street Press.

A NEW BEGINNING, A SECOND CHANCE:

Johnson, Jim. 2000. *MTV's Real World New Orleans*. MTV.

A GATE OPENS:

Raghavan, Gautam. 2021. "10 Years Later: Looking Back at the Repeal of 'Don't Ask, Don't Tell.'" The White House. September 20, 2021. https://www.whitehouse.gov/ppo/briefing-room/2021/09/20/10-years-later-looking-back-at-the-repeal-of-dont-ask-dont-tell/.

Stout, David. 2004. "Bush Backs Ban in Constitution on Gay Marriage." *New York Times*, February 24, 2004. https://www.nytimes.com/2004/02/24/politics/bush-backs-ban-in-constitution-on-gay-marriage.html.

A WORLD TOO PERFECT:

Szostak, Natasha. 2022. "Give Kids the World and Childhood Cancer Society Are Making Magic for Deserving Families." *WDW Magazine*, December 16, 2022. https://www.wdw-magazine.com/give-kids-the-world-and-childhood-cancer-society-make-magic-for-deserving-families/.

BECOMING AN ACCIDENTAL ACTIVIST:

Carey-Mahoney, Ryan. 2016. "Almost 30 Years Later, People Are Still Affected by the AIDS Memorial Quilt." *The Washington Post*, October 11, 2016. https://www.washingtonpost.com/news/to-your-health/wp/2016/10/11/almost-30-years-later-people-are-still-impacted-by-the-aids-memorial-quilt/.

Dreyer, Chris. 2004. "Marriage Petitions Spark Conversation on Campus." *The Gonzaga Bulletin*, April 21, 2004. https://www.gonzagabulletin.com/marriage-petitions-spark-conversation-on-campus/article_f0399346-0d38-5c0f-b548-9f2e09bf5d6b.html.

Elliot, Jane. 2016. *A Collar in My Pocket: Blue Eyes/Brown Eyes Exercise*. USA: CreateSpace Independent Publishing Platform.

Kinsey, Alfred, Wardell Pomeroy, and Clyde Martin. 1948. *Sexual Behavior in the Human Male*. Philadelphia: W.B. Saunders Ltd.

Laughlin, Sheana. 2004. "Judy Shepard Speaks against Hate." *The Gonzaga Bulletin*, Apr 28, 2004. https://www.gonzagabulletin. com/judy-shepard-speaks-against-hate/article_2817da8c-3b76-59ef-a439-3d5c9b28c555.html.

National AIDS Memorial. n.d. "About the Quilt." Accessed April 2023. https://www.aidsmemorial.org/about.

Olson, Ryan. 2004. "Student Calls for Greater Tolerance in Controversy over Sexual Identity." *The Gonzaga Bulletin*, March 17, 2004. https://www.gonzagabulletin.com/student-calls-for-greater-tolerance-in-controversy-over-sexual-identity/article_9d074ea8-f13e-56cc-8f37-f1d80a1dad32.html.

Ott, Tanya. 2005. "50th Anniversary of Second 'Brown v. Bd. of Education.'" *NPR*, May 31, 2005. https://www.npr.org/2005/05/31/4673379/50th-anniversary-of-second-brown-v-bd-of-education.

FIGHTING DRAGONS:

Frankl, Viktor E. 1959. *Man's Search for Meaning*. Boston: Beacon Press.

Ward, Vincent, director. 1998. *What Dreams May Come*. Universal Pictures. 1 hr., 53 min.

DEEP SECRETS AND HOMOPHOBIC REALITIES:

Moreau, Julie. 2021. "Nearly 1 in 5 Young Adults Say They're Not Straight, Global Survey Finds." *NBC News*, June 9, 2021. https://

www.nbcnews.com/feature/nbc-out/nearly-1-5-young-adults-say-they-re-not-straight-n1270003.

NATIONALLY RECOGNIZED:

Associated Press. 2006. "Basketball Fans Asked to Stop Chanting 'Brokeback Mountain.'" ESPN, February 11, 2006. http://www.espn.com/espn/wire/_/section/ncb/id/2327562.

Broverman, Neal. 2005. "Future Gay Hero: Ryan Olson." Advocate. December 19, 2005. https://www.advocate.com/politics/commentary/2005/12/19/future-gay-hero-ryan-olson.

Grant, Jenna. 2006. "Bell of Peace Awarded to Senior Involved In HERO." *The Gonzaga Bulletin*, March 29, 2006. https://www.gonzagabulletin.com/bell-of-peace-awarded-to-senior-involved-in-hero/article_5d2e4ead-d271-5ec1-9f98-2f43eda414af.html.

Inlander Staff and Joel Smith. 2008. "20 Under 30." *Inlander*, April 9, 2008. https://www.inlander.com/news/20-under-30-2129500.

Kobos, Genesis. 2005. "MTV Follows Students to Gay Marriage Proceedings." *The Gonzaga Bulletin*, March 23, 2005. https://www.gonzagabulletin.com/mtv-follows-students-to-gay-marriage-proceedings/article_7ac90d78-6718-5d13-9301-fc65844459dc.html.

Lowry, Steve. 2006. "Students Challenge Military Policy." *The Gonzaga Bulletin*, September 26, 2006. https://www.gonzagabulletin.com/students-challenge-military-policy/article_d0a578f1-186c-5e15-a851-ee9a29cb68b5.html.

NBC News. 2006. "'The Situation with Tucker Carlson' for Feb. 14." February 16, 2006. https://www.nbcnews.com/id/wbna11365925.

Ring, Trudy. 2022. "Focus on the Family, an Anti-LGBTQ+ Group, Defaced in Wake of Club Q." Advocate. November 28, 2022. https://www.advocate.com/news/2022/11/28/focus-family-anti-lgbtq-group-defaced-wake-club-q.

Roesler, Richard, and Travis Hay. 2005. "Same-Sex Marriage Case Stirs Passions on All Sides." *The Spokesman-Review*, March 9, 2005. https://www.spokesman.com/stories/2005/mar/09/same-sex-marriage-case-stirs-passions-on-all-sides/.

PRAY THE GAY AWAY:

Vestal, Shawn. 2005. "GU Hosts Anti-homosexuality Speaker." *The Spokesman-Review*, October 29, 2005. https://www.spokesman.com/stories/2005/oct/29/gu-hosts-anti-homosexuality-speaker/.

CIRCUMNAVIGATING THE GLOBE:

Sherriff, Lucy. 2022. "The Romantic, Heartbreaking Love Story behind the Taj Mahal." Discovery. August 23, 2022. https://www.discovery.com/exploration/the-taj-mahal-s-love-story.

NDIBONA UBUNTU KUWE:

Leibovitz, Annie. 2007. "The July 2007 Africa Covers." *Vanity Fair*, July 2007. https://www.vanityfair.com/news/photos/2007/07/annie-leibovitz-africa-covers.

VILLAGE LIFE:

Human Rights Watch. 2008. "Gambia: President Should Disavow Reported Homophobic Threats." Human Rights Watch. June 11, 2008. https://www.hrw.org/news/2008/06/11/gambia-president-should-disavow-reported-homophobic-threats.

Operation Crossroads Africa. 2017-2023. "What Is Operation Crossroads Africa?" Accessed April 22, 2023. https://operationcrossroadsafrica.org/what-is-operation-crossroads-africa.

Rerimoi, A.J., J. Niemann, I. Lange, and I.M. Timæus. 2019. "Gambian Cultural Beliefs, Attitudes and Discourse on Reproductive Health and Mortality: Implications for Data Collection in Surveys from the Interviewer's Perspective." *PloS one* 14, no. 5 (May). https://doi.org/10.1371/journal.pone.0216924.

ABANDONED AND ESTRANGED:

Bieber, Christy. 2023. "Revealing Divorce Statistics In 2023." *Forbes*, May 4, 2023. https://www.forbes.com/advisor/legal/divorce/divorce-statistics.

Kosakowski, Paul. 2021. "The Fall of the Market in the Fall of 2008." Investopedia. February 10, 2021. https://www.investopedia.com/articles/economics/09/subprime-market-2008.asp.

OVERCOMING DARKNESS:

Bradley, Cole. 2018. "People's Power: Memphis' Early History of Race, Resistance, and Black Political Power." High Ground. June 28, 2018. https://www.highgroundnews.com/features/SlaveHaven.aspx.

Keyes, Allison. 2017. "The Youngest of the Little Rock Nine Speaks About Holding on to History." *Smithsonian Magazine*, September 5, 2017. https://www.smithsonianmag.com/smithsonian-institution/youngest-little-rock-nine-speaks-about-holding-onto-history-180964732/.

National Civil Rights Museum. n.d. Accessed April 24, 2023. https://www.civilrightsmuseum.org/.

Vang, Amelia and Emma Bowman. 2021. "For the First Time in 56 Years, a 'Bloody Sunday' without John Lewis." *NPR*, March 5, 2021. https://www.npr.org/2021/03/05/974035873/for-the-first-time-in-56-years-a-bloody-sunday-without-john-lewis.

Waxman, Olivia. 2021. "How One Atlanta Church Impacted Martin Luther King, Jr., the Civil Rights Movement and Incoming Sen. Raphael Warnock." *Time*, January 14, 2021. https://time.com/5927777/martin-luther-king-warnock-history/.

Williams, Nikesha. 2020. "Katrina Battered Black New Orleans. Then the Recovery Did It Again." *The Washington Post*, August 28, 2020. https://www.washingtonpost.com/outlook/katrina-battered-black-new-orleans-then-the-recovery-did-it-again/2020/08/27/193d2420-e7eb-11ea-bc79-834454439a44_story.html.

CLINTON SCHOOL:

Clinton, Bill. 2007. *Giving: How Each of Us Can Change the World.* New York: Alfred A. Knopf.

Donohue, Gráinne, Edward McCann, and Michael Brown. 2021. "Views and Experiences of LGBTQ+ People in Prison Regarding Their Psychosocial Needs: A Systematic Review of the Qualitative Research Evidence." *International Journal of Environmental Research and Public Health* 18, no. 17 (September). https://doi.org/10.3390/ijerph18179335.

Sawyer, Wendy. 2020. "Visualizing the Racial Disparities in Mass Incarceration." Prison Policy Initiative. July 27, 2020. https://www.prisonpolicy.org/blog/2020/07/27/disparities/.

Simpson, Steven. 2022. "Recidivism Rates in Arkansas Prisons 'Unacceptably High,' Department of Corrections secretary says." *Arkansas Democratic Gazette*, March 29, 2022. https://www.arkansasonline.com/news/2022/mar/29/department-of-corrections-secretary-recidivism/.

LGBTI RIGHTS IN KENYA:

afroqueerpod. 2018. "An Imam, a Bishop & the Rumour That Started It All." *AfroQueer Podcast*. Released July 9, 2018. Accessed April 22, 2023. 19:08. https://afroqueerpodcast.com/2018/07/09/an-imam-a-bishop-the-rumour-that-started-it-all/.

ARC International. 2016. "The Yogyakarta Principles." Accessed April 22, 2023. https://yogyakartaprinciples.org/.

Buckle, Leah. 2020. "African Sexuality and the Legacy of Imported Homophobia." Stonewall. October 1, 2020. https://www.stonewall.org.uk/about-us/news/african-sexuality-and-legacy-imported-homophobia.

Human Rights Watch. 2019. "Kenya: Court Upholds Archaic Anti-Homosexuality Laws." May 24, 2019. https://www.hrw.org/news/2019/05/24/kenya-court-upholds-archaic-anti-homosexuality-laws.

RELIGIOUSLY BASED HOMOPHOBIA AT THE UNITED NATIONS:

Associated Press. 2010. "UN, US Officials Call for Gay Rights." *CBS News*, December 10, 2010. https://www.cbsnews.com/news/un-us-officials-call-for-gay-rights/.

GLOBAL ADVOCACY THROUGH THE INTERNATIONAL DAY AGAINST HOMOPHOBIA:

Cochran, Susan, Jack Drescher, Eszter Kismödi, Alain Giami, Claudia García-Moreno, Elham Atalla, Adele Marais, Elisabeth Meloni Vieira, and Geoffrey Reedi. 2014. "Proposed Declassification of Disease Categories Related to Sexual Orientation in the International Statistical Classification of Diseases and Related Health Problems (ICD-11)." *Bulletin World Health Organization* 92, no. 9 (September): 672-679. 2014. 92:672–679. https://doi.org/10.2471%2FBLT.14.135541.

Human Rights Watch. 2012. "US: Obama Statement on LGBT Rights." May 9, 2012. https://www.hrw.org/news/2012/05/09/us-obama-statement-lgbt-rights.

Lee, Barbara. 2013. "Congresswoman Barbara Lee Introduces Resolution Recognizing International Day against Homophobia and Transphobia." Lee House. May 17, 2013. https://lee.house.gov/news/press-releases/congresswoman-barbara-lee-introduces-resolution-recognizing-international-day-against-homophobia-and-transphobia.

DIVING INTO DEVELOPMENT:

Macinnis, Ron, Taylor Williamson, and Britt Herstad. 2013. "Vice President of Ghana Oversees Launch of Online System to Fight HIV-Related Discrimination." *Impact Blog* (blog), *USAID*. December 6, 2013. https://blog.usaid.gov/2013/12/vice-president-of-ghana-oversees-launch-of-online-system-to-fight-hiv-related-discrimination/.

United Nations Human Rights Office of the High Commisioner. n.d. "Criminalization." Free and Equal. Accessed April 22, 2023. https://www.unfe.org/system/unfe-43-UN_Fact_Sheets_-_FINAL_-_Criminalization_(1).pdf.

FINDING OMAR:

McConnell, Tristan. 2015. "Close Your Eyes and Pretend to Be Dead." Foreign Policy. September 20, 2015. https://foreignpolicy.com/2015/09/20/nairobi-kenya-westgate-mall-attack-al-shabab/.

US Supreme Court. 2015. "Obergefell v. Hodges. 576 US ___ (2015)." Justia. June 26, 2015. https://supreme.justia.com/cases/federal/us/576/14-556/.

PARADIGMS FOR UNDERSTANDING GENDER AND SEXUAL DIVERSITY:

Clinton, Hillary. 1995. "Remarks for the United Nations World Conference on Women." United Nations. September 5, 1995. https://www.un.org/esa/gopher-data/conf/fwcw/conf/gov/950905175653.txt.

Clinton, Hillary. 2011. "Remarks in Recognition of International Human Rights Day." US Department of State. December 6, 2011. https://2009-2017.state.gov/secretary/20092013clinton/rm/2011/12/178368.htm.

Kalbag, Chaitanya. 2006. "Gandhi Peace Prize for Tutu." *Hindustan Times*, October 3, 2006. https://www.hindustantimes.com/india/gandhi-peace-prize-for-tutu/story-2gip795TenEhZRmQAQe1XP.html.

Padget, Tim. 2006. "The Most Homophobic Place on Earth?" *Time*, April 12, 2006. https://content.time.com/time/world/article/0,8599,1182991,00.html.

Poteat Tonia, Chulwoo Park, Diego Solares, John K. Williams, R. Cameron Wolf, Noah Metheny, Andrea Vazzano, Juan Dent, Ashley Gibbs, Bareng Aletta Sanny Nonyane, and Nora Toiv. 2017. "Changing Hearts and Minds: Results from a Multi-Country Gender and Sexual Diversity Training." *PLoS ONE* 12, no. 9 (September): e0184484. https://doi.org/10.1371/journal.pone.0184484.

UNAIDS. 2022. "Fact Sheet 2022." Accessed April 22, 2023. https://www.unaids.org/sites/default/files/media_asset/UNAIDS_FactSheet_en.pdf.

WHAT THE FUTURE HOLDS:

Angelo, Paul and Dominic Bocci. 2021. "The Changing Landscape of Global LGBTQ+ Rights." Council on Foreign Relations. January 29, 2021. https://www.cfr.org/article/changing-landscape-global-lgbtq-rights.

Guzmán, Esteban. 2022." LGBTQ Lawmakers in Latin America Pledge to End Conversion Therapy in Region." *Washington Blade*, May 26, 2022. https://www.washingtonblade.com/2022/05/26/lgbtq-lawmakers-in-latin-america-pledge-to-end-conversion-therapy-in-region/.

Villarreal, Yvonne and Matt Brennan. 2020. "Timeline: The Horrific Story Depicted in Netflix Doc 'the Trials and Gabriel Fernandez.'" *Los Angeles Times*, February 26, 2020. https://www.latimes.com/entertainment-arts/tv/story/2020-02-26/netflix-the-trials-of-gabriel-fernandez-docuseries-coverage.

Wang, Xintian. 2022. "China's Government Is Targeting 'Sissy' Men, with Devastating Consequences." openDemocracy, January 26, 2022. https://www.opendemocracy.net/en/5050/chinas-government-targeting-sissy-men-devastating-consequences/.

Yurcaba, Jo. 2021. "Gay Iranian Man Dead in Alleged 'Honor Killing,' Rights Group Says." *CBS News*, May 11, 2021. https://www.nbcnews.com/feature/nbc-out/gay-iranian-man-dead-alleged-honor-killing-rights-group-says-n1266995.

Made in the USA
Middletown, DE
14 March 2024